Reasons and Feelings

Write Like You Teach
James M. Lang

The Business of Being a Writer
Jane Friedman

The Craft of Research
Wayne C. Booth et al.

The Chicago Guide for Freelance Editors
Erin Brenner

The Design of Books
Debbie Berne

Developmental Editing
Scott Norton

The Dissertation-to-Book Workbook
Katelyn Knox

The Chicago Guide to Fact-Checking
Brook Borel

The Chicago Guide to Copyediting Fiction
Amy J. Schneider

Where Research Begins
Thomas Mullaney

On Revision
William Germano

Listening to People
Annette Lareau

Storycraft
Jack Hart

Writing Your Journal Article in Twelve Weeks
Wendy Laura Belcher

Writing Fiction
Janet Burroway, with
Elizabeth Stuckey-French
and Ned Stuckey-French

A complete list of series titles is available on the University of Chicago Press's website (www.press.uchicago.edu).

REASONS

WRITING FOR THE HUMANITIES NOW

&

SARAH MESLE

FEELINGS

THE UNIVERSITY OF CHICAGO PRESS CHICAGO AND LONDON

The University of Chicago Press, Chicago 60637
The University of Chicago Press, Ltd., London

Published 2025
Printed in the United States of America

34 33 32 31 30 29 28 27 26 25 1 2 3 4 5

ISBN-13: 978-0-226-83203-6 (cloth)
ISBN-13: 978-0-226-84362-9 (paper)
ISBN-13: 978-0-226-84361-2 (ebook)
DOI: https://doi.org/10.7208/chicago/9780226843612.001.0001

Library of Congress Cataloging-in-Publication Data

Names: Mesle, Sarah, author.
Title: Reasons and feelings : writing for the humanities now / Sarah Mesle.
Description: Chicago : The University of Chicago Press, 2025. | Series: Chicago guides to writing, editing, and publishing | Includes bibliographical references and index.
Identifiers: LCCN 2025009523 | ISBN 9780226832036 (cloth) | ISBN 9780226843629 (paperback) | ISBN 9780226843612 (ebook)
Subjects: LCSH: English language—Rhetoric—Handbooks, manuals, etc. | Academic writing—Handbooks, manuals, etc. | Scholarly publishing—Handbooks, manuals, etc. | Communication in the humanities—Handbooks, manuals, etc.
Classification: LCC PE1408 .M51726 2025 | DDC 808.06/6378—dc23/eng/20250514
LC record available at https://lccn.loc.gov/2025009523

♾ This paper meets the requirements of ANSI/NISO Z39.48-1992 (Permanence of Paper).

For Luna’s whole pack

Now that my ladder's gone,
I must lie down where all the ladders start
In the foul rag and bone shop of the heart.

WILLIAM BUTLER YEATS

Contents

PREFACE

Who

This book is for writers with deep expertise in the humanities who also really love writing as a personal creative act. It's for people who value precise and even rarified language and who also want multiple fire emoji!!! responses in group texts and online. It's a book for deep-feeling nerds who want readers to respond in a deep-feeling way to their written manifestations of nerdery. For such a writer, intellectual, aesthetic, and institutional desires blend together. This book aims to keep company with that affective state.

Writers who want these rewards face choices—choices about styles, practices, and platforms—that this book navigates. But this book takes a different approach than many other writing guides. First, it doesn't assume that its reader wants advice on a specific form, a term I'm using to comprise both aesthetic formal elements (voice, tone, style) and publication formats (review essay, Substack post, monograph). Instead, this book imagines its reader weighing many possible written forms. As anyone reading this book knows, humanities experts head toward an unpredictable future. The forms of the past, and the institutional, editorial protocols rewarding them, will not proceed forward unchanged. So, a second unusual feature of this guide is its speculative relation to the changeable landscape it explores. It's a writing guide keeping its own lookout for new paths toward meaningful writing, in uncertain territory.

Everyone writing in these conditions, myself definitely included, knows that the choices available aren't often good ones. They're just the options we have, right now. The daily negotiations we carry out with ourselves about sentences and diction and citation—about even sitting down to the page—exist always in the face of strange and swirling precarity. So a personal commitment to writing's pleasures isn't the only quality readers of this book will share. More infrastructurally, this writing guide addresses writers in the humanities as the institutions that have conventionally sheltered the pursuit of humanistic writing—universities, newspapers, magazines, more—sag, strain, crumble; variously reconfigure, reanimate, or give way. Yet as these institutions, and the world around them, seem on many days to be ending, we seem to find ourselves everyday within them, trying to find a way forward. Living through it feels equal parts horrifying and annoying, despairing and absurd, eye-rolly and weeping on the floor. Obstacles to our writing, our survival, loom; bad feelings whittle away at our energy in all we try to do. Still, writing draws us. Somedays, sometimes, some configurations of words seem to offer a way to be, or a place to go.

I hope this book will be useful for writers who are just starting out into this uncertain territory, as well as for writers who are, in several ways I could imagine, *re*starting in the midst of institutional upheaval. It's a book for everyone who loves humanist study looking at the shaky forms around them and asking: Well, what can we make of this? What can I do?

I ask these questions with some intensity because for me they're not hypothetical. Structural crises in the academic humanities have played out in the real time of my days. I can measure the fissures of the whole system in the number of job interviews I've had canceled, the sets of keys turned back in, the sympathetic furrows in the foreheads of beloved mentors who have asked, "Do you find people look down on you?" The problems aren't about me, but they're still my problem. They've manifested as a crisis in my identity. In conference registration forms, fellowship applications, hallway interactions, and my own head, I've felt unrecognized, even unrecognizable, and in that I am not alone.

Expert humanists face a general crisis, but the material differences in how that crisis plays out means that our experiences of it are highly personalized, hard to generalize from. As any glance at a day's headlines will show you, crises almost always affect the most vulnerable soonest and hardest. That is true in higher education as in anywhere else. I imagine that the variously vulnerable readers of this book are, as I can be, highly sensitive to misrecognition or misrepresentation, particularly in response to any proposal for action we don't have the resources (material or emotional) to implement. That makes writing this book a challenge. It makes circulating this book a challenge. In this emerging context, what optimism wouldn't be cruel?

This book is on the hunt for a version of optimism that could sustain a community for writing without ignoring the lived differences of the present's reality. So in the following chapters, I keep returning to a series of questions. How can those with resources—such as myself, and the press distributing this book—inhabit opportunities without hoarding their rewards? How can we establish collectivities that reckon with suffering without either universalizing it or allowing it to trump other experiences, of insight or pleasure? How can I—how can the readers of this book—inhabit our struggles, in their intensities and diversity, learning ethics from them, without operating as though only our suffering authorizes us?

For my own part, a surprising thing happened to me at the very moment I gave up the hope that an institution might give me a job doing the writing I had trained to do: I started to care *more* about expert writing as a source of emotional, social, intellectual pleasure. When my sense of scarcity made many kinds of writing harder—particularly the slow, sustained kinds that academia is best at "counting"—I came to prize most the moments my writing did find someone and move them, especially if that someone was also deeply knowledgeable, and perhaps even more so if they understood something about why a sense of hurt made my knowledge valuable to me. In the years since then, I've co-started and run a magazine, co-started and edited a book series, and contributed as both editor and writer to other magazines, reviews, and journals; I also got a job teaching college writing. For over ten years now, I have trained first-year college students how to imagine themselves into the genres of academic expertise, even as I also worked with academic experts to remake those genres (one might say: to imagine ourselves *out* of the genres we no longer felt served us). I have talked to many people about their words and lives, and how they hope the former might shape the latter. I have also thought about how my words might matter to my life, and to my own hopes and fears.

My view, after all these conversations and dark nights, is that the precarity facing us is best met with a utopian perspective. Or, to conjure a word to describe a quality our actions might take on: we should encounter the future utopically. By this I don't mean acting with a naive idealism, or a heroism, or a denial of feeling, or even a particular belief in a future-oriented hope. I don't know what, as people with deep expertise in the humanities, it is possible for us to accomplish on this darkling plain. But I do think it's possible to inhabit our cracked shelters as though the vulnerability of this new exposure might enable more than fearfulness, more than anger. What I want to offer in this book is an alternative way of thinking about our options, one that doesn't forget that they are limited. I have found it better—better for style, rigor, and ethics—to write while remembering that vulnerability creates not only reasonable fear and anger but also opportunities for different kinds of connection, consolation, pleasure, even transformation.

If these transformations do not save us—and who knows, that might not be within our grasp—they might still make the present meaningful. The question we face, as writers, is how to encounter destruction as a formal problem that could, ideally, produce more than itself. What can we do with our writing besides cling and smash? I feel the weight of this question every time I walk into my classroom, introducing "academic writing" to young people who may well live past the humanities as we know them and who may already have outlived "writing" as the art and labor it was; I feel it in my editing; I feel it when I sit down to put some words together, myself.

It's a good question, one that might be ballasting, and because I take it seriously I hope to forgo, in this book, taking the comforting avuncular posture of someone who knows what they or you should definitely be doing with the time you give to your words. Acting right now as though the capacities of these forms are predetermined would be in bad faith, and worse, it would miss the chance I want this book to take: to remind its readers that with every act of writing and publishing—and, for those of us who teach, with every assignment given and evaluated—we're actively reworking the conditions of writing's possibility. Our forms shift or sediment with every performance of them. We're all making, all the time—I'm making, right now—the forms through which our writing becomes legible, the worlds that value or don't our legibility.

And so this book about writing during the collapse of the humanities is not about abandoning our attachments to the institutional humanities. In my experience as an editor and as a professor and especially as a university-trained writer myself, I have often encountered the fantasy that outside academia, writing can be free and powerful and beautiful. I don't think that's how it works. I don't think this fantasy serves our writing; I think it distracts from the responsibility to make academic writing itself freer and more accessible in its creation and its effects. While this book grows out of my own experience creating alternate forms for expert writing, it resists the temptation to believe that "public" address or journalistic, trade publication can solve all our problems. It's not true, in my opinion, that our investments in more equitable, accessible worlds require us to stop nerding out with other weirdos who've devoted huge swaths of their lives to our specific branch of nerdery.

I'm writing this book in the way I am because I believe our most nerd-specific forms can hold our ardent attachments, and because I believe that narrow, specific forms of address can have as much world-making value as broad ones. Creating spaces, convening communities, in which expert writers can flourish is a difficult and often discouraging labor that nevertheless has been shot through, for me, with intense joy and connection. Working hard at world-making makes me better, I hope, at appreciating any scene of intellectual intimacy, even provisional, awkward, or imperfect ones. I like careful conference papers; I also like the spontaneous jazz hands about *this word, this one word!* at the bar after the official panels are over. These scenes feed each other. I'm a believer in many forms of mediation and in all the ways they allow us to iterate ourselves, fabricate ideas, read each other differently.

It's because I'm curious about being read with different stakes and different standards, and thus as different versions of myself, that I'm here, in peer review, looking for you. The possibility that we might find each other in a space like this—a book from a university press, seemingly so far away from the blogs where I first really learned how to think about passionate writing—is one point of evidence that it's worthwhile to work in both modes, and also to work *on* both modes.

Okay, but: What does all this alleged "form-sedimenting" and "world-making" look like in practice, on a given morning spent chafing against the abrasive textures the apocalypse seems to be generating as it unglamorously unfolds? Why would we pour ourselves into writing at all? And even if we wanted to, literally where is anyone supposed to find the strength?

Those questions percolate throughout this book's two sections. The first, "Why," is more existential. It asks why expert humanist writing might be valuable, now. Or, put differently, by working through my own questions about the political economies, publication strategies, and prose styles we navigate, it tries to propose some metrics of value, of understanding what's worth doing, that are better suited to the futures we might encounter. The second section, "How," takes a more practical approach, although, as I explain, "practical" can be an awkward standard for the eccentric performance art I find much expert writing, at its best, to be. The chapters in this section consider how pedestrian-seeming decisions—about nouns and verbs and bad moods and times of day—enact the existential questions about purpose and form that the first section introduces. In them, I've tried to consider "finding the strength" a task whose difficulty and intellectual complexity are equal to those of other creative labors. Some of the chapters are shorter and bossier, while others are more recursive and self-reflexive. Many of them draw attention to the jaggedness of the swiftly tilting timescapes in which they were composed. In these ways, they represent my own scene of writing as an active dialogue with other writers, thinkers, and versions of myself. They are not theory or abstraction. I see them as a sort of performative "book act" that hopes to be participating in the world-making they also call for.

In that sense, the very fact of this book feels to me not a theory or wish but actually practice, in that it's an idea I had about what kind of academic writing might be possible, put into action. All our forms, this book proposes, are up for negotiation. If they don't allow us to say what we know or want to understand, no one but us can make them new.

PART ONE

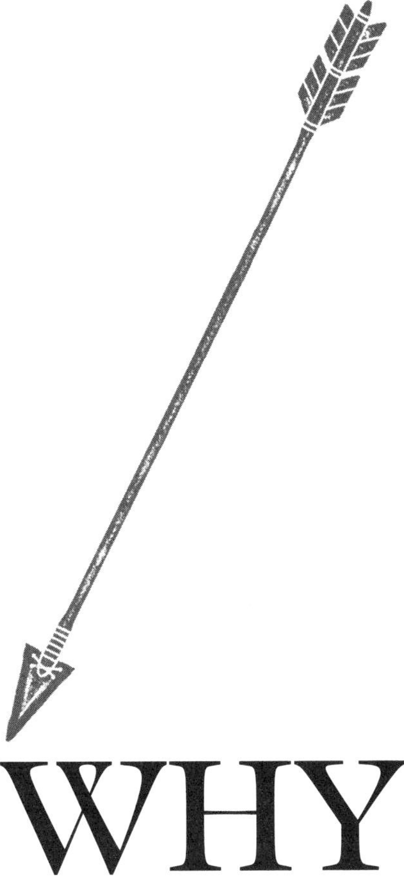

WHY

ONE

Reasons for Writing

Why should we write, now?

I'm writing this on a Friday morning. Let's say it's your Friday morning. Maybe you have taught your classes for the week; maybe you are floating in the enduring weirdness of a sabbatical or fellowship; maybe you have gotten your kids to school; maybe the slow mornings at your nine-to-five job mean you can steal an hour; maybe you are on the bus. You have something that my group texts will sometimes refer to as "my precious writing time," as though it were a plastic toy pony, which, let's imagine that it is. There you are, currying My Precious Writing Time's silky rainbow-colored mane, considering whether and where to go for a ride. On a given Friday, with one hour or two or six or twenty-four, what hope, what inspiration, what need, what goal, might spur you to write?

Some answers come readily to mind. We write for professional necessity. Because we love reading. Because we have an attachment to, a delight in, our own scene of narration. We desire status, authority. We desire having that authority recognized, reflected back. Because we're irritated that everyone else is getting it wrong. Because we're worried that without our writing, no one will get it right. Because we read *Little Women* or Proust and we seek the scene of composition like a lost manuscript or a madeleine's scent. Because we love the world, and words. Because of spite, fear, fascination, the spirit.

It's easy to wax poetic. Sitting down to actually write is harder. Writing happens word by word and minute by minute. For me, the minutes aren't all the same. Writing warps them. My own personal Precious Writing Time continues to be an unpredictable means of transport. I never know how fast or slow it will go, which makes for uneasy traveling. In the slow moments, worries fill my mind. Is *this* direction the best one? Did I pack the right tools and snacks? Is the weather clear? Why, why, did I take *this* toy pony from all the choices in life's stable? Why, in a historic moment like the one I inhabit, would writing time be precious at all?

When I ask, then, why we should write now, I'm talking about a particular pressure I feel in writing. It comes when I'm trying so hard to toe the line of this moment—which, I know, is the only one in which writing can actually take place—and the seconds stretch out, empty of words, and the weight of the world crushes in. I'm in a long-term relationship with my habit of procrastination, so I'm well acquainted with this experience. But in the last several years, its texture has changed. My whole relationship to time has changed. The existential dread I have always felt hovering around any writing journey feels more oppressive, now, because time in general feels scarcer. Like glacial ice or public university funding, time feels like a resource it's increasingly difficult to renew. I don't want to spend it on something that doesn't matter. Yet the worry that I will spend time on something wrong eats at my decisiveness. I'm trying to figure out the right thing to do, to write, and I'm watching the seconds on my laptop Pomodoro timer—I'm using it right now—go tick, tick, tick.

Hence this writing guide, which aims to help you develop your own personal reasons for writing, in the rapidly changing compound that is the dark room of the "now." This word names both a historical surround—here picture me gesturing broadly at the landscape from My Precious Writing Time's back—and the specific minutes each of us get to work in, on Friday morning. How can we best use this minute or that to make the broader now feel, or be, better or more secure? What would that even mean?

In answering these questions, I've tried to be guided by theorists of writing practice who keep existential and ethical considerations—and one of these, I should say, is simple enjoyment—at front of mind. This book exists the way it does, for example, because of the intellectual and stylistic space opened up by Tressie McMillan Cottom's multiplatform expressions of expertise. It shows, more and less explicitly, my ongoing engagement (and negotiations) with questions about writing raised by Virginia Woolf, Alice Walker, and Patti Smith.

To the extent that I've succeeded in keeping my compass aligned with these theorists, I often find myself scoping different territories than those mapped by writing guides directed at humanists particularly. Eric Hayot, for instance, provides clear formal advice in *The Elements of Academic Style: Writing for the Humanities* (2014); this book you're reading, in contrast, aims to help you consider whether academic style—used in pursuit of publication in an academic venue—is the one you want to use. More fundamentally, this book heads a different direction than Joli Jensen's wonderfully helpful *Write No Matter What: Advice for Academics* (2017), which begins from the not-untrue claim that "Rightly or wrongly, the measure of our professional worth continues to be our ability to write and get published."[1] The phrase "get published" has, in the context of Jensen's book, an implied meaning: to produce academic writing that universities perceive as such, to aid in our pursuit of university-based goals. I agree with Jensen that most of us who have spent time in universities have felt ourselves measured in such a way. We have felt that measure spur our writing; that through writing we might, for instance, as Jensen writes, "finally—if we are fortunate—achieve tenure."[2] I certainly agree with Jenson that academic writing has an immense value; it creates a specific intellectual experience that I'll go to the mat (you can find me there in chapter 4) to defend. Like Hayot, and like many others, Jensen delivers truly helpful strategies to help you commit to substantive academic projects, many of which I've used. In this book, I'll have some tips in that direction myself.

But for my own part, I simply can't start from the assumption that a specific form of professional-status-driven writing, or any kind of writing, is the best thing you can spend your Friday morning doing, as though there were no future in which our expert worth might be measured differently. In fact, that future has already slipped into the now of my mornings. Institutional uncertainty means, among other things, a proliferation of metrics by which our worth might be valued—and, much more importantly, by which we might value ourselves. In such a circumstance, the consolidated category of the "professional" or the "academic" weakens; it might already be irreparably damaged. I have some sadness about this state of affairs, but I'm not interested in pretending it hasn't taken place. And if we admit it has (admit the unlikeliness of finding even "finally—if we are fortunate" some kinds of professional security), how might our reasons for writing change? Can we still motivate our writing with some teleological hope of inchworming our way up a depersonalized professional measuring stick as it splinters around us? Why would we even want to?

I don't mean that last question rhetorically. Even as professional standards diminish in the material resources they promise, they remain psychically powerful. It's worth considering why. The answer has something to do with how our received fantasies about writerly talent costume a stark individualism of our moment. Humanists admire "good writers." We have been trained in institutions that praise individual voice, personal brilliance, admirable discipline in producing words on the page. In these same institutions, courses teaching writing often spin away from other scenes of scholarly expertise, indicating to humanists that writing skill is something we should have, rather than learn. (Jensen, with admirable forcefulness, rejects this dangerous act of mystification.) In conversations with humanist writers, I see how many of us, even when we are critical of professional metrics, share their emphasis on the self-directed individual. This mystical "good writer" figure may feel like a creative ideal. But in our current era, the romanticized visions of our work's production have particular stakes. There is a specific risk to how these visions leave us primed to see ourselves as solitary creative agents, acting for ourselves, rather than *as people in a scene*.

And writing is often a solitary act. It resists abstractions. It takes place in very specific particulars, richly textured negotiations with our individual selves and our embodied conditions. Even when two writers share a passion for a topic, they may have dramatically distinct relations to deadlines, hopes, research dollars, and carpal tunnel. Many humanists worry about the corporatized university, and this chapter will show some reasons we are right to do so. Corporatization may seem opposed to romantic "good writer" ideals. Yet when we focus too much on writing's individualist qualities—in terms of either talent or production—we hasten writing's dissolution, along with other art forms, into yet another form of economically driven practice and competitive social relation structured by what Sianne Ngai describes as the "hypercommodified, information-saturated, performance-driven conditions of late capitalism."[3] To return, then, to my question from above, I think our aesthetic myths about writing and talent predispose our feelings about and reasons for writing to be swept up in the destructive storm of our prevailing ideological weather system. In this maelstrom, writing feels like a tool for conquering the world, rather than comprehending it.

I do think my time is precious, and that writing is too. But our era's emphasis on productivity and privatized success teaches us to treat Our Precious Writing Time—even when we feel the preciousness as one of aesthetic creativity—like a resource we should hoard, something we should accumulate only for ourselves, hiding it away from the grasp of other people or things to do. It teaches us to feel that the best reason for writing is to divest ourselves, individually, of the struggles precarity creates. By this logic, our writing time becomes precious when it helps us shake free of precarious conditions, leaving them for everyone else. Such ideas of "freedom" and "preciousness" we should work to resist. We can't gollum away Our Precious Writing Time, hoarding it to the detriment of the community that might read our work, and expect the preciousness of our writing to remain. Our writing loses value when the world of our readers gets worse.

So in this chapter, I propose that as we, individually, consider why each of us should write now, our answers might depend on the company that writing enables us to constitute, at a time when so many collectivities are shaking. Each of us might write, in other words, guided by a vision of a "we" that our writing could help bring into being. This prospect might mean coming to see writing as a multifaceted set of activities, taking place among many others, in which hard-earned expertise can be turned toward personally and civically enriching comprehension of the world. It could mean recognizing that our lived weird individual writing moments aren't just undertaken at the same time, but also in a shared time—a now that none of us can ultimately escape. What if this now, freed from the false hopes of an obsolete and individualizing set of predetermined professional goals, allowed humanists to use our writing, and our time, to build an alternative, more collective, kind of worth? That might be a reason for writing, now.

*

In this book, I'm addressing readers who face a particular crisis of the "we": writers with expert knowledge in the humanities, defined here as those who have received some advanced humanities training at universities. While readers of this book may not currently write within universities, or at least not in a conventional way, this book's "we" will all have negotiated with how universities, through the allocation of resources, make "the humanities" legible as a category. This book exists in the way it does because of an evolving instability in the conditions such experts face, whereby one set of expectations for how writing might secure individuals to this "we" has eroded while nothing certain has taken its place. I am talking about the crisis in the humanities, as it exists now.

In saying that the now is an era of crisis, I don't mean to be unduly nostalgic for a past that certainly had its own share of bullshit and insecurity. I believe us to be in a crisis of the humanities. I'm also well aware that humanities writers have held this belief for a long time. One researcher tracked the phrase "crisis in the humanities" through JSTOR and found its first use in 1922.[4] Ever since, he writes, humanities scholars have been worrying about enrollment, methodology, and hyperspecialization, noting that "I think this is enough evidence to suggest that there has been a *sense* of crisis in the humanities almost as long as there have been departments of humanities" (emphasis in the original). This phrasing seems to imply that a sense is different from a reality or a legitimate situation; certainly, he's right that a "sense" should be differentiated from, say, a dataset. Yet senses, no less than datasets, demand interpretation, and can have powerful effects.

I know the sense of crisis, for me, has been both enduring and highly variable. When I was in graduate school over a generation ago, in the early 2000s, a sense of crisis scented the entire experience. The first question I was asked in my first graduate school interview was, "Do you know that you won't get a job?" This question does and doesn't correspond with the data of that year. Hiring in the humanities has been volatile at least since the seventies, but in 2001, the number of jobs in English had risen for four successive years, reaching one of the highest levels in a decade.[5] Clearly *someone* was getting jobs, and both the questioner and I knew it. Wanting those jobs was clarifying as a reason for writing. When advisors told me not to count on getting a job, because of the crisis, what I heard them telling me was "the good ones will get jobs, so write to prove you are good." I absorbed the implicit standard—a "measure of my worth," to go back to Jensen—that if I published one or two scholarly articles, I would be a good candidate for a job; that if I then wrote a book, I would likely get tenure. The language of crisis felt less like a call for structural transformation and more like an internal sorting mechanism, or an enthusiasm test. Persisting in the face of crisis, and rising to the writing challenge scarcity created, felt like a way to demonstrate worth and love, a shared sense of preciousness. It was a steep but clear path to a we.

I can remember a specific moment when my own sense of the humanities crisis shifted under me, showing the fissures in the "we" into which I had previously believed I might write my way. It was December 2009, a bright and cold night, and I was bundled into a white winter puffy coat, wearing high heels and thick tights. I stood outside the home of Patricia Yaeger, then editor of *PMLA*. She was hosting the University of Michigan English Department's faculty holiday party. I had been invited to the party because I was spending the year at Michigan on a postdoctoral fellowship. I had gone on the market the previous year with one chapter of my dissertation done; I didn't get a job, but I wasn't worried. The postdoc I later secured at Michigan seemed like a coup, and I was excited to go on the market with Michigan letterhead. In the fall of 2009, I scheduled several interviews, and then felt a slow emptying dread as every single one of the jobs was canceled due to funding reductions. Standing outside Patsy's door—her gracious house under tall trees, silhouettes moving through the windows, everyone so welcoming, everyone so kind—I felt something like terror, and something like grief, and something like blankness.

Everyone at that party knew about the crisis—we had all talked about it for years. So I was uncertain about how to understand this changing reality I felt I was experiencing alone. What would I say when they asked me about MLA? About my interviews? I had long been told that my writing could secure a future in this we, the one whose house I had been invited to visit. My writing was good, but I had not published it. Was that why all my jobs, my future, had gone away? That was part of it, but not all of it. My writing had gotten me interviews. Could it be the fault of my writing, my publishing, if the jobs themselves didn't exist? Was *all* of our writing, the way we wrote, the things we did, the problem? Was it the fault of my love, my commitment, my enthusiasm? I went into the party.

Everyone around me talked in bright tones, and seemed so beautiful, so smart and proud, and they couldn't see the cracks I felt underneath me. Maybe those fault lines weren't there. Maybe the "we" was fine, after all. Maybe I could join it next year. Maybe the humanities, like the crisis, was something that could endure.

Writing now, almost fifteen years later, I can see the ways that we have survived, and also the ways we've changed. I come to this book as one of the many people who trained to be a humanist in one version of the crisis and built a professional career in another. One thing those split experiences can teach is how crisis as a *sense* matters to the ways humanists struggle to communicate across historical divides.

The 2008 financial crisis caused a precipitous decline in humanities tenure-track hiring and enrollments, which a decrease in federal resources following the Bush tax cuts has made harder to remediate. By the time the 2020 pandemic hit, the number of MLA-listed jobs had already been dropping for ten years in a row.[6] It seems that writers coming of intellectual age after 2020—and after 2025, and after whatever new crises will unfurl in the future toward which this book travels—will need to navigate their own decollectivizing ruptures. At the same time, those of us navigating professional worlds now still have much to learn from other ways of navigating crisis, both materially and as a felt sense.

I have always struggled to steer My Precious Writing Time; the 2008 crisis didn't create my problems with writing. But shifting material resources post-2008 made the emotional burden of writing into a categorically different experience for me, one I have struggled to explain to those who came of professional age in different moments. I had to learn a whole new way to engage the act of writing when I realized that no matter how much I loved my topic, there wasn't a way to write my way out of a new global reality into a "we" that no longer had material resources to welcome me, even if it wanted to.

The crisis in the humanities is just one part of a crisis in higher education, and, although not currently my focus, in education across the board. For the last two decades, governments—motivated at least partly by their own financial shortfalls, or their ideological suspicion of educational systems, or both—have decreased direct funding of higher education (indirect funding continues, in the form of government-backed student loans). With direct public funding from national and state governments diminished, eliminated, or at increasing risk, universities must find other funding streams. These funds may come from tuition dollars, from philanthropy, or from other sources such as television rights to sports broadcasts (as most humanists know, none of these funding streams guarantee an investment in educational missions). In any event, these funds are increasingly earned in competition with other universities. In this competition market, even nominally public universities increasingly choose to guarantee their own survival by assuming a market logic in their self-understanding. They create themselves as brands. Within this context, humanities experts, in order to not perish, can't just publish. You also have to post and repost. Post on the other platform, do a podcast, write it up for the blog, put it in your handle. It's not unpleasant, when it's a way to show a passionate commitment. But the pleasure's wrapped up in the pressure to establish brand status—a market's measure of worth.

In discussions of the humanities crisis, villains abound. Sometimes the villain seems to be our own work: the narrowness of our topics and the styles of our prose repel resources rather than make the case for them. Arguments about method and style merge with existential anxieties, as though some change in our writing could remediate a crisis our writing didn't create. Sometimes the villain seems external: from within the humanities, accusations of malfeasance are lobbed at administrations, boards, governments, sometimes our students. These accusations are powerful because they are true. Administrations, governments, and students all regularly devalue humanities work. I can't get over the villainous consultants who leech university resources in exchange for terrible advice, and the business-world administrators who accept the consultant's claims that what university classrooms need is fancy cameras rather than well-paid instructors.[7] At every university I know of, specific bad actors need to be called to task.

Yet the problem of the "we" for us, as expert writers, isn't simply an external villain or prose form. Instead, it's the pervasive ways in which our own thinking and acting become infused with the same ethos of privatization that dominates universities—and the broader world as well. Privatization as an institutional shift means that both the costs and the benefits of university structures are decreasingly managed as public, collective goods: funding for universities comes from private sources (such as tuition, corporate investments, or individual donors), and university success isn't measured by an overall increase in public quality of life, but in alumni capacity for earning and social status. An ethos, however, is different from these measurable changes; by ethos I mean, following Christopher Newfield, that certain principles have transcended the status of economic axioms and become cultures, structures of feeling, that organize prevailing beliefs about what is possible, what is reasonable, and even about our own personal worth.[8] Within the belief structure that Newfield understands privatization partly to be, our experiences of subjectivity succumb to market valuation. This includes humanists' sense of the crisis. Those of us writing in professional contexts, in the aftermath of these recent crises, don't often sense that a collective of scholars can make our writing feel valuable, and we may not be wrong. But a privatization ethos is not a good emotional teacher. In its sway, we feel valuable when the market values us, reinforcing our belief that only the market can make us feel better than we do.

*

On this Friday morning—it's a different Friday, now, because I've been at this a long time—it's strange to remember the clarity I felt about writing and the crisis, that older crisis, back in 2001. Today, while the affective charge of academic publishing has not gone away, other kinds of belonging-through-writing present themselves. In the exact same era that tenure-track jobs have declined, social media and independent media have made—albeit with a zigzagging sort of availability—other kinds of writing and publication available to humanities experts. (A more detailed account of this history appears in chapter 3 of this book.) So, on a given Friday morning, if you would like to join some we, the decisions facing you have multiplied. Not only must you decide to sit down to write, and decide what you want to write about, you face decisions about style and audience and publication speed and strategy. Do you want to work on a scholarly article, or monograph, which you might submit for peer review? Pitch something—and then maybe write something—for a venue specializing in critical nonfiction like *LARB* or *The Rambling* or *Public Books*? Try for something journalistic, at *The Lamoni Chronicle* or *The New York Times* or the *Daily Trojan*? Compose an Instagram caption? Some other social media post, navigating whatever ongoingly evolving communities and infrastructures?

As an expert you could share your knowledge and insights in any of these modes. All of them make demands, present opportunities. It can be difficult to distinguish between a demand and an opportunity. Which, for instance, is the expectation that you will talk about yourself, your life and body and its situations? Which is the mandate for an engaging style, in addition to meaningful content? Moving among these modes will require shifts in the subtlety of informational and argumentative revelation; the approachability of your style; the scope of your "hook."

Decisions about our minutes become tangled because the rewards for writing become nearly possible to arbitrate between. What might be one's aim? A job, an honorarium, a reputation? The nice people at the MacArthur Foundation taking notice? I think about the nice MacArthur people about once a week. It is exceptionally unlikely that most of us are going to be receiving a phone call from the MacArthur people this Friday morning. And yet, conditions on the writing ground are such—and many of you know this, on your Friday morning—that other rewards like "full-time teaching position located near affordable housing" and "stable job in media" are so similarly unlikely that the difference between these previously obtainable hopes (a meaningful job with good insurance) and pie-in-the-sky goals (a "genius" grant) come to feel equally possible in that none of them can be counted on to happen at all. The fractured reward framework, for expert writers across the board, can flatten the external metrics we might use to make decisions.[9] We have to choose without material guarantees.

On this point, I want to clearly position myself against a viewpoint I sometimes hear expressed in graduate seminars I visit. Sometimes I am asked to talk about "the future of academic writing" and sometimes "public writing" and sometimes "pitching" and sometimes "the humanities, now." Regardless of topic, the students in the audience for these visits are all in the process of becoming some kind of subject expert; they are in the audience because they have some commitment to acquiring knowledge. With some regularity, the professor who invited me to the class will express some sense that larger, more difficult, and more institutionally oriented projects are a necessary step toward other kinds of work. Sometimes these professors will say to these students: Write your dissertation, work toward a job and tenure, and then you will be "free" to write more expansively.

This is wrong, at least from my perspective. Watching friends get tenure (from my own position off the tenure track), I have not regularly seen them become "free." I know a certain kind of security comes from institutionally granted stability. But I'm not sure the language of tenure or "tenure track" is the best way to describe humanist hierarchies, given that in this crisis moment, "tenure" fails to name a consistently secure state. I don't have tenure, but I do have the shelter of a wealthy university that leaves me mostly free to develop my curricula and gives me excellent databases through which to do so, whereas many tenured colleagues elsewhere have an experience that looks less like shelter and more like being stuck with a specific institution's own precarity and political struggles. Even in institutions without enrollment crises or salary freezes or a wholesale attack on the liberal arts (or critical race theory or the word "gay"), the administrative demands of tenured positions often lay claim to time that might, in some fantasies, be freely spent. Institutions can do many things for you. At their best, the security they offer shelters a world-building that I prize. But it is not their job to make you free.

The increasing privatization of higher ed, and the specific forms that privatization has taken, have undermined faculty authority to determine what kind of writing matters, or even *that* writing matters. There is no decision about writing—its mode or quantity or quality—that can ensure your safety in a class that can be wiped out at the stroke of a pen.[10] So a better strategy for making choices about your writing time might be to ask: What do you find genuinely meaningful, in the horizontal circuits of community in which you now exist? Rather than reaching up the measuring stick, who is with you in your now?

I say all this realizing that describing what happens on a given Friday morning as a "choice" somewhat misrepresents what it's like to be a person. There are many Friday mornings when I spend My Precious Writing Time composing a carefully zesty text, or a devastating or clever response to someone's social media post, or debating with myself about whether or not to post or respond to a post, and I would not exactly say that this use of a Friday morning's writing time is one that I have "chosen." It's more like I let My Precious Writing Time lead me into some field of delicious-but-of-uncertain-nutritional-value clover of its own choosing. It's really different from the choice I make when I set my social media blockers and a timer and put on my "getting serious now" writing playlist and try to write this book.[11] Choosing to write this book is like urging My Precious Writing Time up a steep and lonely hill. I have to mean it. And sometimes even when I do mean it, it doesn't happen the way I hope.

Yet setting it up this way plays into a long-standing set of *affective* reasons for—and responses to—writing. It's too simple to say that the action of writing a book represents an expression of will, while another type of writing, such as posting on social media, indicates a thoughtless and possibly shameful lapse in purpose, even though I have often experienced it that way. Putting my minute-by-minute hours into long-form writing has felt to me like an admirable investment: harder to do, but with the comforting sense that those minutes would accrue toward something substantive and real and mine. The article or book would create a byline, a CV line, leading to more opportunities. Maybe after that a job, a better job, a bigger bedroom for my kids.

What kind of historical context, what system of value, makes this neat alignment of form with mental faculty with good life outcome feel normal? Feminists and queer theorists have taught us the ethical necessity of asking: Whose social position is served by respecting this norm? What are its costs? When we accept this norm, what experiences become harder to see? I have come to believe that this deeply enculturated structure of feeling that divides serious, reasonable writing decisions from impulsive, trivial ones does not often serve us, as writers. The gap makes the complexity around writing's motivations harder to understand and respect. The more I mark some kinds of writing with shame, the harder it can be to value all kinds of writing for what they most substantively offer, and what they teach us about what we want and need.

When I'm stuck on a difficult sentence and reach for the quick exchanges available on my phone, part of what I'm hoping for isn't merely distraction. It's relief. That relief might be a fantasy, like that of a penny-slot jackpot payout: sudden virality, fame, recognition. That relief might also be more reliably on offer, in the form of social moment, either aesthetic or anesthetic in its pleasures, to suspend the encounter with how increasingly scary writing feels. In the moment of the sentence, I encounter my anxieties about my own abilities, and my desires for my future, and my recognition of the world's uncertainty, in a mutually reenforcing fear loop: as the world around me becomes less secure, the better my writing needs to be in order to protect me, and the more inadequate to the task my abilities seem.

Even as I write this, I am staring at my phone, which I have strategically placed just out of reach by the window. I can feel the pull of its smooth shape, and all the worlds it holds for me. I'm trying not to reach for it, and I'm hoping to continue not reaching for it even past my next Pomodoro break in (I just checked) twenty-two minutes and sixteen seconds. I'm hoping to resist my phone until noon, which is, on this particular morning of Precious Writing Time, still a couple of hours away. I am trying to stay with my thoughts, to finish this project I care about.

But after I reach this goal, assuming I do, I likely will reach for my phone, and spend some happy time there, as I do almost every day. If texting and social-media-ing make you happy, then you should too. When we put the minutes of Our Precious Writing Time into direct exchanges, we're not gambling at the penny slots; we're reaching out into the now, with other people who are doing the same. The only problem reaching for my phone early would create is that it might turn a source of pleasure and comfort into an avoidant act, rather than giving texting (or posting) the space to be a substantive act of writing, of world-making, in itself. Writing should be for the world, and worlds need nurturing. You can't just sit around making some book or some think piece about politics or gender and then send it out, with the belief that a world out there simply waits, in anticipation, for your writing to arrive. In our digital era, for worse but also definitely for better, we depend on communities that we have the capacity to write (sometimes on social media, sometimes in texts, sometimes via other interfaces) into being. Our quick digital exchanges, no matter how improvisational, can find real audiences and have real stakes. It doesn't serve us to cast aside as "not writing" these kinds of writing. It's hard to text or post with wit and empathy and insight, let alone do so with consistency, and the reason it's hard is because these actions carry much of the transformative potential that long-form writing can.

However, this is not to present digital interactions of any kind as a solution to the problem of privatization that has damaged higher ed. Social media platforms can feel like a public sphere, and they have offered bright lights in dark times. But every day brings a reminder of their corporate nature, the dangerous power that their occasional brightness cannot fully eclipse. They make our belonging into "impressions," into clicks and followers we can count. As zones of collectivity building, they are hamstrung by the metrics of private, personal status inherent to their interfaces. By training us to consider ourselves through quantification and ranking, they operate in parallel to the brand logic, the obsession with ranking and scoring, that structures higher ed now too.

*

To describe education and publication as obsessed with clicks and rankings and scores might seem to imply that they are driven by facts—by numbers anyone could count and agree on. Yet this is not the case. Even when specific humanities departments can deliver meaningful economic futures, and even when their enrollments rise, it can be, as the critic and departmental chair (and my frequent collaborator) Sarah Blackwood wrote in *The New York Review of Books*, nearly impossible to make such success, or the need for resources success demands, "rise to the level of fact."[12] The best data we have on university funding and hiring indicates that choices are being made on the basis of fear and projection as much as anything else. Students and administrations have created something of a feedback loop, whereby administrations "sense" that students want career-related majors, thus direct funding to those majors, and thereby intensify students' attraction to those majors, because the students' rightly sense that institutions themselves believe career-related majors are more valuable than the humanities. In this chicken-and-egg game, it's unclear which "sense" came first, but it is apparent that the humanities often lose.

This is perhaps to the humanities' credit. It certainly flatters a long-standing self-perception of humanities experts, as Paul Reitter and Chad Wellmon write in *Permanent Crisis* (2021), that our "we" is constituted by our sense of our willingness to serve as "guardians of meaning, value, and human being" in the face of corrosive forces.[13] A spring 2023 *New Yorker* article shows us this self-perception in action, when it describes Columbia University Professor of English James Shapiro sketching a graph of the downward trajectory in humanities funding and then calling the same timeline a "decline-of-democracy chart."[14] Shapiro's implication, one I have heard repeated at many academic receptions, as we all snack on postlecture mini quiches, is that without the humanities, we will have no democracy, and further that those who hate democracy also hate the humanities, and attack the latter to undermine the former. Few people at these gatherings and in these *New Yorker* articles, even when they have read Kandice Chuh's excellent book on the topic, seem willing to consider the inconvenient possibility that the humanities, since their founding, have been as much a tool for rationalizing social stratification as working against it.[15] "We'd" rather consider how our declining resources offer, in a backward way, an evidentiary sense of our moral worth.

I'm as inclined to self-heroics as any of the humanities experts Reitter and Wellmon describe, and if I didn't feel a full-throttle love for what the humanities can offer, I wouldn't be writing this book. But I'm worried by the impulse to assert our moral superiority, whether it's on display in myself, in Shapiro, or in any academic-mini-quiche situation. Not only do heroic interpretations obscure the ethical complexity of our work, they also naively position humanities experts as outside the overriding values of our world. We are not. We swim in the same water as everyone else. Cultural shifts toward individuation and privatization matter to our reasons for writing; they exert powerful influence over our senses, giving shape to what behaviors and attitudes can carry the force of reasonableness, individually and as we act within institutions.

I said above that universities increasingly collapse their ability to perpetuate themselves into their ability to brand; to sell themselves as a class marker that students, parents, and donors can use to enhance their own social status. In this system, humanists feel pressure to produce enough writing for universities to see our value. But pressure is only one thing we feel, or, maybe, only one way that what we feel might be described. To describe the current system only in the negative erases the tantalizing opportunities privatized logic offers us, as individual writers, to escape the devaluation of the humanities by building a brand of our own.

In the grim archive of recent scholarship probing contemporary universities, one of the most bracing essays comes from Bennett Carpenter, Laura Goldblatt, and Lenora Hanson. Their "Unprofessional: Toward a Political Economy of Professionalism" offers an absolute fire account of the fool's bargain universities offer their faculty in our current underresourced moment.[16] The essay tracks how we're asked to believe and act as though our only hope for professional security is to bolster the university's brand, in competition with other brands. In such a context, not only are we fighting for scraps, but as we do so we're asked to erase any harm we experience, since to make that suffering apparent would be to damage the brand that feeds us, as it were. We expose ourselves to risk and absorb the harm of any risk, because to complain that the university caused us harm would be to endanger what feeble remaining capacity the university has to protect us.

In this excellent essay, I find implications beyond the authors' claims. Their reading of complaint is inflected (as certainly mine is too) by Sara Ahmed's account of how universities contain experiences of the physical, sexual, and psychic risk those within them endure. But "Unprofessional" does not consider the many points of evidence suggesting something disturbing: how full of delight and pleasure risking ourselves can become. As humanities experts, we may feel superior to many of the people—athletes, aspirational sorority girls posting on RushTok—who purposefully turn their bodies into displays for university brands. We're skilled at critiquing the dark logic of identity commodification, the insidious ways corporate motives co-opt personal relations. But I don't think we can consider ourselves above or outside the world of branding in which such actors thrive.

In the ways we maneuver through our changing professional

options, I see our situation as becoming *more* like these athletes, rather than less. This is not only because all of us, athletes and authors, are doing our best with the bad choices available. We authors, too, far too often, internalize uncritically the status pleasures the privatized university seems to lure us toward. In our uptake of new publication options, we create brands that serve a range of resource streams. We write more personally, about more parts of our lives. We create professional value from our intimate experiences of embodiment. Like athletes, we expose ourselves; we compile our stats.[17] Don't many of us—and don't the platforms I've personally fostered help us do it—essentially perform the role of humanities influencer?

To put it that way exposes me to my own cringe responses, even though I know the dire contexts that drive the performance. But I also know that I can't fully play the victim. It's not just bad choices and false consciousness. It's the pleasure of being ideologically affirmed. I wouldn't do it if I didn't, at least to some degree, *like doing it*. And I don't think I'm the only one. Put differently: to meaningfully consider our reasons for writing, in this time of crisis, we need to reckon as honestly as we can with our own investments, so to speak, in the privatized logic of our era. Because central to all this is how administrators' and students' "senses" shape our own sense of Our Precious Writing Time.

Those of us who have inhabited universities during the last fifteen years have felt how the institutions in which we gained our expertise, and thus in which we gained a sense of ourselves as experts, have changed in their relation to our expertise's value. We have felt it in crappy offices and bigger classes and increased publication expectations. Our Precious Writing Time takes place in an era governed by a weird inflationary logic. When our expertise is devalued, so is the writing that expresses that expertise. Perversely, then, we have to produce more of it in order to gain purchase on the security a university can provide. (Here I'm imagining humanities experts, like other historical victims of economic inflation, carting wheelbarrows full of JSTOR printouts to the HR office, trying to buy an adjunct appointment.)

At the same time, humanities experts ourselves are absorbing the lesson—how could we not absorb the lesson?—that we don't matter for each other as an audience. It's not simply that we have to write more for universities to value us. It's also that it's hard for us to value our own writing unless more people, preferably different people, read it.

Like athletes entering themselves in the new transfer portal, choosing to play, as it were, *on but not only for* a university basketball team, many of us humanities experts in our current now imagine ourselves as forces beyond the institutions in which we work, or the various collaborations (teams, departments) those institutions house. In many ways, this is a positive, even necessary, transformation. It would be so even if our institutions weren't so unsteady. But it is not easy, in this context, to find ways to value each other.

*

I tell my students to be cautious of writing "we." As a political gesture, it's a term that can minimize difference, even as it purports to reject abstract or universalizing gestures. I ask my students: Who asked your reader if they want to be in your "we?" Did you? I also keep asking myself. Writers often use the "we" as a scrim, onto which a projected image obscures and aggrandizes the specific contours of the author's individual experience. Jennifer C. Nash is just one scholar to outline recently how often white feminists, in particular, make this move, claiming the feminist "we" for white women's experience.[18] Knowing this is the case doesn't seem to make me immune to the habit.

The stratified crises of the current moment make collectivity ever harder, especially when I consider the "we" of a book that aims to reach readers in the nows of the future. I've felt an inherent incompatibility between "bookness" as an experience and publishing practice (a slow one, easily thrown into upheaval for material as well as intellectual reasons) and the topic of this particular book, which is the collapse of on-the-ground conditions for its readers. I'm writing in the midst of a particular set of historical conditions, marked by war, state violence, environmental and institutional calamity. I am reviewing copy edits here on a Saturday morning in the aftermath of the 2025 Los Angeles fires: incinerated books, bicycles, lead pipes, asbestos, and artworks float in the air I breathe. You will read this book in a different set of conditions. My own sense of climate realities leads me to expect that whatever shape your now takes, it's likely to contain even more disparity, grief, and trauma than mine. I can't know what this future will be, and yet here I am, waving at future you, throwing forward some thoughts about political economy and ponies. I'm gazing at my imagined future reader through increasingly inadequate glasses as the writing conditions around me (and also, presumably, her) continue to shift. What universities will exist for her? What rights of personhood? What summary of this book will AI, which hardly existed when I started this manuscript, read to her, or allow her to access?[19] What will remain of writing as a human intellectual art? I can't begin to know.

One thoughtful account of the word "we" comes at the beginning of Monica Huerta's *Magical Habits* (2021). *Magical Habits* sketches out some strategies for occupying the legacies of violent histories. In its opening pages, Huerta remembers sitting in church and listening to a "we" extended to a gathering of people, some there by pressure and some by choice. Like Huerta, I grew up with a liturgical we, and I know both the pleasures and the pressure it can generate, the competing senses of friction, irritation, and joy that come when one is called. The word "we" can describe, and it can be a performative. It can enact.[20] Huerta sees herself as "alone when I write *we*, but maybe soon with some company."[21] The possibility of company, she posits, makes the "we" worth the risk, for her.

What readers of this book share is a lived relation to a broken time. This is a complicated thing to say. I know that differences in the degree of loss experienced by potential readers of this book are so vast they are better considered as differences in kind. Not all of our losses stem from writing, and it's uncertain how many of them may be repaired by it.[22] Yet for any repair to be possible, this broken time may require our remembering, to paraphrase Dickens, that we are all fellow passengers to the end of the world, not competing creatures bound on other journeys. We also share, in our different ways, the legacies of other writers who used their expertise and their artistry to address worlds in crisis, worlds for which they could not have trained. It's by taking responsibility for each other here, in this particular break, in this provisional kind of together, that we're most likely to access something like freedom in how, and what, we write.

To propose, as I do, that "the humanities" are something worth having in common at this stage of the journey means that one form I believe we should continue to work with and through is the university itself. This, too, is risky, because "the university," I really know, is so screwed. But universities make a particular kind of legibility possible. They are repositories of many resources we should not abandon. And they have, even if despite themselves, been sites where radical approaches to collectivity—what Chuh calls "alternative theorizations and models for ways of being and knowing"—have emerged and been strengthened.[23] Thus the "we" I'm trying to give us a way to imagine is one that must necessarily navigate between the institutional and the utopic. Another way to put this would be to say that writing, as I'm thinking about the practice, always navigates between fantasies of both endurance and transformation. To write is to enact a belief in sustained conditions of legibility; to write is to reach toward a future, one open to whatever change for which writing calls.

I have felt, sometimes, like nothing I could write would ever matter to the world's real problems. In other moments, I've felt like nothing about me or my life could matter if I didn't write. Both of these feelings carry the weight of a cultural order that tells us we can only matter individually. And both of these feelings are among those I hope this book can help all of us learn to resist. Thus the specific advice I give in this book for "humanist writing" often includes strategies for other activities: reading, editing, canvassing, and other forms of organizing, listening, talking, teaching, chilling out. These activities not only improve what happens when you sit down to the page (although certainly they do that); they also teach us how to value the creative labor that takes place in receptive, collectivizing acts. They teach us, as writers, to be in solidarity with readers and other writers rather than in competition with them. They can reenergize our respect for other humanities experts in a world that teaches us to disregard them.

This book draws on my expertise and on my experiences; it proposes that bridging these categories makes stronger company. In the form and the content of what follows, I'm trying to figure out strategies that collectivize rather than universalize or generalize. My hope is that doing so offers some frameworks that help you surface your own reasons and feelings for writing. Writing now is terrifying. But writers have found forms in past conditions of calamity. We come to this moment knowing that if our times are unprecedented, they are not the first to be such. I try to tell myself what I tell my students who feel so unsteady as they look out at the future: amid this uncertainty, we might learn how freedom, in good company, feels.

TWO

Writing About Feelings

In the spring of 2013 I was having big feelings about a new pair of running pants. The pants were from Lululemon, then in the early days of its global conquest. The feelings were delight, in the pants, and irritation, in the way other people talked about the pants. I published an essay about my pants and my feelings called "The Unbearable Awesomeness of Lululemon Pants." In it I wrote:

> I myself have just acquired my first pair of Lululemon running pants and I would like to offer a reason as to why they are worth 88 dollars: there's a seam across the top of the butt that makes my ass look better than it does in any other running pants, ever. That's it. That is the reason.
>
> Here's a reason that has *nothing to do* with why my Lululemon running pants are "worth" 88 dollars: that they will "last a long time." This is a rationale often offered for why we running/yoga ladies should truck off to Lululemon with our hard-earned cash in hand, and hold our heads up high while doing it.
>
> My opinion, and this is the point of this essay, is that this durability reason is bullshit and should be discarded and, let's be clear, *never used.*[1]

My essay described a collision between the feelings that count as "reasons" and the ones that don't. It was an argument against disavowing the emotional content of our motives, and specifically against strategically deploying such rationalizations to justify resource allocation. My essay was not academic writing, as this book will define it, but it drew on my humanities expertise, and although the essay addresses parts of culture—ladies, running, butt flattery—that are easy to dismiss as trivial, we can draw a straight line from its central concerns to ongoing arguments about evidence, style, and argument in expert humanities writing across the board.

A few years later, my essay (the exact first, butt-seam sentence above) was quoted in a *Notre Dame Law Review* article called "Fashion's Function in Intellectual Property Law." To date, this quotation constitutes my only published contribution to legal scholarship. I feel basically fine about a legal publication quoting my writing about my butt to illustrate the argumentative claim that "aspects of garment design are functional not only when they affect the physical or technological performance of a garment but also when they affect the perception of the wearer's body."[2] In fact, my essay argued this exact same point.

Noticeably, however—and here my noticing generates further big feelings—the authors of this legal article don't quote me by name; they refer to me as "another reviewer" of pants (one of several they quote) rather than crediting me as someone making, as they too are, an argument about culture and its resources. Here, too, we see an emergent issue of resource allocation—of authority, rather than of the $88 my running pants cost—in an expert deployment of reason and feeling. Like the legal scholars, I was writing about how self-perception matters to fashion, resources, and power. My essay circulated for four years before their article's publication. Nevertheless, they quote my essay as evidence for their argument, rather than treating me as an interlocutor with an argument of my own. As a writer working in a world where citations are literally counted and where reputation, if intangible, can still have real material effects, I noticed their decision.

Something about my essay narrowed its function. In this narrower function, it did not seem to merit named authorial acknowledgment. Maybe the cause of this narrowed function was my writing voice; maybe it was my choice of venue. Maybe it was my evocation of my own embodiment and my expression of desires about how I wanted my butt, specifically, to appear. Maybe it wasn't about my writing at all. It's equally possible that the legal scholars had their own writing problem, one they needed evidence, rather than an interlocutor, to solve. Some of these motivations might seem like reasons, and some like feelings. In that fungibility, and in its revealing concatenation of embodiment, function, and status, this example presents to us a question about writing that, perhaps strangely, parallels the one I brought to my running pants: how do feelings, style, and feelings about style matter in determining whose arguments have worth?

*

What world—what form of relation—can we make, and with whom, by sharing our reasons, and how might our shared feelings differently build worlds and relations? Over the last fifteen years, part of how we in the humanities have responded to our escalating crises has been to test out answers to these questions. We want a radical, almost impossible-seeming transformation in our conditions. This desire is a feeling. Our historical conditions have intensified that feeling past the point of misrecognizing it as such. At the same time, those historical conditions have exacerbated the pressures around writing, drawing the emotions writing itself generates into heightened relief. Some of us have wondered if infusing our expert reading, teaching, talking, and writing *with* feeling, trying to heighten the affective honesty or effect of our prose, would help reinvigorate our collective relation, while also (bonus!) making writing more fun.

Around this proposition swirls considerable and important debate. If we write with and toward our feelings, our personal

experiences, will we lose the cultural authority that comes from reason, university-trained experts' traditionally understood domain? Will dwelling in the personal make us solipsistic, actually less likely to focus on shared experience? Or will it make our collective stronger and advocating for it easier? We sort out our answers to these questions every time we sit down to Our Precious Writing Time, feeling our way toward what we have to say, and to whom, and how.

I say "we" and it's true, but I'm writing this chapter out of a desire to articulate for myself how I understand the written relations between feelings and expertise. It's complicated. I have a scholarly background in nineteenth-century literature; I am a professor in a writing program; in both my scholarship and my teaching, I'm constantly juggling reasons and feelings as both topic and frame. In 2012 I started a digital magazine with another humanities expert and friend, Sarah Blackwood, in collaboration with our mutual humanities-expert friend Jordan Stein. We called it *Avidly*, a website dedicated to writing "with intense eagerness." We asked all our other friends, many of them also humanities experts, to write for it. The name of this website tells you something about how I'm positioned vis-à-vis the incorporation of feeling into humanities writing: I'm for it. I think that personal, sensory, embodied responses contribute to the collective project of world-interpreting expertise.[3] But no responsible scholar of sentimental literature or professor of writing can be "for" feeling in an unambivalent way. That would be like being "for" power. Just as "reasons" and reasonability can be deployed by the powerful to conceal self-interested behavior, so can "feelings." Rationalizations and emotionalizations, as maneuvers, are equally likely to disguise undesirable and crappy ways of writing about and being in the world.

Some of the first pieces of writing I personally published were about, in addition to Lululemon running pants and nineteenth-century sentimentalism, Patti Smith's stretch marks and Virginia Woolf's need for birth control. There has never been a moment when I didn't ardently believe that what I *knew* about these topics emerged from how my body felt about them. I similarly believe that developing the craft of making writing out of and about those feelings makes for a richer experience of knowing, for both writer and reader. This craft practice is a kind of expertise, one integral to the humanities' worth as I see it, and it's one reason why the study and teaching of writing, itself, merit respect and resources.

This chapter considers how our shared genres and grammars teach us about *how reasons feel* and *which feelings feel like reasons*. I'm interested especially in how the feeling of reason connects to "our" resources and worth. I have come to think that as humanist writers, our collectivity would be best served by reexamining how our craft practices of writing are built to support particular, but not inevitable, standards of what feels reasonable. Such a reexamination would allow for a new and rigorous reentry of the avowedly personal and emotional into expert writing as a strategy for knowledge production—and a more honest awareness of the emotions created in even our most traditional deployments of critical genres. Writing feelingly can seem like a craft problem specifically relevant to those who hope to publish in journalistic or public-facing rather than scholarly venues, but I would argue against such a division. Even when it travels unrecognized, the craft of managing how writing feels, and how writing makes readers feel, gives ballast to humanistic inquiry, writ large.

*

While I was drafting this chapter, *The Guardian* newspaper semi-negatively reviewed a book I had edited. The critic didn't love the book, but his bigger worry concerned my whole editorial project:

> [The book is] part of a series called Avidly Reads, an offshoot of the online magazine Avidly, in which various writers, mostly American academics, talk about how cultural forms and objects—among them opera and board games—make us feel. Is this a betrayal of scholarship? A shift away from sober analysis and professional expertise to

> a more blurry, personal discourse? Professors used to trade in facts; now, almost as often as their students, they begin sentences with "I feel like . . ."[4]

I found it pleasurably annoying to read this *Guardian* reviewer, swimming around as he is like one shootable fish in the crowded barrel of pundits lamenting all this feeling talk. I did not respond to his review with the same delight as a friend who cackled, via text, "I *live* to betray scholarship." But I did roll my eyes, in much the same way I have been rolling my eyes at similar critics since the beginning of my experience as an editor, when I systematically rejected all the many essays pitched to the *Los Angeles Review of Books* making this literally same, as it were, "I feel like" point. Other venues took a different tack, hence the crowded barrel. One especially whipped-up *New York Times* editorial, for instance, went so far as to portray the phrase "I feel like" as a kind of violence. For this writer, confusing ideas with feelings, even just rhetorically, doesn't just blur "sober analysis" (as *The Guardian* critic had worried) but assaults it: "'I feel like' turns emotion into a cudgel that smashes the distinction . . . between evidence out in the world and internal sentiments known only to each of us."[5]

A cudgel! You don't need to be an expert in close reading to notice this editorial's efforts to instill a sense of fear in the reader. The language of feeling is powerful, the editorial tells us, but in a messy way: it threatens a vulnerable distinction the editorial tries to make us want to protect. The author of this *New York Times* editorial teaches history at the University of Virginia and identifies in the article as a humanist, expressing a humanist concern about the power of language. She does not position herself against emotions, but rather against a phrase that (she claims) confuses thought and emotions, perpetuating a world of emotionalizations, and in so doing erodes thought's capacity to produce democratic exchange and to grapple with serious problems. For the writer, feelings can't lead to exchange, and thus they must be kept where they are: safely on their proper side of a vital—and vulnerable—"distinction" between the world and the internal.

I found this a strange claim. In order to support it, the *New York Times* critic quotes several expert sources—a historian, a linguist, a sociologist, a neuroscientist—all of whom share her worry about "I feel like" as a phrase. None of these experts, however, proposes the idea that those of us who evoke feelings (rhetorically or otherwise) in conversations might be doing so because we believe some important social knowledge might be gleaned from feelings. And here is a strange omission, for someone who identifies as a humanist. In the years since 1977, when Raymond Williams introduced the phrase "structure of feeling" to describe "social experience" that is "not yet recognized as social," and 1978, when Audre Lorde parsed how feelings like joy can "bridge" the "threat of . . . difference," some of the most formidable minds in humanistic study have concerned themselves precisely with the social relationships personal feelings reveal and shape.[6] These writers are only two oft-cited examples of the many humanist scholars whose thinking developed in tandem with mid-century feminist and minoritarian political work. Since then, guided by Eve Kosofsky Sedgwick, Lauren Berlant, and Sianne Ngai, among others, humanist study has been marked for decades by "the affective turn," exploring the many ways in which feelings, even when felt individually, are hardly personal. They are, among other things, points of evidence that clue us in to the conditions by which human life is evaluated as resource worthy, or not.

Part of what makes humanists humanists is our orientation toward, broadly conceived, the emotional facets of experience. We write about aesthetics and spiritual experiences and about how cultures organize those experiences into and through structures of value. We write about intangible values that structure performances, interactions, and events. While, certainly, humanists pursue many kinds of scholarship and not all would identify with this characterization, a skilled investment in discerning and describing ephemeral and often emotional experience—in taking emotional experience seriously, as a mover and shaker in the world—distinguishes the humanities from the social and so-called hard sciences, at least in part.

What troubles me about the anti-I-feel-like pundits, then, is not only how their account of rational scholarship discounts my own personal project (although, that is super annoying) but also and more significantly how they draw an implicit and devaluing connection between a venue like *Avidly* and the humanities as a branch of knowledge. If to assert that feelings matter to publics is to "smash" a distinction on which both democracy and scholarship depend, all the humanities are potentially to blame, no matter how reasonably humanists write. To accept that writing *with* feeling, about feeling, can't be scholarship because feelings can't be "evidence in the world" leads pretty quickly to the belief (or feeling?) that humanist disciplines don't produce scholarship, or expertise, because they grapple with something, feelings, that aren't really in the world, and only matter, to the extent they do, personally rather than collectively or socially. By this account, all the humanities are reducible to navel-gazing. And who (to return to the questions of the last chapter) would want to major in that?

The authors of these *Guardian* and *New York Times* reviews don't say, overtly, that they disrespect the humanities. But they don't need to say it. They demonstrate their disregard through their failures to know about (in the case of the *Guardian* critic) or cite (in the *New York Times*) humanities scholarship, even when they are writing about topics within the humanities. They fail to acknowledge humanities expertise as a valuable resource. And thus (rather like the Notre Dame legal scholars who can see my writing only as evidence, not argument) these pundits don't pay citational respect to a scholarly resource they don't see as one.

It's because I feel protective of both *Avidly* and the humanities—and, frankly, of feelings—that I'm spending a long time on these points: first, that feelings are in the world, and second, that humanist scholarship is really good at describing *how* feelings are in the world, partly because we're good at writing feelingly, including the feeling of "reasonable." My concern isn't just with how outsiders characterize the humanities (and *Avidly*); I want also to object to the ways some of us in the humanities can buy into this divide by either disavowing the emotional content of scholarly humanities writing or, conversely, by exaggerating or lamenting scholarly writing's lack of feeling. We can't defend humanities scholarship, and we can't make our writing feel better, if we deny how much feelings matter to what we, in our humanist writing, always do.

In writing this chapter, I spoke to several humanities professors about what it would be helpful for a writing guide to say. Many described a cultural divide in their departments, whereby some faculty failed to take seriously graduate students or colleagues who were writing scholarship in more personal, formally inventive styles, and especially graduate students who aimed to write, with expertise, for nonscholarly audiences. These faculty members did not take such writing seriously and they did not want to learn how to teach or evaluate it. Their job was scholarship: these feelings and styles were not scholarship, and not their job. The professors I talked to, on the other hand, worried about how this judgment transmitted to students, who were hesitant to admit their interest in (or, given the job market, practical need to learn) such styles, because they feared they would lose their departments' respect and the practical resources (attention, funding) that go along with it. As a professor of writing who navigates my university's sometimes unpredictable resource allocation to my program, I am sympathetic to the students; I sometimes feel that there's a strange "not our class, dear" (class, here, as both status and course) taint that attaches to both the teaching of writing and the active *learning* of writing, especially in new critical forms.

To what extent is this a problem? I don't want to attack a straw man and I'm certain that the conversations I have are shaped by my background, position, and social world. The way that humanities professors feel about their students' writing, and the correlation of those feelings with rewarding graduate school experiences, would be a complex and worthy object of study. I certainly don't want to further perpetuate the devaluing of conventional humanities scholarship by implying that professors shouldn't prioritize writing it. But to the extent that humanities faculty fail to take seriously changing, experimental, affect-rich written forms through which humanities expertise can be conveyed, they replicate and exacerbate how culture writ large can dismiss humanities expertise, because of its association with feelings.

For my part, I do see a significant difference between the writing that I publish in *Avidly* (whether I write or edit it) and academic writing. Venues like *Avidly* draw on expertise, but they aim for different editorial standards and durational significance: they are neither peer reviewed nor institutionally archived. These editorial and publication processes carry an affective force, particularly in moments of professional crisis, as the next chapter will explore. But that's a far cry from saying that writing in *Avidly*, or other nonscholarly writing by humanists, is drunk on feelings while scholarship (humanities or otherwise) soberly analyzes evidence. In fact, I would say that sober *is* a feeling, in addition to a biological state, one that our craft practices can generate or not, and that sober is only one of many feelings that infuse academic writing of all kinds, both in its production and in its reception. There are differences between writing feelingly about feeling and writing thinkingly about feeling (both take place in all sorts of venues), but this stylistic variability doesn't produce the same differences in knowledge structures that publication processes do.

A lot of the expert writers who seek out *Avidly* do so because of their hope that writing for *Avidly* will provide a conduit for emotions, in a way that (many of us have been trained to believe) conventional academic forms do not. They may be wanting, for instance, to entertain rather than educate; they may want to express some emotions that they are having about how other people are feeling (or reasoning); they may want to write about an experience or insight outside their expertise. They may want their writing to enter a conversation with a quicker turnaround. *Avidly*'s editorial modes exist to evaluate a piece of writing's skill at accomplishing these aims. What extrascholarly forms don't exist to do, no matter how they do or don't support emotional writing, is to indulge writers who imagine affective writing as a realm of wonderful expressive freedom that scholarship doesn't offer. That's not how it works, I want to tell them. Stepping away from the particular architecture of peer review doesn't free you from all structure, all constraint. Feelings may be different from reasons, and some feelings feel better than reasons, but writing about feelings, or at least writing well about feelings, isn't a less complicated activity than writing about reasons.

Feelings matter, as affect theory teaches us, because they're reactions between our bodies and the world. For writing about feelings to matter, then, it must own its responsibility to bodies and the world. That kind of writerly accountability is hard. It doesn't necessarily feel good. The freedom it offers comes with the necessity of exposure and without the promise of affirmation. It is a craft practice you must rigorously pursue. As an editor friend of mine with whom I discussed this chapter asked me: "Will you please tell people that writing about feelings doesn't mean you can make shit up?"

*

In the '60s and '70s, many humanities experts experimented with how new written forms might integrate liberation politics into institutional structures. Like them, humanists now are renegotiating feeling and expert form based on historical and political motives, as well as intellectual and aesthetic ones. That we can identify the historical motives of affect-rich writing should remind us that reasonable styles are similarly historically negotiated. Despite what some people seem to believe—and here I'll point back at our poor *Guardian* and *New York Times* writers for two examples ready to hand—there never was a moment when a reasonable style was truth universally acknowledged, free from power and history. No matter how much nostalgic yearning you might feel for it, there's no good old days of rational argument to return to, back before all these personal experiences came in to gum up the works.

The best response to such a fantasy that I know comes in *Objectivity* (2007), Lorraine Daston and Peter Galison's jaw-droppingly good intellectual history. The book focuses on the rise of objectivity as what they call an "epistemic virtue." Rather than an enduring human value, or a mode of inquiry emerging simultaneously with the Enlightenment, objectivity was a surprisingly late comer to Western science, appearing in the middle and later parts of the nineteenth century. Observational science has been around for a long time. "Objective" observations came to be scientifically desirable, Daston and Galison show, at the same time that scientists came to understand their own "subjectivity" as a contingency they needed to manage in specific ways. Subjectivity traveled, not always consistently, into science from the philosophy of Immanuel Kant. In the post-Kantian moment, scientists across fields took up the idea that subjectivity existed, that the self of the scientist was active and prone to projecting its own beliefs onto the world, and that it thus had to be managed by practices of self-discipline. The ideal scientific self, at the historic moment "objectivity" emerged as a goal, was both energetic and, with practice, self-controlled.

Objectivity, the book, but maybe also the concept, is also a genre study. Daston and Galison don't use the phrase. But they unfurl an intellectual history of surpassing significance by tracking a particular genre of book, the scientific atlas, as the scientists producing them reworked their generic norms over a few hundred years. Atlases are collections of related scientific images, "they are the dictionaries of the sciences of the eye," and they "train the eye to pick out certain kind of objects as exemplary . . . and to regard them in a certain way."[7] Atlases are thus a genre designed to offer genre training to their readers, who learned how images mobilized (in the words of one useful genre theorist, John Frow) "a shared convention with a social force."[8] Objective images used the genre of the atlas to show how they were different from previous scientific images, in the same way that Bob Dylan (this is an annoyingly dudish example, I'm sorry) famously used the Newport Folk Festival to show how his plugged-in folk music was different from previous folk music. Daston and Galison's book compiles and compares images from books that compile and compare images, in order to show the changes in scientific norms such genre comparisons reveal.

I recommend this highly enjoyable book to anyone interested in the history of ideas and/or good writing. It is not about good writing per se, but it describes the complex problems of representation that have long swirled around scholars as they sought to share what they understood to be true in the world. Representational strategies, Daston and Galison show, change in tandem with historically situated epistemological beliefs about what it's like to be a person, with variously "human" skills and limitations. By attending to these representational transformations, *Objectivity*, a book "about" a history of scientific illustrators, becomes helpful to us, as humanist writers. *Objectivity* helps us see, quite literally, how qualities like objectivity emerge historically as *styles*, that writers and other illustrators can learn, and also learn differently.

Some events in the book's story get at this point and why it matters. *Objectivity* begins in 1877, as the physicist Arthur Worthington drew image after image of falling liquid drops, "untangling the complex process of fluid flow."[9] Worthington, initially, was after "a systematic, visual classification."[10] But then his method for capturing these drops changed. By 1894, Worthington was photographing rather than drawing his drops, rendering them in a different medium and also style. Photographing the falling drops of liquid showed asymmetrical jets and bubbles, not the "perfect" types Worthington had sketched previously. As he gained different ways to represent these distinct moments in the liquids' movement, Worthington gained both new understanding of the liquids *and*, and this is crucial for the book's argument, a new sense of what "understanding" would mean, filtered through a new belief system about what a scientist should be and do.[11] Daston and Galison locate in Worthington and some (although not all) of his peers a "sea change in the observational sciences," which were now motivated by a desire to achieve "that new form of unprejudiced, unthinking, blind sight we call scientific objectivity."[12]

Staring at *Objectivity*'s illustrations, I had a jolting revelation about something that we might call academic style. The revelation was about a parallel—not a causal or historical relation, but a formal one—between how Worthington's photographs sought to capture liquids and how humanists' academic sentences seek to capture our own slippery topics. Worthington, in both his modes of imaging, was trying to understand motion by making it slow down—making it stand still. In his "objective" images, he also wanted to reveal, with precision, the idiosyncrasies of a specific object in a specific moment. This, I thought, is what academic sentences seem also to do.

As an editor who helps writers move between scholarly and other venues, I've often had cause to note some specific prose strategies university-trained writers frequently use. These are our use of deictics (such as the one that begins this sentence), our use of the verb "to be," and our abundant use of prepositional phrases. The effect of these stylistic decisions is to mirror the "epistemic virtues" of "objective" images. These academic deictics, like this one, still the spinning world, making their objects available for description and analysis. The prepositional phrases scrape nouns away from "this," attempting to add precision about where and when this is, often in the unwieldy, unpredictable fashion of Worthington's asymmetrical jets. The key noun of the sentence often doesn't change or change anything else: it simply is.[13] Presenting our evidence in an objectivized form, we strip our will from it. "This is," we write. "There was." Our acts of judgment appear as observations. Our recurring use of the passive voice intensifies our performance of selflessness. Like scientists, we developed representational processes to help us present ourselves as the kind of observers we wanted to be.

A full history of academic style is (is) beyond my scope here. Did the splitting of the arts and the sciences that took place concurrently with the rise of objectivity influence how humanists, in their study of the arts, sought to stylistically represent their study as knowledge, rather than art? How has humanists' long-standing status negotiation with the sciences influenced our changing modes of prose? These are worthy questions to which I don't have the answers. Even presenting my own observations about academic style in a historical context reveals the limits of what I'm noticing: not every academic depends on formations of "to be" (although, if you start watching for it, I promise you'll see it everywhere) and not *only* academics depend on that formation.

What I do think *Objectivity* forces us to see, and this is (this is) why I'm spending so much time on it, in addition to the fact that it's so good and such a completely excellent model of research, is (is) this (this): the sentences of humanities experts have an illustrative, representational function for our knowledge making, and the styles of our sentences reflect our (changing) values of what we should represent and what a "good" or meaningful or useful representation should be like. Comparing humanist sentences to scientific images helps those of us whose examples work through words to consider how our own representational styles demonstrate particular epistemic virtues that establish and enhance our credibility as resource-worthy researchers in a community of intellectual exchange.

I'm taking the long route through this example in the hopes that the windup will drive home a point that many humanities experts accept in the abstract yet seem not to apply consistently to their own practice. The claim, as obvious as it sounds, is that the neutral voice of reason, as it dominates academic writing practice, is neither neutral nor (if we see "reasonable," as I do, as yet another shifting epistemic virtue) impersonal. *Instead, "reasonable" tones and styles enable a kind of epistemic virtue signaling.* They develop from—and when deployed, reinforce—specific ideas about personhood and interpersonal interaction. Those ideas are products of history.

We could put it differently and say: The prose styles currently coded as "reasonable" evolved to manage particular concerns about power, and to bolster particular power relations. In this way they are like any other style. So in making this claim, I'm not implying that academic or reasonable styles have a unique or necessarily more troubling entanglement with power than any other style. I'm asserting my intellectual principles, as a historicist, about how language always works. Epistemic virtue signaling of every kind, whether reasonable, sentimental, or radical, works because it supports the needs of real people, in history, trying to do things with words to make the worlds in which they want to live.

*

Let's go back to butts. In physiology, in feminism, in critical race theory, in plastic surgery, in running pants, butts matter extremely, because, as the cultural critic Heather Radke writes in *Butts: A Backstory* (2023), "Women's butts have been used as a means to create and reinforce racial hierarchies, as a barometer for the virtues of hard work, and as a measure of sexual desire and availability."[14] Radke's book draws on, among other framing sources, Sander Gilman's classic study "Black Bodies, White Bodies: Toward an Iconography of Female Sexuality in Late Nineteenth-Century Art, Medicine, and Literature" (1985), which shows that "the buttocks have an ever-changing symbolic value" in matters of raced, gendered, embodiment.[15] Thus, while sometimes embarrassing to discuss, butts are a good point of entry into the methodologies of reasons and feelings. (Note: we are only one paragraph into this discussion and already I have made two inadvisable puns. Don't worry; more are coming.)

Butts are real; you can see, touch, change, and measure them. They are, without a doubt, evidence in the world. Yet when you see or measure a butt, what are you learning? Of what, exactly, are they evidence? The symbolic intensity around butts means the "structure of feeling" around them remains, to use Williams's phrase, "in solution," shiftingly hard to get a grip on, even for the person who has the feelings, or the butt. Butts transmit such excessive meaning that normal styles of "reasonable" writing start to feel inadequate. It's hard to say "this is" what a butt means, in any particular situation. Puns proliferate (as per the title *Butts: A Backstory*) because they demonstrate fluid signification at play. Despite or because of this symbolic intensity, and despite the extent to which some people (more than others) are judged by their butts, excessive display of butt attention, butt soreness, or butt pride can be damaging to those people's ethos in many discursive situations, perhaps such as this one.

Almost any expert humanist who is writing today, I would guess and hope, has at least a passing knowledge of how pseudoscientific taxonomies of the hips, butts, and thighs have been deployed to support racist social orders. Both Radke and Gilman, for instance, draw on Sarah Baartman's story to demonstrate how butts have been taken as the observable signs of racialized intangible qualities—intelligence, appetite management, and more. It might be slightly a stretch to say that nineteenth-century European scientists appraised butts like Baartman's in order to evaluate the internal capacity for reason, but butts have certainly been measured to evaluate other internal capacities, such as discipline, which are pegged (sorry) to reason. Such discriminatory beliefs were not abandoned in the nineteenth century. Contemporary scholars of racial embodiment such as Sabrina Strings demonstrate how pseudoscientific beliefs about race, reason, and body size persist today, making it difficult for many people, particularly women of color, to gain epistemic authority over even their own experiences, whether visceral or observational.

All this is to say that many people who wanted to prove they were intellectually, civilizationally, or physically/racially superior used butts as the physical evidence to prove that such desires were reasonable. This bleak history becomes useful for our purposes. Butts insist on the embodied history of reason, and on the historically specific hierarchies attaching some bodies to unreason. In the conceptual difficulty of butts, the emotional and self-interested history of reason becomes crystal clear. You might put it this way: reasonable styles feel good to some people for the same reason that some people feel good in Lululemon pants: because they highlight and flatter a comfortable relation to historically powerful types of personhood.

For others, "reasonable" styles will feel uncomfortable. Such discomfort isn't unreasonable. It's a productive feeling that reveals a lived relation to the world's histories. When writers reject the friction of a bad stylistic fit, they design (in both scholarly and nonscholarly writing) stylistic approaches that enable new purchase on the world. To even make this point seems superfluous, given the tremendous amount of evidence that can support it. I am thinking, here, of contemporary writers such as Sara Ahmed, Judith Butler, Alexis Pauline Gumbs, Saidiya Hartman, Cathy Park Hong, Audre Lorde, Fred Moten, Adrienne Rich, Christina Sharpe, Hortense Spillers, and the many others whose work has *through style* as well as through claim expanded the boundaries of what it's possible for humanists to know.

*

To put my political cards fully on the table, here's how I understand the situation that humanist writers face: the debates about reasons, feelings, and representational style we have inherited and that we live out in our writing took formative shape, along with our institutions and our disciplines, across a long human era significantly structured by global slavery, colonialism, and the heterosexist practices that helped rationalize slavery and colonialism.[16] This coextensiveness inheres in our writing and we can't shake it off or pretend it's not there. It shapes how writing feels, for everyone. For some of us it feels enabling; for others, less so. But to say that reasonable writing, or that academic style, as a product of Western-influenced orders of reason, will always carry some legacy of the worst parts of what those orders can do—as, certainly, it does—isn't at all to say that academic style has no capacity to transform or illuminate those orders. As *Objectivity* teaches us, all our styles have histories: none are free of the world, and thus all are at play in the world. In fact, because academic style, like all styles, works generically (which is to say, by evoking and deploying communally held modes of recognition) it's inherently available not only to repetition but also to productive parodic transformation.

From this claim I want to spell out some further consequences for this conversation, consequences that emerged for me as I read scholars whose own styles and practices often run counter to my own, often because of the intellectual differences between us. I cite them out of respect, and as a part of my own project to further dislodge the belief that experimental, radical writing is necessarily more affective than conventional forms. I also want to return to the questions of why what humanists do has worth.

One consequence would be that, as Amanda Anderson so beautifully argues in *How We Argue Now* (a book about argument, not directly prose style, but as I'm saying, these topics intertwine), even the most seemingly depersonalized claims reveal "the aspiration to critical distance as an embedded practice," which for Anderson, much as for Worthington, *Objectivity*'s physicist, represents "an ongoing achievement" of personal, often emotional, effort, undertaken out of a commitment to ethical world-making.[17] Academic style doesn't lack feeling; it displays a relationship to feelings, based on values. Pushed further, all styles enact values of personhood; those values include hierarchies of emotions that might be stylistically displayed. These hierarchies are up for debate.[18]

A second consequence: not only do different styles manifest different modes of embeddedness; they also enable different modes of knowledge production. Styles are methods. "Method stirs the graspable world so that it responds to one's curiosity, whatever that may be, following whatever practices are suited to the task."[19] Here the literary critic Jonathan Kramnik frames out a structure for the multidisciplinary university, with an eye toward situating literary study within it as one discipline with specific methodological skill in discerning "a part of the world . . . important for collective flourishing."[20] I'm extending Kramnik's claims to propose that just as universities (and the world) need many disciplines, so do disciplines need many styles. For humanists, because writing is a key knowledge-making practice, and because writing style embeds modes and values of personhood, and finally because as humanists our task is to explore modes and values of personhood, we're going to need multiple styles if we care, as we should, to explore multiple modes of being.[21]

These consequences may seem obvious. I hope so. If they do, perhaps you will also accept a final argument about our resources and respect, as humanists. It's accepting this final point that has the most consequences for our collectivity, as we find ways to value the work we do. Here we go:

To the extent that writing is where humanist claims about human experience become convincing, or not, if you are teaching your students to understand the world through humanist methods, and to gain or share their understanding in humanism's written forms, you are teaching them writing. You are teaching them writing regardless about how you feel about your own status vis-à-vis your university's writing faculty or your own willingness to learn about writing or the teaching of writing. And, especially if you never address writing or style explicitly, if in your classroom norms of academic style transmit "untaught," then the kinds of knowledge as well as the epistemic virtues that those styles contain won't go unlearned; rather, they'll become naturalized, gaining generic force, with a political purchase on the world. So regardless of how you think or feel about what you do, and no matter what else you do, if you assign writing assignments, if you *assign humanist readings,* you are teaching writing; you are a teacher of writing. And because you are, you are also tasked with the responsibility that comes from teaching your students the embedded epistemic values of how humanist writing either should feel, or can feel, or—when we are at our best and most expansive—*might* feel. In our classrooms, every day, we teach our students and ourselves how it feels for the crafts of humanist writing to have, or not, worth.

THREE

Some Feelings About Writing in Public; Some Reasons for a Counterpublic Humanities

In 2017, I walked to the front of a crowded hotel ballroom. The ballroom didn't swirl with dancers. Instead, filling the room were rows of those ugly round-back convention chairs, the kind made to motivate wedding havers to cough up the extra money for chair covers. In these chairs sat attendees of that year's Association for the Study of Arts of the Present conference. During crowded sessions, those chairs always seem a little too close together, especially for a group of people demographically inclined to carry multiple tote bags. I'm sure that day I was carrying multiple tote bags. I headed to the front because I was one of the several speakers on the roundtable that had drawn together this tote-bag-carrying crowd. We were editors there to talk about the *Los Angeles Review of Books* "at five." The panel was in the ballroom because in that era, and still even now, panels at academic conferences about any kind of extra-academic publication always draw a crowd. One way to make academics crowd together is to offer the prospect of writing for someone else.

This chapter begins to tell a material, even technological, history of that prospect, that hope or possibility, in one era when it was put into action. One reason to recount such a history is to give some guidance and encouragement to writers, now, who are themselves prospecting extra-academic publication as a potential resource for writing that feels meaningful, feels good. But I also tell this history in an attempt to treat an itch, almost an irritation, I have with how the general topic of that panel is often described: as writing for the "public humanities." I'm not the only one to have some level of allergy to the term but, given my biography, mine might seem a strange and unfortunate reaction. I was on the panel because from 2013 to 2016 I was *LARB*'s senior humanities editor, and because *Avidly*, the online magazine I had started in 2012 with Jordan Stein and Sarah Blackwood, and that Blackwood and I then still coedited, was one of *LARB*'s successful "channels." My experience was also unusual on the panel because I had seemingly spun off from *LARB* into even publics that were both broader and, well, different: I had a side hustle (short-lived, it turned out) writing celebrity profiles for women's magazines like *InStyle* and *Self*. The month before the panel, my interview with Gwyneth Paltrow was the cover story in the premier issue of Paltrow's (also short-lived) print publication, *Goop* magazine. The cover of the magazine displays Paltrow immersed in a mud bath, literal goop. It was hard for me to tell, at that ASAP panel, whether interviewing Paltrow put me at a career high or a career low. We were all there because we were interested in writing in new ways, for new audiences. Is Paltrow an interesting new audience? Is she the public? No one was less certain about this question than me.

According to Paltrow, mud baths are supposed to feel healing, and I'm prepared to believe they're great. Yet the mud bath also gives me an apt metaphor for my uncomfortable response to some discourse about the public humanities. Are they the panacea we imagine them to be? Might they also be a distraction, or even an accelerant, rather than a cure?

Today, in the possibility of the public humanities, writers, universities, and grant-giving institutions like the NEH seem to be finding a vision for the humanities' future. We are in a crisis of status, we humanists, and in the public, we can, the thinking goes, be restored. Here's something funny: when *I* was in a crisis of status as a humanist, I turned toward writing for what I guess would now be called the public humanities. I was, indeed, reenergized. But not in the way, or the for the reasons, that some public humanities discourse might lead one to expect.

I am concerned about how, in the last decade, the hopes brought toward nonscholarly publishing seemed to have scaled up, from the personal to the institutional. For all my love of unconventional publication, this transition still strikes me as weird. Or rather, it's not strange to me that universities might want to support scholars in developing the complex skill set of multiaudience critical writing, which after all is a long-standing intellectual craft practice. But I am surprised at how universities sometimes describe such support: as a response to an ongoing crisis in public consensus and the status of university-based expertise. When I find that lofty hope percolating through university websites, it often feels out of balance. It feels inflated, the naively overhyped counterbalance to another mood that, the next chapter will explain, I find equally grating: the mournful dirge university-trained writers can sound when they consider writing for university-facilitated audiences.

Here's the thing: I've spent enough time in the public humanities trenches—enough time writing, editing, wrestling the content management system (CMS), scheduling the social media posts—that the particular mode of hope often traveling along with public humanities interest feels not just naive, but sort of worrisomely so. And so my frustration with the term remains. I find the term infelicitous. I find the idea (speaking my truth, here) unexamined. And thus, I guess as a result, I find the affect surrounding "public humanities" discourse to be . . . well, the word that keeps coming to mind is "irritating." Like mud in weird places, it chafes. What is this public we're imagining? And what version of ourselves—our humanist identities—can we believe might successfully be welcomed there?

*

Almost a decade after that ASAP panel, we are in a new era. In an excellent essay, the critic Ryan Ruby wonders: Might ours be considered a "golden age"? In the essay, Ruby neatly defines a set of central terms for contemporary criticism, "public" among them. "By 'public,'" he writes, "I mean that the intended audience for this criticism is external to academia."[1] Even when the writers and readers of public writing developed their expertise in universities, journalistic histories, rather than scholarly ones, shape the practices and protocols of "public" writing, from prose style to editorial oversight to distribution strategy.

Ruby is extremely correct that the "historical norms of journalism" determine how public writing works, and like Ruby, I emphasize in this chapter that norms and practices matter to what writing can do.[2] I want to highlight, though, along with Ruby, how histories of academia (specifically academic hiring) profoundly influence how public writing *feels* for university-trained writers. For writers who gained their expertise in universities, academic cultures, histories, and hierarchies form the affective backdrop against which most writing takes place. Those cultures and hierarchies are currently undergoing strange transformations (as they were, also, in 2017). Increasing numbers of experts, like myself, remain tethered to academia's resources, but by threads that don't weave into the traditional fabric of a tenure-track faculty. This situation creates new shades of affective experience for extra-academic writing without erasing the university's emotional pull. We don't leave these tethered emotions behind when we enter the public. They shape what we want from the public. And they shape how it feels to craft a sentence, to arrange words around an object or topic we love or hate or have come to understand.

When I started editing at *LARB*, I was in the last year of a luxurious three-year Mellon-funded postdoctoral fellowship at UCLA. The fellowship had appeared in my life like a genie popping out of a dirty lamp. I'd been scrubbing through the detritus of the 2009 job market, trying to find some way to cast some light on my future, when all of a sudden, all my hiring wishes came true. But, as so often occurs in stories, it's hard to know how to make the right wishes. Three years into my fellowship, my life had shot deep roots into Los Angeles (my husband's job, my small children's childcare and new friends, my own transplanted heart thriving in the surprise magic of Southern California's abundant weird soil). I didn't want to move, even if my family could afford to, which probably it could not. But I also knew there would be no job in UCLA's English department waiting for me at the end of my fellowship; they had recently made two hires in my field.

For all the privilege of my position—and a three-year post-doc with low teaching and benefits is extreme privilege, for sure—I still faced an uncertain future. I had always been told that finding a tenure-track job would be unlikely. In 2013, it seemed nearly impossible. I didn't know what kind of job I might find, and that uncertainty made me feel like I didn't know who I was or who I would be. I have compared notes with many people who have endured the ongoing iterations of the job market's collapse. "I was so sad my mouth hurt," I once told a friend, who nodded sagely. Yes. Her mouth hurt from job market sadness too. Neither one of us knew who we would be if our job was not to speak our expertise.

Although academic writing was not the source of the job market crash I experienced, my writing carried a disproportionate affective burden for what it meant to me. Academic writing was not the academy or the job market, but because writing was a practical means by which an academic job was (or in my case, was not) earned, my feelings about the academic job market shifted, through a kind of emotional alchemy, onto my feelings about academic writing. My personal sense of failure and grief attached to a norm of prose, a strategy for publication. My fellowship meant that I had time to write. I couldn't use it. When I sat down to my in-progress monograph, I felt the collapse of the job market at the level of the sentence.

Academic writing gets a lot of grief for being "bad." I don't think it is. I think it's good. But it can definitely feel bad to produce, sentence by sentence, a piece of writing that needs to not only describe its object but also defend your ideas *and* your intelligence, your financial security *and* the value of your expertise—in the largest sense, to make the case that humanities expertise itself is worth having. Here, too, we find a collision of scales. Although no one sentence can push back the tides of neoliberalism as they press into the university, or the university's own hierarchies, every sentence can feel burdened with such out-of-proportion tasks. Even when the sentences produced under these conditions are good to read, they're often terrible to write.[3]

When I started *Avidly* with friends, and when I started editing for *LARB*, I was driven by a possibility I didn't quite have the language, then, to put into words: What would happen if the job of my sentences was to affirm my relation to an object of attention, rather than to protect myself within a precarious system? What world would such writing require, and what worlds could it create? What version of myself could such writing allow me to be? These are questions humanists are still asking. We write to the public to try and answer them. But the public is an abstract concept. Our personal hopes for what the public can offer us are particular. And our practical means of accessing that mysterious thing, the public—the infrastructures along which writing can move—are always historically specific, concrete.

*

The job market crash that significantly determined the shape of my career (which may well be a different crash than the one shaping your career, or your students' careers) took place in 2008 and 2009. It happened in tandem with the banking crisis and the election of Barack Obama. These events, the financial crisis particularly, have a well-documented relationship to university hiring.

Less frequently mentioned in histories of that moment in the humanities is a simple product rollout: WordPress's 2008 launch of its new administrative dashboard.[4] This dashboard, with its suite of easy-to-use templates like "Magazine," made managing a magazine-like website simple, even for non–tech experts. These new website templates allowed their users to signal aesthetically a more professionalized relationship to the material they published. Unlike the simple scroll of most blogs or pages on Tumblr, sites managed through WordPress's dashboard could easily arrange themselves in columns, with the appearance of a magazine or newspaper. They allowed you to highlight authors' names as bylines, showing that authorship, and thus also editorship, mattered to the publication.

Was the new WordPress dashboard smaller potatoes for the academy than the financial crisis or the election of Obama, America's first Black president and the only nerd president of my lifetime? Yes, absolutely. Yet it matters significantly to the history of the public humanities. It meant that all of us nerds, worried about our futures, could take publishing into our own hands. WordPress's dashboard, with its shifts from previous platforms like Blogger, allowed nerds to write expertly, for the benefit of each other, "in public" and also in a venue. We could be niche, without limiting ourselves to nicheness. We could create new editorial standards of expertise, and new modes for its expression.

The early 2000s moment feels like a lifetime ago, I realize. But it's worth diving into that wayback machine, as it were, because the florescence of independent publishing the moment brought into being still registers, if indirectly, in what it's like for expert writers now to sit down to the page.[5] I'm interested in a few specific changes that took place after the turn-of-the-millennium emergence of Web 2.0, which is a now geriatric-sounding term for the shift toward a mobile and responsive internet environment, one that invited user interaction and offered ease of contribution. In that context, blogs and sites devoted to social commentary (of television, fashion, celebrities, politics) flourished. In 2006 facebook became universally available; its newsfeed allowed us to make our public reading public;[6] in 2007, Apple released the first iteration of the iPhone, bringing digital writing into previously impossible-to-fathom interstices of our lives. Suddenly, words could reach readers throughout their days, as they traveled through different versions of (and scenes for) themselves.

It's hard to capture the amount of amazing independent magazines that started right around that time. Facebook and Twitter feeds aggregated into our lives the writing that WordPress made possible to aggregate into magazines, where editorial oversight made individual streams into writerly scenes. A quick gloss of some relevant outlets may be useful here: *Bookslut* was founded in 2002; Gawker Media and *The Believer* in 2003; *Jezebel* in 2007; *The Point* in 2008; *The New Inquiry* and *The Awl* in 2009, the same year that all six of my MLA job interviews were canceled because funding for all the jobs had been withdrawn. Feminist-specific venues like *The Hairpin* and *The Toast* launched in 2010 and 2013, respectively; in 2011 Bill Simmons, that brilliantly loathsome Boston sports fan, launched *Grantland*, which felt particularly significant because his magazine's strategy seemed to involve hoovering up a wide-array of clever bloggers and giving them health insurance in exchange for attaching their cleverness to his masthead. In 2015, MTV News followed suit, hiring an editor, Dan Fierman, away from *Grantland* and announcing a commitment to long-form digital journalism. I was not the only young academic of the moment worried about my own ability to get secure job benefits. It seemed marvelous that such idiosyncratic writers, young smart people on the internet, were suddenly staff writers.

What I'm describing is the emergence of a particular public that was different—and, for humanities experts, had significantly different emotional effects—than the one created by legacy publications. They didn't aspire to general interest or the broadest possible reach. These were publications that, like us, had a sense of specialty. They had deep knowledge of their topics, and a careful practice of inhabiting strong sensibilities. They celebrated nuanced ways of looking. Where did they look? At granular details. This was a habit of attention that had grown out of two powerful internet cultures: the world of recaps and the world of blogs.[7] While these are distinguishable spheres, they share a habit of intense looking and commenting, whether at television shows (even bad ones) or lives (even unremarkable ones). They demonstrated that acts of attention, especially when those acts of attention were filtered through a strong theory of value (such as feminism), can endow facets of life that had seemed mundane and minor with great fascination, interest, and even pleasure.

This moment in independent publishing—and its cultivation of distinct, particular audiences—felt tailor-made to both the skills and the desires of those of us trained in the critical humanities. We were good at paying attention. And we wanted to find parts of ourselves—and write toward parts of others—to which our sentences had previously not had access. So it's perhaps not surprising that underemployed academics followed magazine-making suit. In the wake of the job market crash, public-facing digital venues created by academics surged into existence—*Bully Bloggers* (2009), *Tropics of Meta* (2010), *Avidly* (2012), *Los Angeles Review of Books* (2012), *Public Books* (2012), *Aeon* (2012), and the rest of *LARB*'s channels. We had witnessed bloggers establish themselves as viable, communal *worlds*. Why couldn't we do the same?[8]

Publications like those listed above are definitely public-facing. But it's important to recognize their shared aslant relation to both mainstream journalism and academic publishing. Avowedly niche and nerdy, they remain at the fringes of the sanctuaries that either university archives or a more clearly for-profit structure might provide (*LARB* and *Aeon* are nonprofit; I believe the other publications listed above draw significantly on volunteered labor). Even while owning their relation to institutions, they improvise their own shelters. While these shelters take different forms and have different, we might say, vibes, all of them ask their authors to draw their expertise outside institutional hierarchies. Obviously, publications generated at the fringes of university life remain influenced by academic status. But, just as a bar or a pool or a coffee shop or a gym or a camping site (which might be the spatial analogues of various publications I can think of) might be influenced by, yet different from, the wood-paneled and unfortunately carpeted academic conference rooms I have known, academically aslant publications unsettle institutional authority and modes of engagement. Such an unsettling in fact provided an opening for transformation in how we understood the community our published writing hailed. It's not that we were writing for different audiences, it's worth saying directly. We were writing for the same people we might have otherwise—the same readers who might have read our scholarship—but we were writing with a changed sense of what drew us together, and how we might feel about that connection.

To implement this transformation, we needed new skills beyond our expertise. To put it in the words of my friend and frequent collaborator Phillip Maciak, the present iteration of the public humanities emerged the way it did because "we wanted writing to feel different, and we back-engineered forms to produce those different feelings."[9] Here, Maciak connects an emotional state (one created by economic and professional precarity) to a shift in craft and technological access.

Those of us experts involved in editing and writing for public-facing venues weren't wrong to think that our habits of granular attention could serve us. But we had to learn how to write sentences, paragraphs, claims—to craft structures—that could connect with people in different places than the ones where we were used to finding them. I mean both different parts of their lives and also visually and physically different interfaces and screens. What did an iPhone's screen mean for a paragraph? What did a changed job market mean for a reader? Most of the readers who cared about our topics maintained, as I did, ties to universities. But we wanted to reach the parts of those readers that existed outside university-granted authority and judgment. Knowing that academic contexts felt bad to us didn't mean we had the skills to write the sentences that would feel good to our *readers*, also mostly academics, in other times and places and screens, in other parts of themselves.

It's the slow and ongoing work of learning to make such sentences that explains the emergence of what has been called, as a catchphrase for a general stylistic shift, the "*LARB* voice." A 2016 *Chronicle of Higher Education* feature described this voice as "more personal, sometimes impressionistic, and more lively than typical academic fare."[10] The feature quotes me, saying something that still feels important: "As Mesle told me, writing for *LARB* 'gave me back to myself my own opinions as a reader.'" What I am saying here is that the new forms I was developing let me care about reading and writing and assert the worth of my own taste *outside* academic significance. I still valued academic institutions. I just wasn't sure whether, or how, they valued me. Writing felt better to me when I wrote toward people who might care about me even if institutions did not, and who would evaluate me and my opinions outside whatever institutional life they, themselves, had. Here, unburdened by the need to earn institutional approval, my sentences could carry their own weight.

*

In 2016, the National Endowment for the Humanities established a fellowship for "Public Scholars."[11] This fellowship was a visible marker of how dramatically institutional understandings of public-facing writing had transformed. It's my sense that grants and programs of this kind came to be partly because the universities and grant-giving foundations that now seek to fund public humanities work were attracted to that moment's vibrant energy. For those of us who were at the time working to create new venues for expert writers, this was a wonderful kind of validation, and it also felt strange. Many of us had invested huge amounts of time in creating nonacademic worlds of value making. We had done so because we wanted to be able to recognize each other *outside* institutions, independently. We had found ways, in a time of scarce economic resources, to back the currency of our attention to each other. What would happen now that those institutions were paying close attention to us? Could we—would we want to—use those skills to bolster the same institutions whose resource distribution had made us feel so uncertain about our worth?

The matter became more complicated as it became clear that

2016 would bring about a sea change in how "the public" understood itself and what kind of communities and consensus "public" dialogue might create. There was Trump, of course, and the Cambridge Analytica scandal, but I mean other things too, small and large.[12] New software transformed digital publishing all over again: most importantly, the rapid adoption of AdBlock Plus devastated revenue streams for independent websites.[13] There was a moment in independent publishing when digital worlds seemed able to offer sustaining resources to writers and editors; after AdBlock Plus and in line with other economic developments (and a change in public attitudes toward media and social media particularly), that moment didn't last. In the first years the NEH was giving public scholarship grants, independent digital media was collapsing: by 2019, *Grantland*, MTV News, *Bookslut*, *The Awl*, *The Hairpin*, *The Toast*, *Pacific Standard*, and *Gawker* had all closed.

When universities and departments consider training writers to work in new contexts and for new audiences, I always hope they know they cannot simply outsource the platforming of these writers to a media sphere with such a fragile economy. For writing to appear anywhere, to any group or public or collective, so much work has to be done—work done by people who edit and email and post and email about the edits and the posts and who wrestle the CMS and manage the servers. I am always glad when institutions like the California Humanities Counsel and the Whiting Foundation and others devote resources to *venues*; I am also so saddened when I see budgets for publications put on the chopping block. This book is a guide for writers, rather than a funding program for universities, but if any university administrators read this, I hope this request registers: for the resources you grant to writers to matter, you must resource venues and presses too.

The language of many public humanities websites often addresses grand scales. Regularly they will mention, as the Council for Independent Colleges does, that "leaders in higher education and humanities scholars have worried about a 'crisis' in the humanities,"[14] or that, more generally, as the University of British

Columbia's Public Humanities Hub has it, "We live in a time of crisis."[15] The crises are broad-reaching, and so these institutions hope the public humanities will be. "Public humanities" as a term can comprise institutional-scale endeavors like museums and databases, not just writing, but the same language of "broad" appears in reference to writing: the NEH's "Public Scholars" grant page describes its aim to reach "the broad public" and "the broadest possible range of readers" in the same opening paragraph. This is just a sampling from a few public humanities and public scholarship pages.

These expectations emerged, temporally if not causally, in a previous era, the early 2010s moment I have described. In so doing, they pay respect to that era's accomplishments, even as they somewhat misrecognize what was achieved. Although some publications for humanities experts, like the *Los Angeles Review of Books,* often work at a large scale compared to academic publishing, the *size* of their reach wasn't their most significant accomplishment. It was the transformed sense of relevance. The independent sphere of digital publishing had eased the emotional burden under which humanities-trained experts, in the wake of a hiring crisis, wrote, by presenting us back to ourselves as a worthwhile audience even when institutions were not affirming our value. Though that independent sphere no longer exists as it did, its standards are transmitted back to us in institutional hopes for public-facing writing today.

The problems facing us *are* broad, and so are institutions like universities and the NEH. Institutions should develop large-scale, institutional solutions to broad scale problems. I am, I'll say again, *so glad* that public scholarship programs exist so much more robustly than they did ten years ago. Increased resourcing—in the forms of grants, classes, and recognition—provides incredible opportunities. They help enable the current renaissance of writing; they respect the labor it requires to practice an expanded range of writing's crafts.

But it's worth remembering: institutions can't easily give us a noninstitutional version of ourselves. My journalistic or "public-facing" writing didn't become powerful in comparison to my more conventional academic writing because there was something wrong with academic writing as a form. Rather, the feeling of academic writing was troubled by the political economy in academia. That economy has not significantly changed. As "public" writing moves into a closer affiliation with universities, my hope is that we can continue to craft sentences (both academic and journalistic) in which we can, above anything else, affirm each other's worth, regardless of whether university-based resource allocation affirms us, or our modes of judgment. I worry that by emphasizing broad scales and external affirmation, the shift toward public audiences will become another vehicle for undermining humanists' collectivizing respect for our own expertise.

*

While I've been drafting this chapter, at least five senior academics have approached me for advice about writing books for trade, rather than academic, presses. A few have asked me if I plan to reopen submissions for the crossover book series I cofounded and edited. Several have asked me about writing for *Avidly*. I myself have been, in the background of working on this project, accumulating materials and ideas for my own trade-press book. What are all of us hoping for, as we turn toward nonacademic audiences?

I can best speak for myself, of course. For my other book, I made a deliberate choice to write for trade publication rather than peer review, even though the topic, a media history of white femininity, racism, and white women's hair, emerges from my field of scholarship and even though the book requires a considerable amount of research, research I hope scholars will respect. I am writing the book for trade publication because it's a collection of essays that I hope, above all, will be pleasurable to read for a particular kind of reader.

I imagine the reader of my trade-press book wearing grubby soft pants at night, after the kids are in bed, feeling some kind of ambivalence about whether she did or did not clean the kitchen.

Or maybe, at another time, she is standing on a train at rush hour, bracing her work bag between her feet and looping her arm so that the train's support pole rests in the crook of her elbow, keeping her hands free to hold my book. This is, as my later chapter describes her, "my girl and where she's going." I want my other book to engage my reader as she navigates those material parts of her experience.

And that means I need to have this other book vetted in an editorial process that focuses on pleasure and accessibility, above knowledge-building significance. When I faced the choice between an editorial process centered on meaningful peer review of my scholarship (enacted in both content and form), and one centered on an editor who would comment on how my content and form integrated reader pleasure, I chose the latter. And I chose an editor who had the same sense I did of my imagined reader. In order to write a book for that reader—interrupted by questions about whether she remembered to buy the milk, or jostled by other bodies and staring around the train at other women navigating the world of femininity the book describes—I need to have an editor whose primary job is to tell me: Sarah, your sentences are too long. Yes, Sarah, this sentence too. And this one. Also, this paragraph, which you clearly think is funny, is not.

My reader, I want to say, may well be an expert in the humanities. But I want to reach the part of her that's reading somewhere outside her scholarship. Unlike in my academic writing, which I write with the expectation that a reader wants a complex understanding and thus will tease out a demanding sentence, in my trade-press book I want to tell my reader, with the structure of my sentences, that more distracted parts of her matter, because they do.

Providing sentence-level support is not necessarily an academic press's job, because the academic press provides resources for different, although just as important, readerly needs. For this other book I chose publication with a trade press—you might choose to write trade books or nonacademic essays—because your girl is on the train, rather than in the classroom, too.

But, okay, something important to admit: another part of my decision, existing alongside these noble goals for readerly intimacy and affirmation, is my desire for a kind of quantifiable, immediate status: followers, recognition, announcements, some kind of "nice" or "significant" deal. I want to write "in public" because of how, my world has told me, doing so will contribute to my personal success—which is to say, my *private* success, or, as I described in a previous chapter, my *privatized* success. Uncertain about academia's ability to value me, I've also absorbed a devaluation of academia; to some degree that my therapist and I will have to parse, I've made publishing decisions based less on data or tangible resources and more on my felt sense of trade publishing's glamour. And because I know this to be true, I'm wary about the rhetorical sleight of hand that happens when anyone juxtaposes "public" writing to academic writing, making all university-based publishing seem like a private, more self-interested affair.[16] The phrase "public humanities," in this way, can put a virtuous gloss on complicated ambitions, making it harder to recognize how they fit into infrastructures of value we otherwise question.

All ambitions are complicated. I'm not trying to disavow mine. I do hope to examine them with some kind of honesty. And doing so makes me want to remind myself, and you, and the people who've asked me this summer about trade-press publication and public writing, that we'd probably do well to check our sense of what we're hoping for. I'd like my books to change the world, and I'd also like them to change my life. Both or neither might take place. But extra-academic publication, no less than academic publication, is a fragile economy, in terms of attention as well as other resources. And I don't think publication strategy is the difference maker in either case. I'm not sure how we'd run the numbers on that, what ratio of attempt-to-accomplishment we'd need to plug in, but I don't think it's the shift from academic to public or trade that flips that mystical life-altering, world-changing, switch.

What I do think is likely—almost inevitable, in fact—is more intimate transformations. These come through developing, sentence by sentence, a version of yourself who can stand next to your reader on the train and say something that explains that train car, or makes the ride there more pleasurable. This is a different goal than the scholarly one of adding something new to human knowledge, shifting the conversation about your topic in an ongoing way, and because it's a different goal, you will be writing with a different part of yourself. The version of you whose voice takes shape amid the thrum of the train, or on a quiet tired evening—or wherever and whenever *you* speak to your imagined reader—will be nourished and strengthened. If you have spent most of your days nourishing the parts of your voice that speak in the classroom or the conference hall, that speak into another academic's imagined future prose, then nourishing this train/evening voice will change you.

You are part of the world, and so is your reader, and the relation you make together—academic or journalistic—is a change in the world. It's a narrow, not broad, change. That is a change worth writing for. And it's a change scaled to the level of the sentence, something (unlike many infrastructural changes) writers can craft and control—the substance of which writing is made.

*

Pretty regularly—it just happened yesterday—students want to talk about how I got into editing. They're looking for ways *they* might get into editing. I tell them the story I've told you here. I say: "It was a different time." The technologies and economic structures and emotional intensities of the moment made particular kinds of circulation and connection possible. It's not that we don't have technologies and economies and intensities now, I say reassuringly, but they're different. I can give them tools for crafting writing and relationships they find meaningful, but this isn't the same as offering them a clear career strategy. They'll have to improvise with venues and platforms, trying out the available infrastructures to see what they can make possible. I think a lot is possible. I also think we're in a historical moment in media technology when much remains unclear. I'm trying to tell these students, individually, what I'd like all advocates for the public humanities to register.

Sometimes I feel nostalgic for the world in which I would have known how to help them. Sometimes I wish I could go back. In one of those moods, I felt myself drawn toward a particular kind of time machine: a precise theory of publics, which still exist, written in a moment in public life we've left behind. In 2002, the same year that *Bookslut* launched and right before Gawker Media did, in the moment of a surging Web 2.0 and before the various consolidations of facebook and the iPhone and WordPress and *Grantland*, the queer theorist and literary scholar Michael Warner published a book called *Publics and Counterpublics*. Considered from our current vantage point, two decades and several iterations of discourse-circulating technology later, the insights of *Publics and Counterpublics* take on a new cast. It's a bit like reading some especially prescient speculative fiction. I went back to it looking to see if it could explain what it was about public writing I valued, and that the phrase "public humanities" didn't seem to capture. A public, Warner argues in the title essay, isn't constituted by its size or scope. Instead, a public convenes around a discourse, one circulated via open invitation. It's "a relation among strangers" who are drawn together by their shared attention.[17] Thus within any kind of "public" nests the capacity of writing toward a potentially unlimited other, because anyone interested can join in. This is the magic the word "public" names: the hope that a new and transformable "we" can be, might be, activated through a shared encounter with a circulating discourse. A public comes to be, in Warner's lovely turn of phrase, through "a poetic world making."[18]

When I told *The Chronicle of Higher Education* that writing for *LARB* "gave me back to myself my own opinions as a reader," part of what I meant was that before *LARB*, my reading, and my writing too, had become overly determined by my professional, obligatory-feeling relation to institutions. One way we might describe the fluorescent feeling of humanist writing outside academic publication—the writing that took place in *LARB* and elsewhere in the early parts of this century—is that such publication allowed humanists to reconnect *outside* professions and *inside* genuinely offered attention. To use Warner's terms, it gave us back to each other as strangers. It reintroduced us. And this, it turns out, gave us something more important than the possibility of *more* readers. It also gave us a new way to be better, more invested readers—readers who might become a community. To become, maybe, friends.

In 2002, no one could have anticipated the glorious and highly temporalized social media events like the "what color is that dress" moment of 2015 or the fake @MayorEmanuel account of 2010. We couldn't have known how powerful digital circulation could become, or how quickly its pathways would be short-circuited by villainous agents (Zuck, Musk), bad regulation, and our own bad feelings. This is as good an account as any of why it's hard for me to give advice to my students, who weren't even born yet when Emily Nussbaum was posting about Buffy on *Television Without Pity*. And it also helps explain why our fantasies of the public humanities get worrisome and mud-bath-y when they fail to take precise, historicist account of the messy, real-world infrastructures (on social media? In publications, and if so, which? Via email, or Substack recommendations?) through which writing, and some kinds of writing more easily than others, actually moves.

In particular, I'm invested in the circulation of writing that contains the rarified and experimental styles in which humanists express humanist knowledge. In the previous chapter I proposed that styles are methods; that the ways humanists write can't be separated from *how* we come to know. I'd add here that styles are equally methods for determining *whom* we come to know, and on what grounds. In efforts to make ourselves accessible, what versions of our knowledge and our sensibilities might be lost? I might just be expressing the worry of someone who once tried to convince *InStyle* magazine to publish a celebrity profile criticizing the conflation of consumerism with feminist agency, which, it turns out, is not something *InStyle* thought its "girl" really wanted to hear about in the middle of a December gift issue. This is not a slight against *InStyle* magazine. But it is a true story about how humanist ways of thinking, in many broad publics, feel frictional. Arguing with the editor of that essay, I wanted—still want—to keep that friction felt.

My use of the word "frictional" comes from Warner too—from his explanation of his second term, "counterpublics." "Counterpublics are 'counter,'" Warner writes, "to the extent that they try to supply different ways of imagining stranger sociability."[19] The use of their signature styles marks them as vulnerable, likely to draw hostility from the mainstream. Counterpublics persist, in public, to trouble the norms of the public, in the hopes that the "poesis" of their "scene making" might have a relation to the public that is "transformative, not replicative merely."[20] At the present chapter's conclusion, I want to ask: What might this concept offer humanists writing now?

I keep debating this question with friends. By proposing that the "counterpublic humanities" is a meaningful idea, I put myself at some risk of making a false equivalence between groups (humanities PhDs now and queer activists of the '90s) who face categorically different kinds of vulnerabilities. But I keep returning to the idea, partly because '90s queer activism is such a good a model for collectivist response to crisis—even crises of a very different scale—and one that has been personally meaningful to me. But beyond that, the idea of a "counterpublic humanities" helps name the value of ways of writing that feel frictional to what broad publics can easily accommodate. Such friction might be actively aggressive, or it might take the more subtle form of making us feel awkward or nerdy or dowdy. These feelings might exist because, in the public world the far right works to create, our humanities expertise actually undermines our authority to describe what it's like to be human. What would happen if humanists embraced those feelings, finding in them continuing value?

It was as humanists ourselves that so many of us in the past decades developed improvisational ways to write toward, edit, platform, and recirculate each other. We collectively developed new writing styles that could still contain the weirdo idiolects, the poetics, in which humanist thought can take sophisticated, casual, and quickly circulating shape. Our public exchanges didn't have to interest *the* public at large (or, we might say, at broad) in order to transform our feeling about each other's value, as readers. We didn't need to find new readers: we needed to look around and realize we were already filling the ballroom. Our infinitely permeable but also small-scale expressions of excellently nerdy granular attention might, after all, be what has the strongest capacity to sustain a humanist "us" in uncertain times.

FOUR

“But Is It Any *Good*?”

Or, Some Feminist Questions About Academic Writing

> Our first step is to acknowledge the ideological basis of our endeavor.
>
> SUSAN K. HARRIS, “‘But Is It Any *Good?*’: Evaluating Nineteenth-Century American Women’s Fiction”

1. IT’S GOOD

To what degree is it possible, in the infrastructure of the now, to make a feminist case for academic writing? I have a lot invested in this question, so I want to be precise, at the outset, about how I’m using these terms. By a “feminist” case, I mean one testing my claims against a fundamental goal to redistribute the labor of and access to carework, pleasure, and epistemic authority, experiences that have historically been apportioned along gender’s intersecting lines. By “academic” writing, I mean writing that is evaluated, distributed, and accessed via university-based systems of review and archival investment. Given that the resources needed to produce and access academic writing are increasingly privatized and hierarchical, what manner of participation within academic writing’s political economy supports feminist aims?

Set up that way, one answer is *no* manner, *no* support, *no* can do, can't go for that. The very framing of these questions, asking essentially, "But is academic writing any feminist good?," seems to presume the same negative answer as the question posed in the title of the 1991 Susan K. Harris essay from which I draw my own title and epigraph. But like Harris, I'm embarking on an endeavor with an ideological basis. She describes her critical relation to nineteenth-century women's fiction by explaining, "We are drawn to nineteenth-century texts despite their apparently antithetical values and *want to find some way of talking* about them" (emphasis mine).[1] So, too, do I want to find some way, within my values, of talking about academic writing and about its draw, worth, and pleasure. Here is a thing I *like*. I *like* to bring a question to a university database, to run a search for key terms, to download an article bedecked with JSTOR's familiar header, the "J" insignia with its dragon-like vines. I *like* to sit down to my printout of that article with the confident sense that I am reading something tested, something that reaches toward true. I want this experience that I like, that I value—an experience shot through with privilege from start (accessing the database) to finish (having a quiet place to read)—to also be something I can stand with, as a feminist. Is this possible? Or is this affinity, this pleasure, like so many of my affinities and pleasures, fundamentally at odds with my politics?

I realize that when most people take up the question of whether academic writing "is good," the genre's feminism may be a third- or fourth-order concern, lurking beneath a series of negative judgments of a primarily aesthetic order. When I've discussed this book project with friends and colleagues, many of them have cocked their heads and leaned in conspiratorially to whisper, as though we were discussing something no one else had ever dared to say: *Are you going to talk about how academic writing is bad?* They want to know if I'm going to address how academic writing can be variously awkward, insular, boring, hyperspecific, jargony, clotted, depersonalized, alternately arrogant and obsequious. They are right. Academic writing can be all these things. Such qualities exacerbate the niche nerdiness inherent to the genre and the excessive demands it makes in both its production and consumption. Through these demands, aesthetics shift toward the political: they make academic writing exclusive, inaccessible. A professor once told me that reading my academic prose was like "wading through treacle," a phrase I'm definitely not at all still mad about, and that I also feel usefully summarizes many legitimate criticisms of the genre, its labors and absurdities.

As I'll explain, though, I'm not very interested in the claim that academic writing has bad aesthetics. *Most* of the writing produced in this fallen world has bad aesthetics. Most novels are mediocre. Most essays are pretty bad. My poems are really bad. Consider briefly the horrors of corporate memos, marketing reports, consulting-firm websites. If it was our job to dwell in such mediocrity, we might take up its textures as a daily topic of pleasurable complaint. I get it, one hundred percent. But dwelling on the "badness" of academic prose forecloses our ability to think through the broader question of how this genre works, what we might make with it, and how, in turn, it makes us—our lives, our habits, and our idea-worlds.[2] Those are the questions that interest me when I consider Your Precious Writing Time, or mine. Why would we do this, when we could be writing or reading fantasy novels or whatever genre you think is "good" aesthetically—or, when and if we are concerned with the practice of political good, taking up that labor more directly?

Again, I'll return to this fundamental tenet: the world pressures none of us into humanities expertise. That we've chosen academic worlds in the past really truly does not require us to pursue them now. But in reading this book, this chapter, you offer me some evidence that you share my affinity, my desire, for academic worlds, at whatever level of ambivalence. It's that desiring part of you this chapter addresses.

In this chapter, I try to make an affirmative case for academic writing, and to affirm it alongside my feminism. I don't see academic writing as a superior form of writing, feminist or otherwise, across the aesthetic or political or intellectual board. But I do find it to be a genre of expert humanities writing with unique capacities that are worth fighting for. Given my own writerly track record, you may be surprised—certainly I am—that *this* hill, this famously mucky and bad-weather landscape, is one I'm willing to die on. But here I go, running right up.

Academic writing is, for me, a kind of utopic practice that can't be fully contained by the worst failings of the institutions that facilitate it. It offers the potential of a uniquely rewarding shelter for being as an expert—being in words, being in readership, being with the weird and beautiful and infuriating materials we love and hate and care about. And as such, especially when we can detach its value from the ever-dwindling possibility that academic writing might procure for us particular kinds of jobs, academic writing holds out the *possibility* for a pleasurable and socially significant way of relating, in the unsteady now.

In short, academic writing: I think it's good.

2. SCRIBBLING

There's an iconic imagined scene of a nineteenth-century woman writing, or, as she has more famously been described, "scribbling." This woman, depending on which observer you ask, may or may not be happy about her situation: putting pen to paper in moments stolen from the distractions of her children, her domestic scene, her husband, or the bill collector.

I often think of this woman—both her ideological function and her many real-world antecedents—when I encounter the assertion that academic writing is bad. You can find this claim all over the place. Google "academic writing bad" and you'll find many versions of this conversation, from blogs to podcasts to *The New York Times* to *The Chronicle of Higher Education*.[3]

The phrase "scribbling women" comes to my mind because it describes another genre often casually assumed to be bad—nineteenth-century American sentimental fiction. The phrase comes from a letter that Nathaniel Hawthorne famously sent to his editor railing against the success of what he described as "these innumerable editions of *The Lamplighter*," Maria Susanna Cummins's 1854 novel. Of this novel and its kind, Hawthorne wrote, "Worse they could not be, and better they need not be."[4]

The Lamplighter, a best-selling novel, tells the story of an orphan with good hair finding true love.[5] In all these aspects, it seems the opposite of academic writing, which rarely finds huge audiences, maybe because its stories too rarely feature good hair or happy endings. Yet to my ear, what Hawthorne disliked about sentimental fiction strangely echoes contemporary criticisms of academic writing. He hated that it was repetitive, rule-bound, poorly edited market fodder produced ad nauseam to no meaningful end. He hated feeling that in order to achieve professional success, he would need to limit his creativity and churn out a degraded version of something he loved: yet another "innumerable" version of the same story.

Hawthorne's phrase comes from a letter, written in a condition of irritation and frustration (relatable). I know it's something of a mistake to consider it as representative of nineteenth-century attitudes or even of Hawthorne himself. I'm now going to double down on that mistake, by connecting Hawthorne's letter with a claim made on facebook, the correspondence genre of our time. In the summer of 2022, a facebook friend whom I very much admire, the eighteenth-century-literature scholar Blakey Vermeule, posted that she had "finally figured out why academic writing (the reading and writing of it) is so awful."[6] In the sixty-two-comment thread, many academics weighed in, commenting on problems from the sentence level ("floppy verbs," which I agree is a total problem) to institutional stress. Vermeule's own provocative thesis—one worth considering—was that academic writing's awfulness came from its knotted attempts to meet two conflicting demands: obedience, which she identifies as the "overriding value" of academia, and emotional honesty, which she asserts as a necessary quality of writing that "actually moves people."

It may seem strange to take as an example this off-the-cuff discussion, when so many more formal discussions of academic writing's problems are available. I choose this particular thread precisely because of its casualness, its spontaneity, and its pile-on effect. In it, a powerful academic (and beautiful writer) chats semi-publicly with many other academics, many if not all with some power of their own (some of the comments in the thread, for instance, are mine.) Social media conversations give their participants a chance to try on claims, to feel out those claims' stakes. The claim tried out here, about academic writing's knotted values, also tries out a grounding premise, a claim held in common: that we've all been wondering, Why is academic writing so awful?

Even if we concede that most academic writing isn't very good, the rhetorical gesture of this opening premise bears attention. The claim that "academic writing is awful" works here as both a premise and a joke (as the "laugh emoji" responses testify). No one in that thread, I'm sure, thinks that *all* academic writing is bad. Instead, it's a move like other sweeping genre dismissals (sentimental literature is bad; yacht rock is bad; soap operas are bad) that function as a kind of pleasurable community making. We, these claims imply, who identify the badness, may not be good, but at least we are above that bad thing, and together in our shared judgment. We have, whatever else, a genre sensibility in common. The desire for a shared sensibility that this facebook thread captures is one citable instance I can offer of all the moments I've had with people leaning in to ask me about the badness of academic writing. These moments are casual, but they are not free of significance or power. I want to ask: How does it serve us, as an academic community, to distance ourselves so insistently from one of our central activities? What kind of "we" do these gestures of superiority ferment?

I may be the wrong person to answer this question. As a Midwesterner, I'm not a great reader of complaint as genre. I respect complaint as a politics, and I know that complaining about daily experience serves a consciousness-raising function and as an enjoyable social glue.[7] But I'm not great at hearing, within complaint, the often-present expressions of love. (Midwesterners express love by stiff-upper-lipping and with the phrase "no worries either way," both of which are basically the opposite of a complaint form.) There may be more love than I'm hearing in the "academic writing is awful" social banter around me. "Where love is concerned," writes Lauren Berlant, "disappointment is a partner of fulfillment, not an opposite."[8] But not all complaint forms work the same, infrastructurally, as feminism knows. So I still want to point out the troubling (to my mind) effects of how we academics consistently distance ourselves from academic writing through particular kinds of complaint and criticism.

Academic writing, the thread says, capitulates endlessly and obediently (to the market, to hierarchies), to the detriment of its aesthetics, its insights, and its ethics. In this way, and despite important differences, the sweeping dismissals of academic writing replicate the move made in dismissals of women's sentimental literature. In its assumptions, the thread positions its speakers on the side of a series of qualities that American culture has long coded as male—authenticity, self-determination, generally being real. In this conversation, a person who dismisses the genre gets to be on the side of honesty, rather than the side of obedience, and therefore affiliated with a particular idea of freedom. Academic writers, this thinking goes, are unfree because they are obedient and confined. They can't *move*, whether themselves or others. This idea of freedom is one that feminism teaches us to question. Academics criticizing academic writing in this way assert a melodrama of their own beset style. They would like to be free from those scribblers, with their norms and rules and "innumerable editions." Academic writing itself becomes feminized. And perhaps because this is the case, I become motivated (ideologically?) to recognize the politics inherent in underexamined taxonomies like "academic writing" and "bad."

Certainly, much within humanist writing and publishing should be criticized from within a feminist perspective. That doesn't mean that all criticisms of academic writing are feminist; in fact, what I'm saying is that many criticisms take antifeminist forms. To endorse or imply the fantasy that our writing might be good, if only we could get outside academic forms, buys into an unhelpful light-out-for-the-territory way of thinking that fails to recognize something those of us who show up for the PTA meetings, the food trains, the committee meetings, know: even when they're annoying, communally recognized forms can be a kind of care practice. Genres and their procedures help us negotiate the daily practices out of which collectivities are made. And whatever constraints collectivities impose, without them how could a world of readers be made?

As to the idea that rule-bound, obedient writing can never be emotional or move people, I just disagree. Many generic "rules" are designed to move people: Even those of sentimentality can be a real source of power and agency. Even taking into consideration the pleasurably punchy tones through which the idea is expressed (the tones that give the genre of the social media post its useful capacity for provisional meaning-making), I wonder to what extent Vermeule really believes it.[9] It would be a strange claim coming from the same person who helped me understand the eighteenth-century origins of the rom-com, a genre that definitely makes me, at least, cry.

3. ACADEMIC WRITING

What makes *this* book academic writing? Not the fact that I am an academic and not the fact that I want to say something real and meaningful and true based on careful reading and thought. Many kinds of writing are produced by such people and with such aims. What makes writing "academic" is the author's decision—here, mine—to enter their words into a system whereby claims are tested for truth, generativeness, and significance, by the "best standards" a given field has to measure those qualities. We call the process that evaluates these qualities "peer review." If these qualities are anonymously evaluated to be sufficiently present in the piece of writing, and if it is collectively determined to merit inclusion in the archives universities create and the databases universities fund, it will pass a threshold and be granted long-term status as a meaningful, identifiable, and, crucially, *findable* building block in the long construction of human knowledge.[10] This book, if you are reading it, will have met that standard.

I include several other kinds of writing, besides those put through peer review, in the category of academic writing. Lectures, conference papers, readers' reports, lesson plans, emails upon emails upon emails connecting drafts with Reader #1 and Reader #2 and following up with both readers and reminding the speakers to submit their W-9 forms with legible addresses and to not go over their limit, please, and to send their draft on time, and to reassure them that their rudeness on being late with their response and their report and their draft and their form is okay, really, we're all tired, thank you!

These kinds of writing are "academic writing" because they take part in the creative work that springs up around the peer review as a process, standard, and ideal. Much of this writing I also consider to be carework. I don't think that conference papers or class lectures need to become published in order to count as academic and to matter, because even in their untested and unprinted form they assert their worth in relation to the process of peer review, the university's standard of knowledge production. They serve it and engage it and are sheltered by it.

So, it is not the desire to say something true that makes something academic; it is the willingness to submit your truth to a specifically academic process of testing. What this means for you, on a given morning with Your Precious Writing Time, is that you must not only discern and express your truth (hard enough activities, by any measure) but also do the work required to make your truth and its innovation *legible to the existing testing mechanisms*. And you must be willing to wait, on a series of other mornings, while those mechanisms—the emails, the reading, the reminder emails—slowly turn their testing wheels. If you are willing to prepare for and undergo and endure these tests, your work will be rewarded; its words will be inscribed, for example, in JSTOR's ledgers and able, from there, to reach out to the mornings of future researching writers, as though traveling to them by unprogrammed satellite.

So, the question of academic writing's value boils down to our faith that this great system of peer review—all the writing it endorses and demands—offers us, or someone, something that we, at least sometimes, want. Note, here, that unprogrammed satellite is probably our *least* efficient mode of travel. And at this moment in history, the question of *whether we want* what peer review can give us takes on a different kind of texture, because of how dramatically academic writing has entered an era of decommodification. I draw this term from Leigh Claire La Berge, and I was encouraged to place it in relation to academic writing by Michelle Chihara. La Berge's 2019 book *Wages Against Artwork* explores how contemporary artists stage the decommodification of their labor as a part of their art practice.[11] Chihara has extended La Berge's line of thought to ask what emerges for humanities-trained writers in an era when our writing and our labor (as writers, professors, and thinkers) has dropped out of market regard.[12] It was, as we know, previously the case that we might want the authority of peer review because that authority credentialized us for jobs that still existed. Peer review, whatever else it was, was the coin of the nerd realm—the mark of our authority within a professionalizing, market system.

It is not reliably that marker now. So: What *else* was it? And do we want that? Do we want authority, outside a securely professional structure of work? Another twist of the screw, as we consider these questions: Remaining committed to peer review means cultivating a relation to universities as archiving, if not hiring, institutions. Peer review, in some ways, is a durational art of authority, bound, through institutional practices, to the future researchers our writing hopes to reach. Thus, to advocate for peer-reviewed academic writing is to advocate for a lived relation to institutions, even when we are suspicious of them, and even when we have been damaged by them. The writer entering peer review, like Marina Abramović entering MoMA, commits to being present in the institution because it's the dialogue with institutionality that makes the art, the academic writing, what it is. Do we want such mediated encounters? What can emerge through their crucibles? Another way to put

that would be, Is there a "we" that each of us wants to be a part of, a sustaining one, that peer review can help us produce?

If you look at my CV, with its solitary entry under "peer-reviewed articles," you'll notice that what peer review offers me I don't want very often, compared to other things I could have. I usually prefer starting a project when I'm excited about the idea, and getting it into circulation immediately, rather than impatiently waiting the who-knows-how-many years for an essay to slouch toward JSTOR to be born. But this time, with this project, the one you're reading, peer review was essential to what I wanted. I want to be tested in this way; I want to talk to this particular testing machine. I wanted to know if it can read the words and styles that are my method for describing the worth of writing: I want to ask peer review if it knows about Jessica Wakefield and midi-length skirts, about terms like jerkery (*n.*) and jazz-hand (*v.*) and jazz-handsy (*adj.*).[13]

So at least in this instance, my answer is yes. I want *that* we, I want its shelter. I am here to send you some emails on its behalf. I am ready to fill out my forms.[14]

4. BEEF AND PRUNES

What are the best ways to write in tandem with an institution whose aims are not necessarily yours? With an institution that depends on your labor yet may often refuse to acknowledge the range of labor that you do, an institution that places the idea of you, of your caretaking labor and your insight, at the center of its proclaimed values while often disregarding or ignoring your material needs? These questions, very real ones for those of us writing professionally within universities, will feel familiar to those of us who have also faced them privately, within the many institutional scenes (marriage, America, PTA meetings) where women and other feminized caretakers have sometimes struggled to find creative ways to work and live.

As a feminist writing in support of academic writing, it may not surprise you to learn that, alongside my attachments to peer review, I have a series of feminist concerns. Peer review functions to the extent that we believe those who participate in it are committed to evaluating writing, research, and ideas in good faith. By "good faith" I mean that they (or we) are acting with integrity and generosity. Peer review needs people who don't hide petty jealousies behind nitpicky intellectual objections; who don't get huffy about hard-to-hear criticisms; who don't expect the worst. It needs people who neither commit acts of sabotage nor expect them.

This is a tall order. I can here reverse my own maxim and say that because it's hard to consistently act in good faith, it's also hard for peer review to function in the way I imagine most of us would like it to. The gears of the system are scholars who are also actual people like you and me, and also like you and me they are flawed and exhausted. Sometimes they are extremely kind and helpful and at other times they are lazy and misguided. They are, on occasion, riven with grudges and possessed of insecurities of a more or less toxic nature. Their tests may be unfair.

But the problem isn't just personal. Here's the thing (or *a* thing) about peer review: It's a system that depends on institutions but aims to produce knowledge that matters in excess of those institutions. The knowledge peer review aims to find and distribute should be true, be generative, *everywhere*, or at least anywhere, regardless of where it was produced or who produced it. In an ideal world, we might create a hierarchy of knowledge, ranking the usefulness of some new book or article above others, but those hierarchies would develop independently of the ways we might rank institutions. To put this simply, we shouldn't value a book or article just because it was produced someplace with a high *US News* ranking; we should value it because of what it says.

But this fantasy of ideal engagement will never fully be reached, because peer review will, by definition, always remain tied to institutions with different resources. Some institutions have huge endowments and powerful reputations. Some institutions pay salaries whereby faculty can teach a 2/2 schedule, while others, to put it mildly, do not. Some have powerful faculty senates and secure tenure lines and money to bring in speakers and to pay for research time. Others, again, do not. Higher ed's institutional hierarchies become ever more stratified. So even when peer-review tests are undertaken in good faith, even when all the reviewers and editors and scholars and conference organizers want all that's best for everyone as we, collectively, hew laboriously toward the best that's thought and known, problems in good-faith equity persist. Increasing stratification means we move farther from, rather than closer to, an environment conducive to producing the good faith peer review needs. Noticing, describing, and pushing against this stratification is a feminist practice.

Here I'm trying to say something more complicated than the simple point that people with more time to write will write more—although that's one thing that's sometimes, although definitely not always, true. I'm trying to get at how writing in stratified institutions can make writing toward peer review feel. Those feelings put pressure on how peer review functions.

When I think about the complexities inherent in the act of feminist writing in institutions, my mind often turns to Virginia Woolf eating lunch. There's one lunch in particular, which she describes in the first chapter of *A Room of One's Own*. In gorgeous prose, Woolf describes a luncheon at "Oxbridge"—sole, partridge, cream and more cream, "a confection which rose all sugar from the waves."[15] Here, at lunch, sated, she feels a special state being reached:

> And thus by degrees was lit, halfway down the spine, which is the seat of the soul, not that hard little electric light which we call brilliance, as it pops in and out upon our lips, but the more profound, subtle and subterranean glow, which is the rich yellow flame of rational intercourse. No need to hurry. No need to sparkle. No need to be anybody but oneself.[16]

"Rational intercourse," in Woolf's account, emerges not specifically from the intelligence of the speakers, but rather from the careful tending to the speakers' appetites and tastes. "The human frame being what it is, heart, body and brain all mixed together and not contained in separate compartments . . . a good dinner is of great importance to good talk."[17] Full of good food, the speakers are freed of grudge and grievance and the need to posture. They are confident in themselves; they glow.

Later in the day, Woolf dines at the new women's college, Fernham. It is a dinner of beef, a dessert of prunes. It's dreary, and everyone knows it; everyone knows the difference between their dinner and what's eaten up the road. "The lamp in the spine," Woolf writes, "does not light on beef and prunes."[18]

Is she right? The whole story could be taken as merely more evidence that Virginia Woolf, genius feminist and beloved maker of sentences, was also a great and abiding snob. But precisely in her snobbery, Woolf becomes articulate about an unfortunate truth: When your actual diet is lacking, part of what you're fed is the sign of your unworth. Your well-being suffers, and your writing can too.

We don't have to condone Woolf's snobbery to recognize the significance of her point and how it matters for those of us encountering peer review. Humanists all come to the same peer-review machinery, while only some of us dine on sole and cream. Many of us, and more all the time, produce our prose in conditions of beef and prunes. Does this disparity matter for our writing, for how our writing feels, for how it feels to confront peer review? Yes. It fucking does. It does in the exhaustion of efforts to write free of the daily reminders of second-class status. It does in rushed sentences and late emails and (sometimes) begrudging jerky reader #2 evaluations or crabby responses to them. It does in anxious attempts to write arguments that will shine in competition with the sole-and-spine-light table, arguments that in their twitchiness betray, like Julia Roberts's escargot in *Pretty Woman* or Silas with his *Rise of Silas Lapham* ham fingers, an ambivalence about sole-and-spine-light-table etiquette and silverware.

It's this moral trouble that our rhetoric obscures when people with secure university employment say that academic writing is "bad," because it follows rules and is too distanced and isn't moving—

because it reads like the psychic damage of beef and prunes. The claim mistakes the quality of writing for what's bad in the infrastructure. It fails to consider the experiences of everyone thrown up against peer-reviews gears in a world of increasing scarcity. Perhaps the problem lies less in the quality of the writing and more in the context-recognizing capacity of our reading. Like, *duh*, why wouldn't writers emotionally distance themselves from judgment? Why wouldn't they be careful of rules? Why *wouldn't* they couch intellectual discoveries in the generic forms that are most likely to make them legible to a perceived sense of the sole-and-spine-light table manners? And how *could* anyone produce unhurried, glowing, nonperformative writing, when they're worried that even the beef-and-prunes budget might be cut? It seems impossible. What's astonishing, then, isn't the "badness," but rather the dazzling fact that, in such dire conditions, so many writers produce writing that's *so good*.

5. TOOLS

How do they do it? Where does the good writing come from? And what should those of us who care about academic writing do to protect it? Given that the whole peer-review process depends on choosing and lifting up some writing above other writing, how can those of us participating in this system do so in the best interests of our genuinely best ideas, and all their makers? Put differently, how can we participate in the systems of evaluation peer review demands, judging intellectual contribution, without perpetuating institutional hierarchies?

I ask the question pointedly because it's so easy to do the opposite, to harm the system and most of us within it rather than to help it work better. Many of us don't seem to have very good tools—a phrase I'm drawing from Audre Lorde's ever-useful maxim that "the master's tools will never dismantle the master's house."[19] How does Lorde's metaphor of the tool help us understand the problems of peer review?

A tool, according to Wikipedia, as good a source here as any, is "an object that can extend an individual's ability to modify features of the surrounding environment or help them accomplish a particular task."[20] But that it not all a tool is. "A tool is someone who lacks the capacity to realize they're being used by someone else. A fool."[21]

The original context for Lorde's claim was an academic conference on *The Second Sex*, organized by the New York Institute for the Humanities in 1979. Lorde was writing to a group of feminists about the failures of white women within that group to attend to difference. She had something to say to women like me who, despite all our righteous anger at the harm institutions have caused, often rush to protect those institutions, especially when women of color criticize them. Lorde's point, as I take it, was not only that white women used conventional and exclusionary mechanisms—the master's tools—to organize the conference Lorde was attending, thus reproducing the very structures they nominally hoped to upset. Her point was also that these white women were themselves the master's tools, his fools.

A tool in the derogatory sense accomplishes the goals of the person (or system) whose tool they are by standing in the way of other, more interesting work. They may think they are meaningfully participating in whatever work has been undertaken. Instead, they impede the real work that could be taking place. White feminists often miss the work we're doing as tools because of how busily we resist the idea that our own role is decorative, a civil facade over more brutal power. But often that's exactly what it is. We perform the feminized labor of making things look like progress while keeping things running as they were.

This is the specific caution I take from Lorde. I bring it to the question of how to engage peer review in good faith. It's very easy for people (not only white women) to engage in what can feel like the carework of peer review—the emailing, the organizing, all its labors—while missing the fact that what's being cared for is the *institution*, and at the expense of its inhabitants.

To help develop a language for a better standard, I went and talked with Roderick Ferguson, who is in no way responsible for anything that I'm saying, but who was gracious enough to help me think through being "in and not of" institutions, as he describes it in *The Reorder of Things* (2012).[22] Several years before, in an interview we did, he said something that has stayed with me. Ferguson said that we need to "take care" in two senses: We need to take care of the people around us, and we need to take care to do the work right. He said:

> You know, when I was writing my dissertation, I was trying to figure out what kind of standard I wanted to hold myself to when I sat down to write. And I thought: I would like to take as much care in writing this dissertation as granddaddy—my father's father, Granddaddy Willie Marvin—took in cleaning fish. Or the amount of care that my mother's mother, Grandma Willie Mae, used to make her lace handkerchiefs, that she sold to people. And I have always thought that that kind of will to integrity that we deliver to the work has to be part of any progressive practice.[23]

What's been invaluable to me, over the years I've spent remembering Ferguson's comment, is how it links "progressive practice," as he says, to a "will to integrity"—to deliberately considered standards of rigor. In the more recent conversation Ferguson and I shared, he emphasized again that an essential practice of ethical intellectual life is both to avoid internalizing, unquestioned, the norms and styles of your own institution—wherever it may be on the sole-to-beef spectrum, which is not the words he used—and to establish "your own protocols and ethics" for writing, teaching, and interacting. Our terms of order, he said, are like terms of ardor; they are ways of showing love.[24] In this way, Ferguson offers a model of ethical evaluation: one that enacts a "will to integrity" without presupposing that integrity can only be found in a particular set of materials, styles, or scenes. Excellence doesn't hew to institutional norms; in fact, it is a constantly renegotiated creative practice.

6. POEMS AND CITIES AND BUGS

In 2014, the critic Emily Lordi published an essay with the wonderfully provocative title "Why Is Academic Writing So Beautiful?"[25] The essay responded to some then recently published essays about why academic writing was detached, turgid, "academic." Lordi responded to this moment of discourse by pointing toward an entire scholarly tradition, Black feminism, that purposefully forged a style committed to both intellectual complexity and aesthetic pleasure. From the abundant examples of writers in this tradition—Hazel Carby, Cheryl Wall, Farah Jasmine Griffin, and more—Lordi easily culls support for her main point: that while one certainly can find bad academic writing, to say that academic writing as a whole is bad is to ignore all the academic writing that's good, and doing so often has exclusionary politics, implying that the "good" writing (often writing directed toward minority communities) isn't actually "academic."

For a long time, when I thought about the value of academic writing, I thought about a particular vision of what universities could be. To me as a young person, universities seemed like sites of exchange outside the larger world's conservative market hierarchies—spaces for weirdos and nerds and feminists, like me and the people I felt lucky to be around. I've come to see, as I've grown up and more clear-eyed, and as the world of higher ed has changed, how entangled universities have always been with the very systems I was trying to escape.

But here's the thing: I still think academic writing has the potential to be the outsider path I imagined. It can be a creative act with the capacity to participate in the same world-reorientating tradition that Lordi's essay describes. What Lordi and others have found in the world of these Black feminist critics, often writing under conditions of existential threat, is what we might call, riffing on a beautiful essay by Fredric Jameson, a "utopia as method."[26]

"Utopic" might be a strange word to bring to academic writing, with its often-grueling labor and institutional indignities. But I'm using it on purpose. Jameson describes the method of utopia as "neither a hermeneutic nor a political program" but instead the inverse of a "genealogy."[27] A utopic method isn't to investigate the past, and it isn't to map out precisely how to get to the future. It's to act as though something in the present might, in some way yet undetected, be the precondition of a different future. It is to reanimate in us the capacity to imagine a future.

When I try to explain to students in my freshman writing class what they are doing, I find myself drawing on this language. I say: the goal of the university is, slowly and carefully, to increase our knowledge of ourselves and our world. The university asks: What do we humans not know, yet, about this poem, this city, or this bug? The university shelters those who want to learn about the poem, the city, the bug; it shelters them without concern for whether this poem or this city or this bug will solve any immediate crises facing the rest of humankind, but rather because it is built to believe that poems and cities and bugs are worth knowing about, in sum. Some poems and some cities and some bugs may in fact be able to help us in crisis. Some may not. We can't know in advance which. Regardless, their existence merits our understanding.

Academic writing is the writing that aims to enter the great ongoing conversation about poems and cities and bugs, by making a claim that something new, something true by our best current standards of knowing, has been learned. The great gears of the peer-review machine turn with the goal of ensuring that a piece of writing meaningfully participates in this work of universities: to know what is known, and to add to that knowledge, so that future scholars of poems and cities and bugs can see this good-faith attempt to add to the knowledge of the world. It is how we show our work to each other, so that others, too, can work, in a project in which we all believe.

I'm advocating for academic writing because I see it as a place where the utopic and the institutional meet and are negotiated. While the connection to increasingly corrupt institutions can warp and limit and make miserable the access to that portal, this is not to my mind a cause to abandon or discard academic writing. Peer review, a process by which we write toward the future, matters partly because of how that writing remains umbilically attached to the present. Institutions, made conservative by their mandate to conserve, may try to limit what we do and how, and they may succeed in limiting what we do, but then again, *they might not*. Instead, *we* might teach these institutions to conserve more than what they need or imagine or fear. We might teach them to conserve a seed of something new.

Or we might not. Committing your life to academic writing, or academic institutions, out of a hope that some poem or city or bug knowledge might generate a new world is a strange and extravagant practice. Because academic writing's value comes from its unknown potential, it's the opposite of on-the-ground political labor. It's precisely because most academic writing doesn't or might not (but in an uncertain way) have an immediate use value that it performs the particular utopic function I see in it. The inaccessibility of academic writing to your average on-the-ground person is not a failure of politics; it is a necessary risk of utopic politics. Likewise, the limited quantity of readers academic writing may find in the now is not a failure of social effect; it's a gambit toward what *might* be read, might be needed, in the future, a future we can't imagine, but which can't use our knowledge if we don't produce it.

"This kind of prospective hermeneutic," Jameson writes, "is a political act only in one specific sense": "as *a contribution to a reawakening of the imagination of possible and alternate futures*, a reawakening of that historicity which our system—offering itself as the very end of history—necessarily represses and paralyzes" (emphasis added).[28]

Here I could line up Jameson with a series of other thinkers: Theodor Adorno, who argued that "only what is useless can stand in for stunted use values,"[29] or La Berge, who characterized the aesthetic as a part of the world "that offers a fleeting respite—even for a moment, even if contingent, . . ." from both political economy and reasoned certainty.[30] To these theorists I will add another, knowing that her own life has veered toward the dystopic: Alice

Walker, who described the imperative, in the darkest conditions, to keep "alive . . . the notion of song."[31]

7. READER #2

I'm writing this, now, on a Monday morning. This particular morning of My Precious Writing Time has broken open a space for me to think and write as what feels to me my best self.[32] As such, this Monday morning feels entirely unlike last Monday morning, which was a real grind of beef and prunes, and also unlike the beef-and-prunes Monday morning before that. If you had come around either of the last two Monday morning and asked me—in the midst of making lunches, responding to papers, filling out forms, the DMV, the IRS, the pharmacy, the committee—to "keep alive the notion of song," I would have told you to keep alive the idea of my eyes, rolling out of my head.

Alice Walker, in the same essay quoted from above, wrote that song mattered because the "life you save may be your own," and she was right, and we should remember it, because all this utopic methodology comes into being, or doesn't, at the level of the personal. I believe what I've said here about the world-making potential of academic writing, and I also know that many of our, or my anyway, actual writing experiences take shape amid very specific hopes and ambitions and dreads. Academic writing may keep alive the idea of song, but it can also hope to keep alive, for instance, a particular professional goal, or, in my experience just as importantly, a particular sense of identity.

I remember, several years ago, reading an essay of "quit lit" wherein the author, full of visceral grief, mourned the future where all she had worked so hard to learn would matter directly in how she spent her days. I've felt that grief, like I've said. What we want is the very personal recognition of our capacity to participate in knowledge making, in the soul light of the future. When a piece of writing does not make it through peer review, or even *to* peer review, the loss is and feels personal.

This is partly why so much of our *talking* about peer review orients around the idea of "Reader #2." I'm talking here about a caricature as much as a sometimes-occurring phenomenon, one that provides an important psychic service. Reader #2 is the imagined peer reviewer who reveals in their report all the worst of our university-trained (or, maybe, university-indulged) behaviors. In conversational deployments, Reader #2 is a bad reader, not caring to understand or accurately grapple with our claims. They are a selfish reader, punishing how our writing doesn't affirm their own importance. They are cutting in their judgments, cruel in their prose. Their sentences stick in our 3 a.m. minds and appear in our aggrieved social media discussions. They take the narrowest possible view of what is known and understood, impeding the possibility that something new might come to be known.

The force of Reader #2, as a villain we probably conjure more often than we actually encounter, crystalizes in us because we come to Reader #2's report as a person, here in the world, and we receive in that report the words of someone we know is also real and in the world, but whose anonymity expands the horizon of their forcefulness. We can be as mad at them as we would like to be at all institutions, at all politics. And we also know that, while we can never actually hurt an institution's feelings or sense of self, because an institution has no feelings or sense of self, this Reader #2 might experience some pain, or some remorse, some shame or some harm, from the way we complain about them. Yet because Reader #2 acts anonymously, institutionally, we are protected from thinking of ourselves as being hurtful even though our complaint aims at hurting them.

There are, it's true, some seriously bad-faith readers out there, acting out their own damage upon other people's writing. I think about Reader #2 sometimes when people complain about cold and impersonal institutions. I, too, can dislike cold and impersonal institutions, but then: I also sometimes prefer the coldness of *im*personality to the actual personalities of a whole lot of people in this world.

Earlier I said that I thought it was weird to criticize academic writing for being bad when basically all writing is bad; here I'd say that anytime people claim to want more personalized systems, I always wonder: Have you met people? (I feel more cheerful about people than I do about writing, but I still think most of us have extraordinary capacities for jerkery.) The personal hurt Reader #2 can cause is the risk of dealing with people. And, as feminism has taught us, those who have been damaged by institutions (such as women) are often most likely, when in a place of security (such as when given the opportunity to be Reader #2), to reenact the institutional judgment by which they themselves were harmed. Put differently, when we encounter Reader #2, we're likely to be the worst version of ourselves, and we're also likely to encounter the worst version of this anonymous reader, who, given the opportunity to judge on behalf of the future, our best hopes, is just as likely to speak on behalf of institutional standards, pressures, and insecurities in their worst form.

I'm ending this chapter here, in the uncomfortable company of Reader #2, because here is a place—unlike our unknown future, unlike our idea of song—where, in a practical if unglamorous way, we can do some work to make academic writing better. By better I don't mean more aesthetic or more directly politically efficacious; I mean better at making knowledge for the future, which is the good that academic writing is designed to do.

The wisdom I've gleaned about what Reader #2 can do hasn't come from my experiences as an academic writer. Instead, it has come from my changing relationship to *teaching* writing. For a long time, in my assignments and my grading, I experienced myself primarily as an intermediary of a vague, depersonalized, authority. Rather than assigning projects that might create new ways of seeing poems or cities or bugs, or rewarding students for the surprising strategies they generated themselves, I positioned myself rigidly along conservative generic norms. I responded to papers as I imagined the institution would, forgetting that no institution can ever read a paragraph, let alone a paper. When I responded to papers in this institutional way, I eventually realized, what I was essentially doing was injecting my own fear of Reader #2 into my students' psyches. There are standards!, my comments implied, not specifying who had the standards or who cared about them or why.

This was wrong. There are genres, of course, and we can help our students navigate them. There are gates and they matter. But I have learned to claim my standards as my own. Freedom doesn't have to mean lighting out for the territory. And staying within an institution shouldn't mean our stillness or subservience, our consent to uncritically using (or being) its tools.

Instead, we have to act, with integrity, on behalf of the way we would like the institution to be, and what we would like the institution to be able to read. In this way, through us, the institution, although always imperfectly, might conserve the conditions of a future in which a sustaining "we" could thrive.

PART TWO

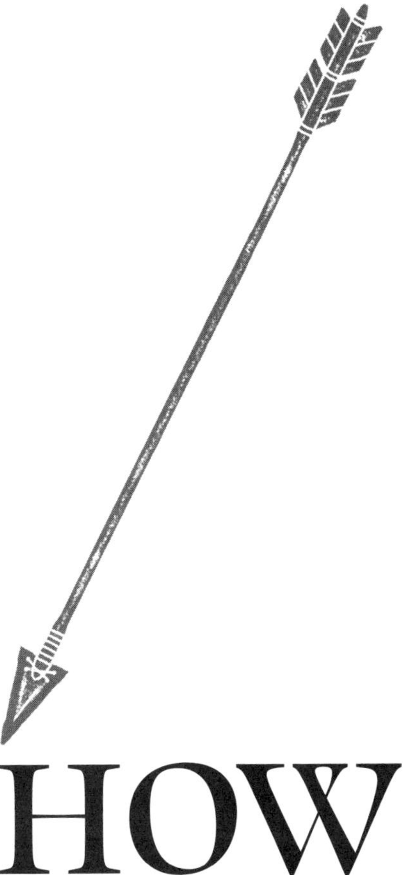

HOW

FIVE

You Have to Practice

It's discouraging. Who wants to practice? I hate to practice. I want to sit down to the page and experience something I tell my students never to expect: "flow." When writing doesn't "flow" for students, they think it's because they're not "good writers," as if "good writer" were a genetic marker or a blood type, something you can be in the way that some people are double-jointed or type O−. I tell them that's not how it works. I tell them: No matter your native affinity, writing will always be labor. I tell them: You have to practice. I have a whole speech. But I don't want to practice either. I want to be an exception to the world I prepare my students to inhabit. I don't want the dreary practicing truth to apply to me. I want to be a "good writer" too.

A Good Writer: What is that? What, in my fantasy, happens when A Good Writer opens a file, picks up a pen? A Good Writer knows how to use all Their Precious Writing Time. They wouldn't fritter it away, like I do, snarfling and pacing around my writing table, phone in hand, like a truffle pig trained to hunt cute dog videos on Instagram. No! The good writer would spend their time choosing the perfect luminous word or wrestling a complex idea into submission. They would work hard on interesting new challenges, not, like I do, always on all the same old challenges. Even now, writing this paragraph (it's a Thursday morning, and My Precious Writing Time feels particularly limited), I'm resenting every moment when my fingers aren't moving elegantly across the keyboard, generating lovely Good Writer prose. Even now, three times in a row, I tried to write a sentence, and what emerged took exactly the opposite form to what, a few paragraphs from now, I plan to advise you to produce.

I know a lot of good writers. None of them actually experience the ongoing paradise I imagine; all of them, even the real genius ones, bang away at the same repeating problems. But the fantasy of breaking free from such tedious actions pulses within me. It's like I've been paying psychic tithe to the cult of the Good Writer for years, since childhood, and every day when I sit down to write I *still expect* the emotional snake oil I have purchased to lubricate the production of words on the page. Instead, here I am: not A Good Writer, just a writer, a better one than I used to be, because I have practiced. I'm not too good, or too smart, or in whatever way too *beyond*, the slow practice it takes to manage writing's basics, let alone to learn more versatile skills, or wrestle my enduring tics. This mythic "Good Writer" looms over my writing. Every day when I write, I have to wrestle him (it's definitely a him) to the side. This personal act of deprograming is yet another activity I have to practice.

The "how" section of this book offers some strategies for inhabiting writing time, for considering sentences and essay structure, and for building the networks that make expert writing valuable. Many of its chapters aim to help writers who have developed their intellectual habits within universities, where the craft of writing is often deemphasized. I'm imagining readers who, regardless of whether they hope to write inside or outside academic publishing, would like to be more thoughtful and dexterous in their prose, working outside a received and often unexamined "academic style." I'm starting with this chapter, about practice, because most of the concepts in what follows aren't hard to explain. Truly: The concepts themselves do not require the stack of pages still before you. I described the qualities that mark what many, pejoratively, call "academic style" in chapter 3, and it only took a paragraph. If you want to know "how" to write beyond academic style, you just ("just") have to avoid those qualities. Avoid the passive voice. Choose more descriptive verbs than "to be." Avoid pileups of prepositional phrases or complex modifying phrases. The chapters that follow give some additional, related advice: Moderate your impulse to "talk" at the lengths of an academic lecture—in the length of your sentences or your paragraphs—unless you have reason to believe that your reader feels willing, at this time, to sit through an academic lecture. Clarify your focus by putting your key noun in the subject position. Remember your girl, I will advise, and where she is going! Some of these points I explain in separate chapters. Others, such as "use a more interesting verb than 'to be' at least most of the time," don't need to be a whole chapter, because that's really the only advice, and now I have given it to you.

What *is* (is!) hard *is* (is!) developing new habits. For instance, I know that one of my tics is overusing the phrase "I think," yet even when I was *revising* this chapter one of the new, improving sentences started with "I think." (My first draft of this manuscript used "I think" eighty-three times.) I *know* that my drafts need more interesting verbs, and I still have to practice finding them, and I don't want to, ever. Yet my process of becoming a more versatile writer involved a lot of printing out drafts, circling all the "to be" verbs, and then going back to replace them with verbs that made more clear who was doing what. Now often I'll catch myself in the act of "to be" writing—"this is," "that is," "we are"—and change my verbs as I go along, so my process works somewhat more organically, but let me tell you: NOT MUCH. And the slow work of putting myself in a place to recognize what my writing has done, so it might be done differently, remains.

Printing out a "to be" draft is one good way to practice, a good drill. It's a way to help build and maintain a habit. Here are some others you might use, to practice the writing advice the following chapters give:

- Take a draft, paste it into a new file, and press return between every sentence (literally every one, I'm sorry) so that you can see them as individual units. Have you a mix of sentence lengths? Are some sentences short and direct? How deep into the sentence must a reader wade before they come to the resting point of a verb?
- Italicize the abstract nouns and underline the concrete nouns. Imagine your girl, which is this book's term for your reader, hopscotching from concrete noun to concrete noun. Remember that reducing the distance between these concrete moments will moderate the demand you make of your girl. Are there places you could help her out?
- Email your draft to yourself. Go to a coffee shop and read your draft on your phone, while in line. Where do you get distracted or bored? Do you need to divide your paragraphs to offer your somewhat distracted reader the assist of some soothing white space?
- Take a paragraph describing a scene and add specific, visceral details to each sentence. Use the thesaurus. Load the paragraph not just like an overstuffed shelf, but like a high-piled oaken rolltop desk, so wedged with details that the tambour top gets stuck when you try to pull its steel handle down to the desk's surface. If you don't know the name for the tambour top, google "what is (is) the top of a rolltop desk called." Then take out all the details but the most surprisingly visceral one, so that the top rolls smooth, the desk contained and clean.
- Consider the scenes your essay seeks to dramatize. On a piece of paper, *draw the scene!* I know, I know, that's crazy, you can't draw, you're a bad artist, you feel dumb. But I swear this really helps, and also is a great classroom activity. When I do it in class, my students look at me in dumb horror and then get all giggly and their drafts improve. (I ask them to draw a scene from their own draft, and then have them swap with a classmate, who tries to put the drawing back into narrative form.) What you're trying to discover about a scene by drawing it is, What's most important within it? What perspectives are there? What details can fall away?
- Print out three similar essays that you like from a publication you'd like to appear in. Reverse outline the essay. How many paragraphs

does it have? What are its sections? What verbs appeal to you? What words jump out? When and how does it use the first person? After annotating these published essays, annotate your draft. What can the published essays teach you? They might teach you that you don't like any essays in a publication, which is good to know! If so, then that publication is not for you.

- Say yes when friends ask you to read drafts and do it in good faith. Reading makes a world of readers, a world in which your writing might be read. If friends don't ask you to read drafts, offer to read drafts. Offer again. Offer and ask to read sentences. If you don't have time, make time. Reading is practicing writing. Learn ways to articulate what qualities help you get where you want to go.

What makes these goofy and annoying practices helpful, in the end, is (is!) your, or my, willingness to repeat them, over and over and over and over. There's no quick fix, no adequate tithe, no devil at the crossroads, no sea witch with a bad feet-for-voice bargain, who can deliver you through the practicing valley. You have to practice it by yourself, and practice it again, and still practice it, forever.

SIX

Who Is Your Girl and Where Is She Going?

Who is your girl? Where is she going? I learned these two questions from *Project Runway,* the fashion reality show, which I watched delightedly for several early seasons before realizing that the show's design advice could be upcycled, as they say, into writing wisdom. In my memory, these questions were posed with some regularity by one of the show's judges, the austerely glamorous Nina Garcia. Garcia's faint Colombian accent twisted the questions with skepticism. Who is your *girrrl*? Where is she *goooing*?[1] When a designer on the show faced these questions, the scene could get antagonistic and twitchy. But don't be defensive when I pose these questions to you. They are real questions, not criticisms, and the best way I know to guide the decisions you make about how style matters in the scene of your writing.

You, my girl currently, may never have watched *Project Runway,* so you may not be familiar with Nina Garcia or these questions. Don't worry. There's still time, and meanwhile I can help. On *Project Runway,* clothing designers compete for the chance to produce a full fashion "line." Each week they square off by designing and fabricating a "look" for a specific challenge. They design for an event, for a client, from a particular fabric. At the end of each episode, models wearing each contestant's look walk the runway, where the clothes are judged for their perspicacity and appeal. It's at this moment of judgment when a contestant might face Garcia's questions. Who is your girl? Where is she going? Garcia would pose the questions to a contestant who had designed an outfit appropriate for no recognizable context. When Garcia asked about your girl and where she was going, Garcia wanted to know: Who, actually, would wear this? *Where* would someone wear it? An outfit might be clever or well executed. But most clothes aren't novelty acts. The judges want designers to remember: Clothes are made to be worn.

So, too, with writing that aims to be read. Reading, like wearing clothes, is an embodied act. It's undertaken by real people, making choices in real places. Those places offer different pleasures, pressures, and distractions. In asking us, as writers, to envision our girls and their goings-on, I'm encouraging us to consider specifically—and with some pragmatism—our desired reader and her scenes. Picture her, your reader, in the path of her life. She is in line at the grocery store or she is at a bar. She stands over her stove. She sits alert at her desk; she lounges on her couch. Consider the style that will fit her there. Your writing decisions about diction, sentence structure, citation, compression, and more matter to your reader's functioning; they do so, much like a designer's choices about fabric, cut, and fasteners. Your writing should absolutely express your own personal style. But if you want your writing to matter once it goes out into the world, it must hold itself accountable to real readers' desires, conscious or not, for self-fashioning.

I'm writing now for you, an audience of humanities-trained experts who are considering an expanding range of publishing options. My own university training rarely addressed how my prose style might address my reader's embodied experience; this is partly because my university training relied on a series of (not always correct) assumptions about my girl and her destinations.

Writing for an academic girl poses several rigorous demands. But repeated practice meeting those demands—even without being taught, explicitly, that they are one set of demands, different from others—normalized them to the extent that I had little sense of how to meet or even recognize the challenges posed by readers in other contexts. Asking myself, or you, about my girl and her destinations—asking myself early and often—helps make sure that my writing makes its best offer to a reader, who can feel well-suited for where she wants to go, and recognized as herself in where my writing asks to take her.

Let's consider the questions separately.

Who is your girl?[2] Probably you imagine more than one person reading what you write. But just as probably, each reader will encounter your prose alone. Maybe, if she likes it, your reader will share your writing with someone she imagines to be, in some ways if not others, like her. It's in the movement between this solitary reader and her own sense of a potentially shared self that you will find "your girl": a collective hailed one by one by one.

What do you recognize about her? Her demographics: her age, gender, race, geography? Her fondness for Jane Austen novels or Rams football or Sasha Colby? Her investment in local politics? The deeper questions here might be: What are the names, concepts, places, and cultural touchstones her world has taught her to remember? What are the values she takes for granted, the ones she fights for, the ones of which she is uncertain? Of what has her world made her proud, and what insecurities has it fed her?

No reader is neutral, although some may believe themselves to be, and because "your girl" names a sense of self recognizable in common, no individual reader will be your only girl, or only your girl. Ethical writing respects the aspects of your reader that your writing doesn't hail.

Where is she going? No one way of writing will always suit your reader, any more than one outfit would always make her feel comfortable, even if "comfortable" was how she always wanted to feel. Speaking for myself, in some contexts I like high heels and tailored dresses and their compressive, demanding power: So, too, might I like your densely wrought sentences. I choose thick work gloves for garden labor, and although I might wish they accommodated themselves a little better to my fingers' shape, I don't mind the rough fit when they do the work for which they are intended: So, too, might I appreciate your incommodious sentence that safely manages a thorny point. When I am relaxing, I want soft, flexible fabric. I have soft pants in three levels of softness and reading materials that match each one. Which version of my moving selfhood does your writing aim to shape, display, hail, endorse, reform?

The key part of all this, as writing advice, is to think of your reader on two axes: identity and context. Or rather, I'm advising you to think of your reader's identity in motion, on the way toward somewhere else. On *Project Runway* they mean, Is your girl going to a party? A coffee shop? Prom? Walking, subway, or valet parking? Your girl, your reader, may or may not be moving physically toward similarly different places. But regardless of whether she is reading at the coffee shop, her kitchen table, or a bar, she may hope her reading brings her closer to different collectivities, or different affinities with them. She is moving toward a new version of herself, or affirming a part of herself. At the end of the reading experience, she will at a bare minimum be a girl who has read this thing and—depending on where she wanted to go—successfully felt herself become a more cognizant self, or a more glamorous one, or more knowing, empathetic, comforted, or (re)assured. It will be a part of what she's experienced, and therefore of who she is.

As writing instructors, we often say that a piece of writing should *travel*, a metaphor I've had students struggle to understand. This sense of transformation is one thing we mean. It's not so much that the writing itself moves, but rather that you've taken a reader toward a new version of themselves, who understands the world differently. A reason many students find this so inscrutable is because so much writing—and so much of how they've been taught to read—works differently, simply by encouraging or allowing a reader to be who they already were, with more affirmation. And this is a fine thing to want from a reading experience! It is basically what I want from my softest sweatpants, a swaddling accommodation, with no hint that any way I manage myself might be subject to judgment or discussion. But there's a wide range of experiences that readers are after, and challenges come in many forms. If you, as an academy-trained writer, are hoping your demanding idea will reach toward readers in their leisure, you should think about what comfort you confer, or what pleasure or reward you offer to compensate for leisure's withdrawal.

Posing these questions to yourself may have a few practical effects on your writing. Here's how knowing your girl and where she's going will help you.

YOUR DICTION

What words does your girl know, and how does she feel about knowing them? The answers to these questions help you consider which words to use, which not to use, which to define. Which dropped names work like the mention of a shared friend and which like a flex?

Your girl, no matter where she is, and no matter what version of code-switching she may currently be employing, will always have the same vocabulary. I make this point because many writers seem to think that the primary change they need to make, when writing for nonacademic contexts, is to use simpler words. You might need to do so, yes, but "simpler" words aren't a sufficient writerly shift. Whether I am at my desk or in line at the grocery store, my knowledge doesn't change. I'll know the same references—poststructuralism, melancholy, midi-length skirt, Jessica Wakefield—regardless. I have just now created a list of words I might use to hail the girl who, like me, is a middle-aged white lady with voracious reading habits trained first in the white mediascape of the Scholastic Book Fair and later in the white mediascape of a 1990s English department. Some of these words register as sophisticated and others less so, but their complexity matters less to your audience than the baggage attached to them.

If I dropped a reference to Jessica Wakefield in a piece of writing, as I have just done, without explaining that she is one of the twin sisters at the center of the long-running 1980s YA series Sweet Valley High, many girls might be confused. But others familiar with that reference might become very excited. I would, with my word choice, have affirmed the specific knowledge of avid Scholastic Book Fair Readers as common sense; the reason the girl would get so excited is because the sense of SVH readers is rarely affirmed as common. More so (or, at least differently so) than a reference to Proust, such as the one made in this book's first chapter, SVH feels particular and limited, requiring explanation. If I were to title an essay, as it now occurs to me would be an excellent idea, "The Melancholy of Jessica Wakefield," a smaller group of reader girls would get even more excited, because to consider Jessica Wakefield in light of psychoanalysis (or Keats, or black bile) would be to affirm to this girl that she could go to a very particular place, where a word she has been told is collectively worth humanist knowing ("melancholy") is brought into intimate contact with a reference she has been made to feel is niche and vaguely embarrassing ("Jessica Wakefield"). My diction would be an act of hospitality to a particular kind of girl, and an act of estrangement to other ones.

In a truly invaluable podcast interview, conducted by Tressie McMillan Cottom, the writer Kiese Laymon describes this act of hospitality as acknowledging the writers in your "first row."[3] In the podcast, Cottom and Laymon share their strategies for navigating white editors who insist that the diction of white readers be affirmed as common sense. Laymon gives the example of an editor asking him to define the word "switch" in an essay. Laymon refused. The readers in "the first row" of his audience know the force of that word, he tells us; to define the word would be to signal to those readers "that they're not reading something that is directed especially to them." Laymon's analysis shows diction's politics. Even if you're not writing "about" politics, your word choice extends (or doesn't) the resource of your welcome, by affirming the centrality of particular kinds of knowledge.

It's maybe worth saying directly: This book's consistent references to popular feminized aspects of culture are part of its politics.

I'm on purpose crafting this writing guide, directed at all humanists, through an idiolect specific to a subsection of those humanists. It's a risk, one I've thought about a lot. My idiolect is marked by Gen X–ish Midwestern white-lady experiences. Many, for good reasons, might find it abrasive or problematic, in the same way that some might be bothered by other feminized style markers carrying an aslant relation to their own social privilege, like vocal fry or uptalk. But it seemed a different kind of risk, and a worse one, every time I tried to write in a more "neutral" and writing-guide-y voice. That neutral voice, as I could manage to produce it, seemed about as neutral as one of those old "skin color" Band-Aids—which is to say, just as inflected by my proximity to power as my Gen X white lady references to Jessica Wakefield, jean jacket queen. So I'm going this route, instead, in the hopes that if my diction feels surprising or narrow, other parts of my writing—such as the ones I mention in the following—offer more broadly comfortable seating.

YOUR SYNTAX

Okay, really picture your girl. Where is she? Is she reading on her phone, on her laptop, from a magazine, printout, or book? Does she have a free hand to hold a pen? Is she alone? On the train? How long can she expect to read without interruption from a train stop, her child, a pop-up ad for shoes? You can fantasize about (as I fantasize about) an infinitely rapt reader, but there are just not very many of those, despite the number of people who fantasize about achieving that state (as I fantasize about achieving it). Most of the people for whom I want to write are tired and distracted and reading anyway. I want my sentences to respect this girl's interruptions, rather than making her feel worse about them.

I try to show that respect by making my sentences easier to wrangle. This may mean making them shorter. But, as I discuss in "The Subject of the Sentence," a longer sentence can still be reader friendly when you organize it around vivid, concrete nouns. Expert humanities writing, in its efforts to make nuanced points about abstractions and to create (as I have discussed) particular tones of objectivity, tends to deploy some demanding syntactic properties. It uses complex noun phrases to capture its topics. It deploys prepositional phrases and passive voice, to home in on a particular state of things, considered in its stasis. Has your girl cleared out a quiet space in her day to absorb a nuanced point, rendered in a demanding stylistic mode? Then go for it; proceed apace in your sentences loaded with prepositional phrases to explain abstractions of thought under the assumption that your reader's motivation to understand your insight will carry them through the nuances of your point, like I'm asking you to do in this sentence, this paragraph, with this point. Otherwise, maybe don't.

But then: Maybe do! As I've said, comfort isn't what all readers want, and comfort can come in many forms. Ease might not offer comfort. Many people in the midst of busy life *want* to remember the tremendous capacity of their minds for rigor. Reading hard beautiful things can be one of the most spectacular forms of self-making; the pleasure of it can, strangely, open up time and mental space in a hard day.

YOUR USE OF SOURCES

Here is an experience I regularly face when editing expert writers who hope to write in journalistic venues. They submit a draft to me about their topic—a photo in *Time* magazine, a funny movie, their mother's death (these are real examples)—and in the midst of the essay I find a complex literature review about how the author's thinking about *Time* magazine, or the funny movie, or death, came into being through a particular academic exchange, which the author I am editing feels determined to cite in depth, or at least by beginning a paragraph by writing, "A recent article helps explain . . ."

My friends! I, too, am a nerd. I am famous in my (nerdy) family for, at age three, declaring to my mother that I wouldn't eat the banana she was trying to feed me, because "I read in an article that bananas aren't good for you." I absolutely understand the intense desire to spell out, in what you are writing, the insight of some other piece of writing, especially although not only a scholarly piece of writing, and how your own perspective relates to that other piece of writing. If this desire motivates your writing to the point that you can't let it go, you have definitely learned something about your girl, and where she is going. She is an academic reader, and you should write, to reach her, in an academic context.

Holding in tandem multiple pieces of writing, their qualities and ideas, is a readerly skill specifically cultivated by those of us with expertise in the humanities. I have that skill, and if you're reading this, so do you. I am glad to have it. I profoundly endorse the citational ethics of writing in dialogue with other thinkers; that's part of why I went to graduate school. But I don't necessarily want to use that skill when in my soft pants or on the train, which are the times I am most likely to look at nonacademic writing. Mentioning your really important article in the nonscholarly reading scenes where I might be reading your nonscholarly essay is a related kind of party foul to mentioning Žižek at a bar. In a nonscholarly scene, what I usually want from your story is *your* story. Tell it to me.

YOUR VENUE

Everything you publish will be shaped, in its reception, by the specific visual and cultural markers of its venue. This is true whether we are considering a PDF downloaded from JSTOR or the fonts, ads, color schemes, and layout decisions made by most nonacademic platforms. These qualities condense into a reader's expectation for a certain publication: She comes to this publication to travel toward this venue's prized version of selfhood. Most venues are good at thinking about their girls; if you've stood at a magazine stand trying to choose between, say, *Vogue*, *Self*, and *Martha Stewart Living*, you've given yourself a crash course in the "who is your girl and where is she going" lesson this chapter tries to teach (and which I return to in the chapter on pitching). As a writer, you have only some control over your venue. But as you write (or pitch something to write), consider how your essay will interact with where a particular venue aims to take its readers, and how your diction and syntax should change accordingly.

Two other notes: First, the same essay will have a different meaning in different contexts, and as you write, you can use this to your advantage (creating either surprise or affirmation). Second, as I spell out in "Know Your Noun," it's not always the case that a more conventionally prestigious venue will best serve a particular piece of writing. A more niche venue that has specifically affirmed the girl you want to reach can often do more for you than a bigger venue with a history of condescending to her.

*

Within this advice, I hope you'll see a polemic against the implication that when experts shift from academic audiences to other ones, they'll endure the indignity of "dumbing down" their writing. I am not immune to this way of feeling, but it's one we should resist. Not only annoying and smug, this belief also misdiagnoses the situation. It conflates a reader's desired destination with a (reductive or false) assessment of her identity.

Here we come back to the question of academic writing and academic readers. If your girl is a scholar and choosing to read your scholarship, you can expect that she has a particular destination in mind: deeper into expertise. To reach this place, this version of herself, she's probably willing to work for your meaning, even if you don't articulate your points in an entertaining or even welcoming way. But almost no other girl—and *not even this girl, in any nonacademic context*—will be so accommodating. This same girl who will willingly detangle your complex prose in the service of information or insight that peer review tells her she can find nowhere else may prove unwilling to stay with your sentences, if she's reading for other goals

When public-facing writing by an expert fails to connect with an audience, it feels reassuring to the expert, often me, to conclude that the misfire happens because of too-simple wiring in the reader's brain. What's more likely the case is that I have coughed out a deeply idiosyncratic paragraph whose clear-to-me intricacies looked to everyone else about as legible as an owl pellet. You can call the reluctant reader of this paragraph "dumb," but the more likely situation is that dissecting your half-metabolized thoughts is not the science project your reader is hoping for, at least at this time.

So in this advice is also some guidance about being edited, yet another skill that academic training could better provide. Grades, dissertation defenses, and peer review—evaluative processes of academia—carry the force of judgment, and they can train writers in "my writing vs. them" feelings that impede the collaborative work of editing. An editor's job (they may be better or worse at it, of course) is to understand their venue's girl and where that girl is going. While part of the editor's role is, like Nina Garcia's, to judge, once they've accepted your piece, an editor's job is to work with you, behind the scenes, on tailoring and styling, because they believe in their girl and they believe in what you have to say to her. Here's my last use of this metaphor: Editing can go best when a writer sees an editor as an ally in finding the best fit.

SEVEN

You Write with Your Body, Which Keeps the Score

According to a best-selling book on neuropsychology, the body "keeps the score." Our bodies, this book tells us, carry the traces of our experiences. Our selfhood—however you think of that self, as a soul or a mind—can't be separated from what has happened to our bodies, or how our bodies have been taught, looked at, loved, hurt.

Let me say this: Nobody's eyes roll further out of their head than mine do when I hear a phrase like "best-selling book on neuropsychology." My life's work is to train eighteen-year-olds how to engage in humanistic methods. I hate when they show up, as so many of them seem to, reaching for all of life's answers in psychological "studies" they know how to quote but seemingly not to question. I spend hours every semester extracting, more or less gently, pop-psychological, neurobiological accounts of personhood from student worldviews, like a doctor tweezing gravel out of a scraped knee.

Yet here I am, bearing the to-me-irritating news that I found this particular best-selling book about neurobiological personhood full of useful thinking. As someone who has read a lot of feminist theory, I didn't need Bessel van der Kolk to convince me that our writing bodies keep the score. ("She was snubbed, slapped, lectured and exhorted," writes Virginia Woolf of the woman artist; "Her mind must have been strained by the need of opposing this, of disproving that."[1]) But reading about van der Kolk's therapeutic practice did help me find a new language for, and approach to, a writing practice within my score-keeping body. I'm interested in using van der Kolk's practices to understand how the act of sitting down to write, before you even get to formulating sentences, will be shaped by your embodied experiences of talking, reading, listening, and, crucially, being read or listened to. The act of sitting down to write will also be shaped by what has happened to you when you have sat down to write before. "How" we write starts before the writing. Or at least, that's how it works for me.

What does it mean for writing that our bodies keep the score? "The critical issue," van der Kolk writes in *The Body Keeps the Score* (2014), "is allowing yourself to know what you know." He goes on: "That takes an enormous amount of courage."[2] Van der Kolk here writes about facing knowledge of trauma—for instance, reconciling yourself to your own self-shattering experiences of abuse. The problem I face most often as a writer exists at a far remove from the trauma van der Kolk describes. My problem isn't abuse; it's an experience usually known as "writer's block." But the concept and experience of "writer's block" carries its own historical damage. As the scholar and writing advisor Naomi Greyser has amply demonstrated, "writer's block" is a concept with a specific history—one tied to the postwar university—that has itself worked to reinforce particular norms of confidence and productivity. Many writers Greyser interviews describe becoming chronically unable to inhabit the authority of their field expertise; many also describe the courage (often felt as a lack) it takes to write in our current expert environments, which can feel so precarious and rough. This psychic structure doesn't generate the same traumas as those experienced by the veterans and abuse victims who are van der Kolk's patients, but it shares some of the same patterns. Maybe for this reason, van der Kolk's research has helped me "know what I know," too. He helps me ask: What practical methods for repair can attending to our physical bodies offer us, as writers?

*

In 2014, the same year that van der Kolk published *The Body Keeps the Score*, Eric Hayot published *The Elements of Academic Style: Writing for the Humanities*. These are very different books, but their coincidence seems significant to me, because both of them aim at acts of demystification, explaining, respectively, the psyche's relation to the body and writing's stylistic relation to intellectual labor. Certainly, neither of these experiences were present to my own training. Both writing process and writing craft were skill sets that my own training obscured. We talked in seminars about embodiment as a link to content, which it is. But the practical mechanics of getting my body to start writing—much like the practical mechanics of composing an effective sentence or paragraph—remained underneath the level of curriculum.

Other writing guides, though—and I'll discuss this throughout these "how" chapters—do address the body. They often do so metaphorically, and, to my mind, not always helpfully. For instance, when I began teaching in my current writing program, the assigned course guide for all freshman writing seminars explained that "in a way, drafting is like running: until you establish a rhythm, nothing feels right, but the only way to find your rhythm is to start moving and tough it out."[3]

As someone who both runs and writes, I agree that there's an experiential relation between the toughness each requires. But as someone who has also spent, cumulatively, as much time avoiding writing and running as I have done engaging in either activity, I also know the analogy's truth doesn't do much to help me face the difficult task of starting either of them. In fact, it may discourage me from the attempt. When I'm not able to start, when facing my fear feels too tough, when I don't have—as van der Kolk puts it—the courage to know what I know, or even to learn what I know, what then? How does it help me to be told that I just need to be tough—or to have it implied that, if I'm not pushing through, this admirable "toughness" is something I lack?

I'm speaking here from a position of extreme privilege. I've been loved my whole life, and generally affirmed and kept safe. The world trains everyone to treat people who look like me—white, feminine, smiley—considerately, if not actually respectfully. I don't face the obstacles of writers whose bodies place them at a significantly higher risk of what Miranda Fricker calls "epistemic injustice."[4] Beyond my gender, I don't display sociological markers that can place writers at a "credibility deficit," to use Fricker's phrase; or leave others literally "dying," to riff on Tressie McMillan Cottom, "to be competent."[5]

But even in bodies like mine, bodies with incredible systemic good fortune, feeling like a failed writer (or feeling like a "failed academic," to use a phrase I heard a lot from a beloved professor) can well and truly suck. As I've hinted elsewhere in this book, I went through a fairly debilitating period of writer's block, one that arguably lasted for multiple years of sitting down, being miserable for many frittery hours while wondering if I would ever be able to escape the gravity of my own avoidance, before finally enough time would have passed for me to get up, put on a smiley face, and pretend that it had been an okay day. This was tough, if not "toughing it out." It was a super crappy, if also mostly self-inflicted, psychic pain that I once described to my therapist as having "a rotten core of shame." The same writing guide that used to tell my program's students to "tough it out" also had some advice for procrastinators. The advice: "Don't be one of them."[6] Knowing that I was like "them" was hard to know; for years, I rarely had the courage to do it. And being disgusted at the prospect of knowing the truth about myself—that I wasn't someone able to just sit down and write—made it hard to know everything, or really anything, else that I knew.

Every time I sit down to write, still, my body remembers those many, many bad days of sitting down into my shame. The physical impact those memories have on my body are easy to see, by which

I mean, they are visible. I can see them, and if you came over, you could too. I walk to the table where I plan to write. I sit down. Look: I immediately get back up. Why? Why don't I stay sitting down? Infinite reasons. I forgot my tea; where are my tissues; oh my notebook is over there; this isn't the right pen; I left my phone in the other room on purpose but—ope!—just realized I somehow need to urgently check my phone. Behind these reasons is another: When I sit down, I feel my sense of self protectively scurrying away from the scene. I mean this literally: I get a sensory sensation, as soon as I sit down, like some essential part of myself is draining out of my head, along the ridges of my shoulders, running *out*. It doesn't want to know. It would rather do anything else—pen, tea, phone, tissue, ope! other pen!—even if the anything else it does contributes to my long-term spiraling.

Van der Kolk has something to say about a version of this experience. He explains that people who have experienced trauma often find themselves stuck in "fight or flight" embodied feedback loops in which even basic forms of social engagement become challenging. They don't feel safe, even when the external circumstances are secure, because the experience of insecurity is being perpetuated in their own bodies.

This therapeutic problem is familiar to me both as a writing teacher and as a writer with intense loops of procrastination. Sometimes on the first day of a writing seminar I'll do a poll about the hardest parts of writing. I'm never the only person who puts "sitting down" at the top of my list. Like my students, I know, consciously, that I'm fine; that I'm spooling out the conditions that make my situation worse. I also know that, for both me and my students, recognizing the problem intellectually does not solve the problem or help me tough it out. In fact, understanding the dire effects of not being able to get out of a bad loop can make that loop harder to resist.

Van der Kolk points to a series of studies in which changing the body's activity becomes the best strategy for changing a state of mind: "Severely traumatized people may get more out of simply helping to arrange chairs . . . than they would from sitting in those same chairs and discussing the failures of their life."[7] He describes chair moving like this as a "bottom up" strategy. One of van der Kolk's colleagues, for example, was adept at bringing abused children into a state of engagement. When the children refused or were unable to respond to verbal or social cues, the colleague would "accidentally" drop a ball near the child, who would often push it back without thinking. "From simple, rhythmically attuned movements," van der Kolk writes, the colleague "had created a small, safe place where social-engagement systems could begin to reemerge."[8]

The phrase "small, safe place" stays with me, because the gentle process of creating one offers basically the opposite strategy of the toughing it out that my old writing seminar course guide recommends. That writing is hard doesn't mean that the best way into it is doing the hardest thing first. On the days when I feel the fear of facing myself particularly powerfully, when I am scared to look square at the event taking place on my page, I can use my body in a different way to make myself feel more able to write as the expert that I am.

*

Part of developing some doable accountability as a teacher and editor of other writers, and as a writer myself, means remembering that there's no one "good" or ideal way to write with your body, just like there's no one right way to have a body or to be in your body. We face different challenges, sometimes categorically so. We don't need to come to the same solution, and we don't need to agree about desirable conditions of embodiment, any more than we need to agree about genres or writing styles. There's not one "healthy" way to write. As a friend recently commented to me, writing sometimes goes better if you embrace any weird practice that works. She, for instance, prefers writing with light shining on her *right side* rather than on her left. That this makes no rational sense doesn't stop it from helping her get to what I would call her safe-feeling space.

Another friend of mine, a gorgeous and accomplished writer, reports that he basically prefers to be a head in a jar while writing. His way of writing from his body is to forget his body. I learned this when he had a small panic attack at the suggestion from his partner that they get a cat. How could he write with a cat? Cats live *in your house* and they are there, *alive*, all of the time. He couldn't imagine getting into his ideal disembodied writing state in a house that contained a constant embodiment reminder, there all the time, grooming itself and contemplating small murder and *purring*.

When he puts it this way I absolutely understand, although his attitude toward animals and writing could not be further from my own. I can get so antsy in my writing body that it's virtually impossible to calm down *unless* I am near the breathing body of my dog. She anchors my big animal feelings deep in her fur somehow; she shares my snacks in a full-pleasure way that helps me enjoy them too. The fact that she has zero interest in words or sentences or ideas, that she is so fully in her body, helps me feel easier in mine. And that is what I want, when writing: an easy, aware, bodily sense.

But it might not be what you want. Writing with your body may mean you take all your body's energy and pour it into your writing, neglecting your body's needs and health and pleasure, as though your writing project was a leeching, external embryo you exist to serve. Related but differently, you may, like Mare of Easttown, fuel your research with leftover pizza and Wawa hoagies, meaningfully distilling from your physical discomfort and vague indulgent unwellness an intoxicating illustration of your own drive. That this is "unhealthy" doesn't mean it's not one real way to do hard work.

Conversely, you might prepare for writing as though for the Olympics, like a lawyer friend who cuts out all alcohol, sugar, and junk food starting months before a trial. She doesn't enjoy the Wawa/neglect "nothing matters but the project" approach, although she told me she's tried it. This friend wants to be in peak form. Her arguments are an extreme sport! She trains; she surpasses simple "health."

I absolutely can't do the ramping up toward a high-intensity scene of potential triumph that works for her. *This really matters,* her whole strategy exists to remind her, and getting that embodied lesson is just absolutely the worst for me and my "can't sit down" body. It's terrible to feel that my life or self-worth rides on what I may or may not be able to accomplish in the act of sitting down. My sense of myself as a writer is too fragile from my own self-imposed psychic injuries, and all of these are easily reactivated in times of stress. So—as with my relation to my dog—I need to keep things calm. The more sideways and nondirectionally I get at my writing, the less stressful it's likely to be. If I get really anxious, I stop typing and write with a pencil—it's just a note, a jot! I'll take a walk, and send myself little audio texts, as though I were chatting with someone who I knew was interested in listening to me.

For me, this is a tonal issue too. Anything that indicates emergency measures makes it harder for me to be the version of myself whose ideas I most want to access. The writing voice that serves me best is clear but also lose, inviting. I can't get that way either through ramping up my bodily care or by telling myself that nothing matters but the work.

But listening to my lawyer friend tell me about her personal-trainer approach to intellectual and professional labor helped me realize that certain kinds of discipline really do help me: a clear routine, going to bed early, doing down dog on writing breaks, eating lots of fruit. Being good to myself in these ways helps normalize writing; makes it seem like a regular, unspectacular part of an honest life. Which is what I want my writing to be (and which may or may not be what you want your writing to be).

*

These days when I write, I sit almost every day at my dining room table, which my Grammy bought me twenty years ago at the Cost Plus World Market off the North/Clybourn Red Line stop in Chicago. My apartment is a strange rectangle carved unromantically out of an old house; the small space probably has no effect on the amount of dog hair drifting, all the time, everywhere, but it's true that there's dog hair, all the time, everywhere. It is the best place I have ever written. It reminds me that I am capable of making hard choices for the benefit of the parts of myself I value most, and if hard choices are expensive (literally and psychically), this one at least was worth the cost. When my kids are at school and my shedding dog dozes fuzzily on my bed—perfectly in my line of sight from the table—I feel a sense of control transmit from my writing space because I know it came from me trusting myself, in a world that didn't always teach me to.

I hope that this book feels useful to people who have substantially less control over the spaces in which they write. The forces that limit what you can control will be intersectional and three-dimensional: your region, your economics, your embodiment, your family, your responsibilities, the local governance of your region. Does your city or state pay for long open hours in public libraries, and do you feel comfortable being female/poor/queer/in drag/disabled in those libraries? These are important questions for writing. Does the fluorescent lighting at the university library hum; are there comfortable chairs; can you afford the coffee shop, and how often; can you afford both a snack and tea? Your body will keep the score of these signals. They will shape the work of your writing, the degree to which you feel supported, and the toughness of what the world asks you to "tough out."

I think about these questions because I know that one of the most valuable parts of my writing space is the privacy it offers me to do my very particular morning routine, the one that helps me, more than anything else, find a small, safe place. Here's what I do to bring myself to my table, which for all its bespoke comforts still can terrify me. I wake up, really early, try not to look too long at my phone, put the kettle on and walk the dog while it boils, make tea, and then, while it steeps, I lie on the floor. I start my writing day doing the same hip stretches I have done since my middle school dance class: extend each leg, flex, point, and bend on an eight count, first rotated in, then rotated out.

I am proud of my morning safe-place routine. I got the idea of it from not only van der Kolk's book but also from Twyla Tharp's very enjoyable *The Creative Habit: Learn It and Use It for Life* (2003).[9] Here, Tharp describes her similar morning routine as a ritual. Her point is that you can train your body to respond in an inevitable-feeling way to a sequence of events: for me, from the tea kettle, to the floor, to the hip stretches, to my laptop and the writing. It's like van der Kolk's colleague with the group therapy chairs, or the simple passing of a ball. What Tharp advises is to create the conditions whereby you don't have to *decide* to be creative; the ritual in which you engage enacts the creativity for you. Rather than waiting for the muse to strike externally, your own ritual creates the condition of muse.[10]

Considering Tharp's sense of creative ritual in light of *The Body Keeps the Score* led me to a question about my own writing routine. I wondered: What is it about lying on the floor doing a dance class warm-up that creates a sense of safety for me? What transferable knowledge might I find in my own personal experience? Why am I lying on the floor stretching my hamstrings, rather than brainstorming a list of words and ideas?

Most basically, my dance warm-up takes me back to a very safe and well-loved place, my above-the-library dance studio. Physically repeating the actions I performed in a place where I felt skilled and valued reminds my body that I am skilled and valued, which helps me believe that what I have to say is worth being listened to.

But, of course, I like to stretch, and I feel safe and even powerful when I do so, because I am flexible and believe I can become more so. Stretching is a source of pride. (I wouldn't juggle in the morning, even if my beloved dance studio had held juggling classes: the last thing I need in the morning is to encounter my deep capacity for spazz.) I used to tell my students to stretch to get the words out, before I realized that stretching might not help them feel skilled and powerful. In fact, stretching is just as likely to make them feel stiff. Now I just tell them that stretching helps *me* get the words out. The trick, overall, is to be interested in yourself without judging yourself: to witness yourself in different activities and conditions (coffee shop? soft chair? spinny chair? cat or no cat?) and let yourself learn what you need, and then give yourself that thing to the best of your ability, even if it's not something you want to need, and even if it's something the world has told you that a Good Writer wouldn't need.

Even after all this, though, all the stretching and the ritualized tea, sitting down still feels hard. But I can often make a "small, safe place" with a strategy that's so simple that it's a little embarrassing it works for me so well: I start writing *before I sit down*. Leaning over the table, maybe with one foot flamingoed against the other knee, or maybe standing in fourth position (which every dancer knows is a power position), I start writing while standing up. If I am sitting and a paragraph gets hard, I get back up, find fourth position or flamingo. I feel safer that way. It makes sense to my body, and that makes my writing make more sense.

Not being able, on a given day, to do the thing I think my body should be able to do is not a flaw; it is not a failure. You don't have to tough it out; instead, you can find a way to go around. My point in this chapter is that writing is hard enough without absorbing the "one of them" shame that percolates around humanities experts and makes writing so much harder. The merit of your ideas doesn't depend on already being the always-confident-in-your-words person the world has told you that you should become.

*

I had thought to end this chapter there. But as I revised it, I started to notice a shared way that many writing guides discuss writing bodies. So I want to add this coda of a sort, which takes up a specific issue around bodily score keeping. That issue is the power of what sociologist Sabrina Strings describes as "a philosopher's slim ideal."[11] This ideal associates slim bodies—and the discipline from which slim bodies are falsely believed to emerge—with good thinking and elegant prose. Strings's research describes how such an ideal emerged in tandem with Western culture's gender and racial biases. The philosopher Kate Manne addresses the same issue with a different method, showing the illogic on which this ideal depends. She also shows how such an ideal saturates contemporary academic life in the form of anti-fat bias.[12] Anti-fat bias, often rationalized by overstated medical concerns, manifests in discriminatory practices around hiring and professional respect. It is a structure, not just a feeling, but it is also a feeling, and we experts feel it when we face the page. Our professional interactions have told us that the shape of our bodies reflects both our capacity to write and the quality of what we do write.

One place we may have learned of this ideal's power is in the books (like this one) that aimed to teach us to write. Here are some comments, some offhand and some structural, that I've found in writing guides, comments that link habits of writing to habits of appetite, discipline, and weight:

> So that's it—three tools that let you contain, cleanse, and connect to academic writing. Project box plus ventilation plus fifteen minutes a day. Are these really all you need to write productively for the rest of your life? Yes and no. Just as most diet advice is some version of "eat less, move more," most writing advice is some version of "fear less, write more."
>
> JOLI JENSEN, *Write No Matter What*[13]

> An obsession for writing is good. But then write. Don't let it get twisted into drinking. An obsession for chocolate is not good. I know. It's unhealthy and doesn't help the world the way peace and writing do.
>
> NATALIE GOLDBERG, *Writing Down the Bones*[14]

> For lunch I eat the same thing every day (bagel with cream cheese); likewise for the snack that comes after the second writing section. . . .
>
> . . . Sitting down to write three pages is harder than sitting down to write two, which makes your habit-creating pattern that much harder to begin. Those extra pages have a way of spiraling out of control, leading to a day when, faced with the idea that you have

> to "catch up" by ten pages or so, you simply give up and eat a bag of Doritos instead. (I have done this, by the way. The chips were delicious.)
>
> ERIC HAYOT, *The Elements of Academic Style*[15]

> Incorporating the "other view" into one's writing makes what you have to say more persuasive, and while it may take a few more words to bring in another view, the overall effect is the impression of greater economy: more muscle and less fat.
>
> WILLIAM GERMANO, *On Revision*[16]

> For example, let's say that you have a main character whose feelings can be hurt if he's spoken to sharply—unlike you, ha-ha-ha. Say he is also a little like you in the sense that when he gets a bit depressed or tense, he heads for a rib joint to eat a pound of burned, fatty meat. So he is perhaps also a little overweight—not that you are overweight. I'm sure your weight is just fine.
>
> ANNE LAMOTT, *Bird by Bird*[17]

> Imagine yourself recruiting a long-distance runner to deliver an important message. What kind of person would you choose: a lean, strong athlete with well-toned muscles and powerful lungs, or a pudgy unfit couch potato who will wheeze and pant up the first few hills before collapsing in exhaustion? The answer is obvious. Yet far too many send their best ideas out into the world on brittle-boned sentences weighted down with rhetorical flab.
>
> HELEN SWORD, *The Writer's Diet*[18]

Here are two more-purposeful discussions of weight and writing:

> In the workshops and in the books I read obsessively as a young writer, editing was described in such violent and intimate terms that it became clear to me—though I never would have said so at the time—that the excised material, the "fat," was metaphorically part of my body, my selfhood, which meant the story was my whole body

> ("This essay needs to be put on a diet," one of my first writing teachers said to the class, when I was thirteen.) I've struggled with my weight since high school, so I'm particularly attuned to this correlation: you cut away the parts of the story body you're most ashamed of, the parts you want no one to see.
>
> JESS ROW, *White Flights*[19]

> I was, like many young women, expected to be small so that boys could expand and white girls could shine. When I would not or could not shrink, people made sure that I knew I had erred. . . . I had tried in different ways over the years to fit. I thought I could discipline my body and later my manners to take up less room. I was fine with that, but I learned that even I had limits when—in my pursuit of the life of the mind—my thinking was deemed too thick.
>
> TRESSIE MCMILLAN COTTOM, "Thick"[20]

And here is an offhand comment I myself wrote that appears in this writing guide, revealing my own associations about body and prose and how those associations are working in me, all the time:

> As when, in a clothing store, I have an idea of what size or style fits me that may not correspond to what feels good on an actual day, and I then have to wrestle with how hard it can be to actually *be who I am* rather than who I used to be or might hypothetically become, choosing a noun can be like choosing the *right now-fitting* dress, an act of honesty generating a lot of freedom and also maybe some ambivalence.

And that's separate from my comments in this chapter about dance class and stretching—let alone the whole Lululemon discussion in chapter 3, or the baked goods you'll find in chapter 8—comments that are not necessarily about weight and also *definitely are*. In the above passage and elsewhere, I'm aiming to describe the value of letting go of preset bodily ideals. But I'm also talking about how it's hard to do so. That difficult surely carries its own message.

Bodies write, and so to talk about writing often leads to some kind of expressed assumption or advice about bodily care. What feels to each of us like care will often be a product of ideology we have absorbed. Ideology isn't a switch anyone can turn on and off. It gets in us all. So, I don't offer these quotations as some sort of "gotcha!" or purity metric. I have found value in many of these writing guides. But we should aim to do our very best, in discussions of embodied writing and in general, to block transmission of the "thin ideal." This ideology is dangerous, and it does harm.

EIGHT

Pitches and Abstracts

Or, Some Ways of Building Worlds with Words

I get asked a lot about pitching. You can google "how to write a pitch" and find lots of advice from editors, but I understand why the question feels evergreen. The pitching process seems mystical to a lot of writers, university-trained writers especially. I know, because—despite having vetted hundreds of pitches—I myself have definitely googled "how to write a pitch." I'm hoping to find some universal key to all publishing mythologies. I want pitching to work, by which I mean "lead to acceptances." The fact that it doesn't always work, at least in that way, makes me feel like there's some magic happening somewhere, up someone's sleeve, when I would like it to be happening in mine. When I'm asked about pitching, I feel academics asking for a key that I'm still not sure I hold.

Pitching, like submitting an abstract, isn't magic; it's maybe more like baking, in that there are some basic steps and ingredients and chemistry at play, and if you combine them according to protocols, you'll make something that tastes good. It's also like baking in that, unfortunately, baking something that tastes good in the abstract doesn't mean that you've concocted something that any editor in particular wants to eat, on the day you offer it to them. That editor might not like the flavor you used or might have already eaten some of that kind of Danish, or might be looking for something more substantive or more snackish, or might just be full. None of these mismatches signals necessary flaws in you or your baking! But you may need to look around for someone with different tastes. Sometimes this takes a long, annoying time, and your cookies get stale, and you have to start again. That is how it goes.

What's the chemistry? What are the steps? Pitches and abstracts perform similar work, with some important differences. Consider, first, abstracts, the genre more familiar to university-trained writers. You send an abstract to a specific editor or organizer for a specific context, in a predetermined genre. That specific context will have a specific girl going toward it, and, as you write, you should consider her. The same girl (me) may wish to attend both the Society of Nineteenth-Century Americanists conference and the Association for the Study of Arts of the Present conference, but those are different places to go, with different assumed-shared references; you can guess which would be more likely to catch, in your prose, a reference to, say, *Pierre*. You'll shape your abstract to the conversation your girl hopes to have, in this particular context.

Yet while C19 and ASAP are different places to go—and your success in abstract submission will depend on recognizing that—both places share a common interest in building human knowledge. They are both scenes made around peer review. Thus, when you write an abstract applying to one, you can trust that your reader, if in good faith, will be evaluating your writing on its significant contribution to knowledge. They will look for your archive, your argument, and your method: These are the things your abstract should include. Your reader will expect you to deliver these things in one to two thoughtfully written paragraphs.

Pitches, unlike abstracts, don't come preattached to a genre (the conference paper or journal article) or a goal (expanding human knowledge). So, while a pitch still needs to have a method or approach, it also needs to perform the more basic task of telling the potential editor what it's proposing. Put more clearly: *The pitch needs to make a pitch.* It needs to pitch something specific. A feature? A reported article? A personal essay? An essay for a specific column or vertical? How many words will it be? What will its point or claim or contribution be?

I have gotten many pitches by university-trained writers that completely failed to tell me what they are going to write, let alone why it matters, or to whom. It's like they've said to me, "I would like to bake you something with flour and rosemary," but have not specified whether they're making a country loaf, a focaccia, or a muffin. Are they offering a meal? A side dish? A snack? I get it. When you're a good baker, and you love rosemary, you can bake a lot of things! You might be willing to bake a lot of things! Whatever the editor wants! Whatever piques their appetite! The writer may hope this expression of the urge to please, to make it work, will be experienced by the editor as generous or accommodating. It won't. It creates labor for an editor. Editors have enough decision fatigue. It's not fair to ask *them* to tell *us* what we want to write, on top of everything else.

So again: Your pitch needs to make a pitch. It should tell the editor what you're pitching, and why it's relevant for that publication and its "girl," at this moment in that girl's life, as well as the word length and timeline for submission. The pitch should also make clear why you're the person to write this piece, although it can't substitute status (expertise is not a pitch) or desire (your interest in writing for a publication is not a pitch) for a clear sense of what the piece of writing will deliver. It should do all this in probably three *shorter* paragraphs. It's great to keep a pitch to a couple hundred words total, although I'll be honest that I have a hard time doing so. If you have the essay written already, which can be a good strategy for a new writer, both attach it and paste it into the email. If an editor rejects your pitch but includes an encouraging note, follow up again, but *not right away*. Give it a little time to breath. Wait until the next time you really have something you specifically can add to the conversation. A couple of months is a good baseline.

Another important difference is that your pitch should be written "in voice"—that is, the pitch should demonstrate the writing style and persona that you'll use in the final piece of writing. Abstracts tend to be written in a forecasting mode—"in this paper I will argue that"—whereas you absolutely should not use that formulation in a pitch, because to do so requires seven words, none of which has yet shown us anything interesting about the topic, or about you. It's a missed opportunity, because your primary goal is to demonstrate that you can generate reader interest. If you can do that, you should do it right now.

Rebecca Onion, an editor for *Slate* magazine, has visited my classes to talk about pitching several times. She's a university-trained writer herself, and she likes making space for expert writers in her publication. She's mentioned in my classes that when she's considering pitches from academics, she is looking to see whether that person can imagine a reader outside university-based conversations—who doesn't take for granted that readers are interested in academic theories, topics, or methods. Similarly, she looks to see if the university-trained writer can work in short, clear sentences and paragraphs; if the writer can imagine a smart but nonexpert "girl" who is reading on her phone, or at work. Despite concerns about jargon, this girl might enjoy learning a specialized term of art. On the other hand (and this is publication specific), she might not be in a context where she can stay with a long, abstract, or carefully modified sentence.

Other editors I've spoken with echo this advice, and I try to take it to heart when I'm pitching myself. The best and funniest advice I've ever gotten is to remember: "You may be an expert, *but you're not a special guy*!" This still makes me laugh, which helps it work. The editor's immediate point was that expert writers need to follow the basic protocols of having a clear idea, appropriately articulated, that all writers need to follow. But his lingering emphasis—*special guyyyyyyy!*—hinted at his wearying experiences of managing the emotional demands that "pitches" from academics can sometimes present to editors, who are just trying to get through their busy day.

University-trained writers can experience a huge amount of emotional intensity around our prose and our status, and if we're not careful we're prone to asking editors to help us carry that burden. It's not their job. Their editorial job is to curate a publication. An editor should be caring, but they're not a therapist: We need to manage our own feelings about our intellectual and aesthetic worth. We need to remember: Our expertise is not a pitch. Our desire to write for a publication is not a pitch. Our love of a topic is not a pitch. Knowing about a topic does not substitute for knowing about a publication, its mores and voice and house style. Please do not pitch something without checking what else the publication has already published. Please do not be precious or thin-skinned.

What else do you have to know, if you're a university-trained writer learning how to pitch? Put the word "PITCH," maybe in all caps, followed by a colon, at the beginning of the subject line. Link your clips. I, personally, hate reading any pitch with a "stylish" font, especially Garamond, so maybe change the font to something more standard if you type in Garamond. Before you send your email, look at it on your phone. Is there soothing white space? If not, add some white space! White space encourages everyone to take a breath, a break. It gives your reader an extra few seconds. Everyone needs an extra few seconds. Especially your editor, even you.

Pitches and abstracts are awkward documents, at least they can be, because to pitch or submit an abstract is, essentially, to request an invitation to a party, a potluck. Everyone knows that it's cooler and more exciting when the invite comes to you, unrequested; when someone else imagines their party and pictures you as the perfect guest. We may, very rarely, be in a position where we *are* the special guy, and the host would be happy to have any dish we'd like to contribute, just for the pleasure of having us there. But that's not mostly how it works, and we shouldn't expect that it does.

In the socially weird hosting system of expert humanities writing (whether what's being hosted is a journal, a conference, or a journalistic publication), asking to be asked is a normal form of awkwardness, one it's best to embrace with good grace rather than avoid or whinge through. The trick is to avoid absorbing the social strangeness or treating it as a personal quality. In fact, the most important reminder I'd give is that precisely because pitching and proposing can be awkward, both also give a valuable opportunity to be friendly and straightforward (the Midwesterner in me wants to add, "and decent"). Pitching and submitting may not always lead you to a publication opportunity, but they always give you something else: a chance to be a writer that an editor or organizer remembers as a solid person. And maybe even a funny, insightful, or cool one.

It can feel like a special few have been gifted—by their institutions, or their families, or their place of origin—open invites to the parties we'd like to attend. It can feel this way because it's true. Writers come from different backgrounds, with unequal resources. Publications can be cliquish and editors snobby or overworked or have horizons narrowed in other ways. I have good connections and I know it, but I still feel a sting when I see other writers work better connections that they seem to build more easily. Inequity is a bitter pill for anyone's writing to swallow.

I still stand by my advice: Show up in your pitch, ask, show up again, be gracious. Consider how to learn more about the publications that matter to you and how to support them. Give them your email; support their work. Read and share. Go to the readings and the launch parties, if you can. Build publication opportunities yourself, if you can. As I've learned more about the world of publishing, I've seen some of its downsides firsthand, but I can also affirm that almost everyone who gets into editing and publishing does so because they love reading, they love writing, they love worlds built with words. I know successful editors and writers from a huge range of backgrounds and connection access. The quality that most of them share is their investment in world-building. All of us can cultivate this quality, regardless of our easy access to institutional or cultural prestige.

I've given this chapter a second title, "Some Ways of Building Worlds with Words," because that's what we're doing when we reach out to each other, through the awkward protocols of pitching and vetting and curating. We're building connections beyond a simple ask or offer. I cannot tell you that every editor or conference organizer thinks about pitches the way I do, but I still want to make the strong case for *you* to consider these interactions as world-building gestures, in themselves, regardless of what response they receive. As a humanities nerd I might put it this way: Alongside the proposition of the pitch resides its performative action of building a relationship between you and an editor and their context. When you send the email, you're asking for an invitation, but you've already started the process of building the world, or building more world. This action, if not the curatorial task, remains significantly within your control. Your pitch is its own scene of hospitality, where you have the option of being a gracious host, as well as an appreciative potential guest.

NINE

Know Your Noun

Stalled out and frustrated in the midst of revising this chapter, I made myself stop grinding and do something guaranteed to irritate me further. I opened a new blank document and (worst!) I *practiced*. I followed the advice that this chapter gives. I got stuck, so I listed my nouns. I wrote:

Noun
Love
Choice
Time
List

My list, although veering precipitously close to self-help ("Noun Love List" here a writerly version of "Live Laugh Love"), has some good qualities. It balances abstract concepts like love and choice with more concrete ones, like noun and, in a meta turn, list. This list about lists helps me see the point I want the chapter to make: Make choices about your time based on what you love. To learn what you love, list your nouns.

I mean this statement as a principle that can guide writers as we consider the publication options facing us. It's a question I asked in chapter 1. Monograph? Scholarly article? More journalistic article? What venue or publication strategy will help our writing take us where we want to go? Answering the question can involve negotiating a lot of ego and ambition and daily concerns. I want fame, professional success; I want the joy of writing; I want to still have time to make some headway on my proliferating domestic to-do list. When I have Precious Writing Time, I have laboriously hewn it from the tough material of a busy life. I want it to matter. Is there some way to be strategic about my publication choices that would help me feel confident that the time I spend writing is going to measurably help my life? How can I think through the choice of publication venue in a way that makes me know what to do with My Precious Writing Time?

My list, above, gives my answer to these questions. There is a way to make sure you're doing a right thing with Your Precious Writing Time, to make sure that it's time well spent. That way is to back-burner the fame and advancement concerns and write about what you love, for other people who love it.

I don't mean love in the sense of an easy or pretty feeling. I'm not very interested in easily containable love feelings like the "pictures in frames of kisses on cheeks" vibes organizing pre-*Folklore* Taylor Swift lyrics.[1] To claim that writing should be an act of love means that it will also enact other feelings—urgency, pleasure, vulnerability, fractiousness, curiosity, possessiveness. These are the feelings we're after. From within this complex relation, our best writing will come, writing that both makes the best case for itself to the world and offers us the best promise for being in our time, in a way that makes our time matter.

Is that annoying? On a given Friday morning with some variously crunched amount of Precious Writing Time, when you're conflicted about your ideas and your motives, "choose love" can be a steep and irritating task. When my heart seems buried in the rag and bone shop of late capitalist academic life, it's often unwilling to give me easy answers about its desires. That's where the nouns come in. It's comforting and writerly to focus on a part of speech. Also, it works. In order to learn what you love, list your nouns.

THE PROCESS

I started thinking about nouns early in my career as an editor, when I first had to learn to take more control of sentences. Previously, the act of making sentences had felt mysterious, something that happened purely through intuition or affinity: through being A Good Writer. When, suddenly, it was my job to make sentences more compelling to read—and then, later, when it was my job to teach students how to write such sentences—noun listing became my go-to strategy. It helps me (and my students) when I'm figuring out a paragraph's topic sentence, when I'm trying to organize a section, and when I'm trying to think of a title. In the chapter of this book called "The Subject of the Sentence" I talk more about nouns as a point of style.

But nouns are tricky. At the beginning of a project, I don't always know which is the most central one. In the unruly sea of my inner life, curiosities and uncertainties and ambitions smash-bang against each other. As I work through a paragraph, every noun leads to others that seduce with their own need for understanding and explaining. It's hard to get the small boat of a nascent piece of writing going toward *any* destination in the midst of all this turbulence. In almost every writing project there's a moment when I get lost in the noun-waves and have to stop, take down the sails, and focus. It helps me to write my noun literally on a Post-it note, like a visual ballast or dose of Dramamine. There is not one next to me on this particular Friday morning (it's a Wednesday morning, actually). But many of the pages in this book have been written under the presiding wisdom of a yellow paper flag stuck to the right corner of my laptop, urgently declaiming that "it's about WRITING!"

Other times the problem my noun lists are trying to manage isn't so much a sea of competing interests as—to change metaphors completely—a changing sense of my own self. As when, in a clothing store, I have an idea of what size or style fits me that may not correspond to what feels good on an actual day, and I then have to wrestle with how hard it can be to actually *be who I am* rather than who I used to be or might hypothetically become, choosing a noun can be like choosing the *right now-fitting* dress, an act of honesty generating a lot of freedom and also maybe some ambivalence. I'm trying to get better at choosing the fit that feels good to whatever version of myself, right now, has something to say. I don't want to choose a noun just because I've seen other people style it elegantly.

So, to figure out what noun I really care about, I take some simple steps. I get out a notebook and a pencil. I prefer writing to typing because the pencil, because it seems quiet and intimate, helps me be honest. Sometimes I set a timer, especially if the project is large or the range of possibilities particularly uncertain. Then I list all the nouns that matter to what I'm writing. I try to be comprehensive. I try not to stop after the first one or two, no matter how straightforward the nouns seem to be, because I have learned that I tend to build elaborate structures of misdirection around my closest convictions, so that I can keep them guarded from the slings and arrows of outrageous professional equivocation. For these reasons, the first nouns I put in my list might not be the ones I'm after. Once I have a good long list of nouns, I do my level best to consider them, noticing the swell of feelings I have (or don't) around each one. Which noun makes me feel most full of things to say? When I have found the noun that matters most, I circle that noun.

I have my students do this all the time, at several moments in every writing process. Last year on the final day of the semester I asked one class to list the nouns that had mattered to our work. The first noun on the list was "noun."

THE PROBLEM OF PUBLICATIONS

When I know my own noun, I ask myself: Who else cares about this noun? Who cares about it in the way that I do? What *venues* make readers who *share my noun interests* feel welcome? What venues invite their readers to care, in the way that I care? I want to find a venue with readers who share both my love object and (to crib a useful pop cultural phrase) my love language. Maybe that place is academic and maybe it is fancy and maybe it's my friend's digital magazine, or their class blog. Whatever that place is, the place where I share the readers' love, I try to imagine my writing published there.

I want to be clear that in making this claim I'm adding my flag to a particular writing camp, raising a banner around which writers might rally. I'm offering my perspective on writing choices in order to position myself against other ideas of what we, as humanities experts, might do. This flag I'm raising stands apart from the "write for broad audiences" camp over there on the horizon, and it's especially antagonistic toward the "write to obtain a professional status" crowd. I like having a lot of readers, and I like having status. I'm not trying to disavow those desires or to say that having readers or status indicates a lack of commitment to topic, a troubling replacement of ambition for love. I think, as I'll explain, quite the opposite.

But I do think that the orientation toward a shared and beloved object should come first. I have developed this opinion and this advice after several years as a writer and an editor and a writing professor, who has in all these capacities spent a lot of time keeping company with the *feeling* of writing. It's absolutely clear to me after all this time that writing feels best when I am writing toward readers who love the nouns I love, and the same seems true for my students and the writers I edit. It makes my writing clearer, more forceful, and less defensive. When I choose venues directed at readers who share my passions, my writing turns into the best version of itself.

NICHE NOUNS

If you love a bespoke and specialized noun, writing toward people who share your love may feel like a limited approach. What if you (me) want to evangelize about your noun to people who *don't* already care? I always want to evangelize, and I'm not saying you (we) shouldn't. What I'm saying is: Don't begin by disregarding the people who already love what you do. Instead, validate them. You, as an expert with niche knowledge, passionate about a niche noun, may find that despite the fantasies of a broader audience, your own niche crew offers the most fulfilling readership. Together, you know and care about niche nouns that a broad audience doesn't, necessarily. The more your readers care about your noun, the more your writing can linger with that noun, explaining its complexities, rather than justifying or explaining why your noun matters. The more your readers share your noun concern, the easier it will be for you to focus your writing time, your acumen, on the thing (or person, or place, or idea) that made you want to write in the first place.

I'm returning here to a principle I've articulated throughout this book, and will return to again: For humanities experts, other humanities experts are uniquely valuable readers. It's enjoyable to draw some new acolytes to your noun's flame, but these newcomers are less likely to help heft you into a more complex noun understanding. Fresh perspectives can help us see new questions and articulate fundamental stakes, but fellow devotes offer the rigorous exchange that helps me get to nuance.

Note, too, that you might write toward several different versions of (in this book's vocabulary) "your girl": You can find her in several different contexts. Academic publication, I've claimed, can facilitate a particular kind of noun love; it's the way to find your fellow noun lovers over the longest scope of time. Peer review is time-consuming and particular, but I don't think its constraints mean that you and your noun friends can't be funny or stylish or have noun fun; in its nerdiness, academic publishing might actually be the most fun.

But humanities experts don't only read academic publications. If you have an insight about your scholarly noun that doesn't particularly merit the time or attention of scholarly publication, you still might prefer an expert audience. A good venue can be the blog of a scholarly publication; I'm thinking, for instance, of the excellent *ASAP/J*, the digital companion to the Association for the Study of Arts of the Present journal, *ASAP/Journal*.[2] But many little magazines, digital and otherwise, cater to humanities experts as casual readers. That these are small and improvisational I, again, consider a strength.

POPULAR NOUNS

What happens when, on the other hand, we love nouns that are widely loved? Are big publications and broad audiences a better fit then? Maybe. Here I feel I can offer a slightly different form of guidance, to university-trained experts whose particular interests are shared by the mainstream.

The more people care about your noun, the more people will write about that noun, and thus, the more competition there will be for publication space. This can serve humanities experts capable of making genuinely unusual contributions to the conversation. The more intensely people care about a noun—and the more people care about that noun—the more likely they are to appreciate the specialized details humanities experts can explain.

But remember that writing about a noun that appeals to a wide number of girls doesn't exempt you from considering where your girl is going. You'll still need to write about your noun in a prose style that fits your girl's contexts. And this may mean that despite the wide interest in your noun, a smaller venue will still best serve you, in that it will give you the chance to write about your noun in the way that's most interesting to you.

Political or public events can suddenly direct intense and broad attention to what previously had been a niche noun, and when that happens a humanities expert with relevant knowledge can speak to that broad audience. But to do so, we need to operate on the clock of public attention. While humanities experts have knowledge we acquire in slow, deep time, public interest in nouns surges and retreats, sometimes quickly. It can be extremely hard to predict. Media objects (books, movies, TV shows) can capture broad interest, but you don't always know if they will or how long the interest will last. Often noun interest wanes sooner than you'd hope, and before you have the time you need to write.

So if one of your niche interests comes into broad attention, it's worth asking yourself: Do you like writing quickly, and does your life allow it? These are questions of both temperament and political economy. It's hard for those of us with caretaking responsibilities to respond to sudden barometric shifts in public noun pressure. This is just one of many ways that journalistic publication fails to offer equal access. Academic publication, operating in scholarly deep time, can rarely organize itself to catch a swell of public noun intensity, yet it's also not beholden to that temporal economy, which is its own kind of gift.

NOUN EVANGELISM

OK but: Sometimes you really do want to spread the word. You'd like to write about your noun for people who don't already care about your noun.

One strategy for evangelism is to ask: Does your noun connect to other nouns of more ready interest to your girl? Some practical advice I explore more in the "Arguments and Other Stories" chapter: When you're aiming to get a broad audience interested in a niche or abstract noun, attach that noun to as concrete and human a noun as you can. If you are interested in a place, find someone who lived in that place. If you are interested in a concept or figure, find someone whose life embodies that concept. You can look for related nouns in calendars for forthcoming movies, TV shows, anniversaries. Scan the horizons, as it were, for upcoming nouns in the news that will give you a chance to display the significance of your noun. Reach out to editors *early*. They may say no. But if they know you're out there, with your specialized interest, they may come back around when the nouns you care about become suddenly relevant.

But shifting your focus to a new noun presents challenges of its own. You can't replace your own real noun interest with a hypothetical one your readers might have. If readers come to your piece of writing because of a preexisting noun interest, you do actually have to deliver some understanding about that noun. Their noun needs to be one you can, yourself, come to care about. If you feel their noun isn't genuinely interesting you may not write about it well. So the best strategy for evangelism is to prepare to inhabit as fully as possible your own noun attachments, however seemingly erratic or obscure, and to suffuse that noun with your own passion and frame, so you can make its noun drama visible to readers who lack a preexisting path to attachment. At the level of the sentence, you need to provide your readers a structure that helps them understand how they might come to love this noun like you do.

BEING THE NOUN

There's what we might call a "shortcut" around the your noun ≠ broad audience problem, a route that some writers can take. When writers become characters themselves, they can serve as the conduit between an audience and a rarified topic of interest. In this case, the gateway noun is the author's name itself. I will read anything by Tressie McMillan Cottom or Jennifer Wilson or Naomi Fry (who, I should say, is a friend), for instance, because these are authors whose trajectories I have followed and whose interests I might not share, on the surface, but whose take I know I will care about.

A simpler if more cynical-sounding way to describe this phenomenon would be to say that, if you are famous, you will have more latitude when it comes to your subjects. It's true. If readers care about *you,* they will want to know more about the nouns you love. And this may not seem fair to those of us who aren't famous and don't seem poised to become so, because it's not fair. Status comes most readily to the already well-connected. Many gifted, passionate writers lack the social, cultural, or economic capital that give them ready access to the status-bestowing platforms that can make your every interest seem significant. Cottom in fact wrote about this phenomenon in her essay "Girl 6," which laments David Brooks's capacity, as a *New York Times* columnist, to legitimize as interesting his "mundane machinations" on whatever noun he chooses—in this case, gourmet sandwiches.[3]

It's all true, and it's annoying. But it's also true that what makes a writer into the kind of noun, a character, who can draw a significant readership, is that they work consistently, even on small platforms, and write with conviction about what they most love. The writers listed above (except Brooks) slowly built significant platforms for themselves by writing toward their nouns. Cottom has theorized this herself, describing her commitment to showing up as her best self in all her writing, so as to build a strong, enduring relationship with her readers. Very few people may have the affinity and commitment of these three writers; we aren't all going to reach their levels. "Become more famous" does not sound like practical writing advice, I know. But I have seen a lot of writers, sometimes quickly and sometimes slowly, become both more lovely writers and more famous ones. And what I'm saying is: Writing about what you love, persistently, in a lot of different ways, can actually help you gain more status, in addition to making your writing time meaningful.

COOL NOUNS

I'm not saying we should lock our insights away from everyone who's not already a member of our secret club, as though we were Scientologists trying to milk the world of membership fees. Public writing (and here I'm considering *all* writing that has been through publication as taking place in public, no matter how paywalled) might be directed toward a niche audience, using the codes and expectations of that audience. Yet by virtue of its publicness, it invites a potentially limitless audience to join that niche group. And what makes such an invitation appealing, at least to me, is the sense that the people who are at the noun party are really having fun. To bang again a favorite drum, as I stand here by my noun flag: We shouldn't devalue the people who share our passions. Instead, I'm a believer in creating scenes of intensity. Shared loved creates a gravity well. It draws people in.

To advocate for the alluring power of a shared love of nouns is to risk the possibility of cliquishness, in-grouping, status games. To love in public can be to perform exclusion and hierarchy. Enthusiasm doesn't offer an escape route from Bourdieuian status games, as anyone who has ever been a teenage girl well knows. I'm sure everyone reading this book knows the feeling of wanting to like the nouns that are liked by those people whose status we desire; we want our taste in nouns to give us a kind of distinction from other people who like other, and worse, things.

But I'm not really talking about taste, I'm talking about love, even though I know those can blur together. If our worlds are crumbling, the best way to build more-stable alternatives is to write about something that matters to us, and to say, about that thing, something that feels important and true. For all the truth in Bourdieu's theory of taste, for all the times in my life when I have wanted to like something cool people liked because I wanted to be cool, that is not the only way that appreciation has attracted me. The attraction, the thing I wanted, hasn't been external to the appreciation. It was within the shelter for personhood that appreciation itself offers.

NOUNS? REALLY?

It may seem that I'm offering luxury advice, available only to the financially stable. Isn't it a privilege to write for love, rather than status? In some worlds, that would be true. I know this because I have at least glancingly experienced worlds like that: worlds with better-funded universities and a more stable media-verse. If I thought we still lived in one of those worlds—if I still believed that making professionally strategic choices about your writing would lead you to a financially secure life—I wouldn't be so cavalier about bracketing the question of practical success.

But I don't think we live in that world, at all. In our world, all the institutions and all the reward circuits are fractured. There's not a publication strategy I see available to any of us as writers that guarantees security; I'm not sure there's security for anyone. One benefit of these fractured systems, the increased decommodification of writing that Chihara and La Berge help us see, is that if no one wants any of our writing enough to pay us sufficiently for it, we are distanced, if not fully freed, from the imperative to choose writing that can be commodified. Instead, we can write what *we* want. When we do so, our writing gets better. This may make people want it; it may (who knows) motivate them to pay for it. But their wanting follows ours, rather than the other way around.

The critic Ryan Ruby points out that the current fluorescence of critical writing seems somehow attached to the impoverished structures in which contemporary critics write.[4] Ruby proposes that perhaps the act of overcoming austerity lends urgency to the writing, making it more beautiful and deeply felt. Another possibility might be that the intensity of our feeling around lost institutions could be read as a component of our love, our breaking hearts, and that this intense relation to the rubble, rather than or in addition to freedom from the rubble, enables the swell of our talents.

Either way, I'm not advocating, with this noun advice, that we ignore the pressures of the moment. Instead, I'm trying to change the balance in our equations. We can't repair the collective status of humanities experts or our expertise by writing about what we *don't* care about, even if a broad audience does. When I suggest finding your noun, I'm trying to outline a practical step for writing, one that makes writing both more enjoyable personally and more sustaining collectively. I'm recommending that in Our Precious Writing Time we take advantage of the opportunity for pleasure and idealism opened up by a brutally honest reckoning with the austerity of our time.

TEN

Arguments and Other Stories

Humanities experts who want to talk with me about writing a trade book often start by explaining their argument. I stop them right away. No, I tell them. You're already thinking about this wrong. And then I give them this advice: An academic book makes an argument, but a trade book is different—it tells a story. Is what you have to say served by a story? Does it have a gripping conflict, setting, and resolution? Are your main nouns characters, rather than concepts? Does a narrative arc help reveal your idea? Then your project might be a good trade book. But if your central claim is conceptual in a way a story can't capture, if you are arguing rather than narrating, or, most importantly, *if you don't know or want to learn how to narrate,* a trade book isn't for you, at this time. A story may sound simple, compared to an argument. It is not. Attempting a trade book without a respect for stories and the difficulty in telling them won't lead you to a book that matters. You'll have given up the worth of a well-made contribution to scholarship and won't gain whatever it is—the audience, the aesthetic accomplishment, the pleasure in prose—that academics tend to imagine a trade book might offer.

These are the formal differences between trade and academic

publishing. There are also the editorial differences around peer review and, significantly, a business difference: Publishers (whether academic or not) sell trade books to booksellers at a "trade discount," of 48–50%. The trade discount means booksellers can afford to stock the book. When they do, they give writers the pleasure of finding their book at bookstores, as they mingle among other readers who are looking for something meaningful and enjoyable to read. But publishers, to gamble on the trade discount, have to believe that many browsing readers will find the book meaningful and enjoyable, even if they have no intellectual or professional necessity of reading it (as academics do with books that have been through peer review). Distilling a whole economy down to a few sentences, I'm obviously simplifying many details. But my point remains: Your book, to get on the trade shelf, needs to offer people who aren't obligated to read your book some value in doing so.

Humanities experts often want to write for broad, trade audiences because we want to be on the bookstore shelf: a beautiful ambition, for sure. But as I've said, a generalist bookstore audience might not be the people who let us write in the way we want. We seem to believe we can write for broad audiences when we've got a topic we think "the public" will find interesting, and also when we think we can craft an aesthetically satisfying or emotionally compelling sentence. I'm all here for good sentences and engaging topics, but these aren't, to my mind, the most important factors in helping a wide audience understand why your book is the one, out of all the many tantalizing options that a bookstore offers, in which they should invest their money and their time. It's a good story about your topic, whatever that topic is, that gets your book to the trade-seller's counter. (If that seems mercantile and crass, then the economics of trade may not be for you.)

Stories vs arguments: I make the distinction while recognizing, nerdily, that it might not hold up under close genre-study scrutiny. The better truth claim would be that the arguments humanities experts make in their scholarly writing work like a *kind* of story, a generic form with its own standards, one quite different from the ones trade books tend to perform. But the distinction between "story" and "argument" helps me get at what I want writers to hear. Academic and trade nonfiction books, both of which try to make claims about the world, do so in different genres, with different standards of success. So as people trained in the academic humanities wanting to write in other contexts, we have to prepare to make a deeply structural shift in how our writing works.

That shift requires different affinities and new skills and the time to develop both. It also will produce an end result that will be evaluated on very different terms. Because stories are subject to different standards of evaluation, they also have different ethics, which is not to say that one is more ethical than the other. But thinking through the ethics of new genres is yet another new skill, one that, again, takes time. For all these reasons, the shift to trade only serves some kinds of ideas and some kinds of writers. If your style, skills, and ideas aren't served by foregrounding story—characters, setting, conflict, resolution—then you have two good options. The first is to develop your narrative skills, writing other short pieces, building your skills for a larger project if you find you like storytelling. And the second is to work in the argumentative mode you've spent so long mastering and write a peer-reviewed academic book on a topic that matters, with gorgeous lucid prose.

*

Here is maybe a good place to say that, when I first thought about writing a trade book, I went to the bookstore and bought a whole bunch of nonfiction trade books roughly in the fields of my own interest (feminism, women's lives, race), so that I could have some models of what I was trying to do. I had a hard time understanding their goals. Each of their authors had carefully crafted an account of some concept that interested them and interested me too. But often the writer wasn't using the most precise language available to them. Even when I wasn't an expert in the field, I could tell when the author wasn't putting themselves in dialogue with that field's most advanced ideas. What, I wondered, were they even doing? The question shows I was failing to understand a central formal difference. These books weren't written in a field; they weren't crafting an argument designed to advance specialized knowledge within a disciplinary (or interdisciplinary) conversation. They were writing for a general audience. They were creating a story about their topic on their own terms, often to *create* a conversation.

When I, a nerd, want to read a nonfiction book, I usually want to know that what I am reading is not just educating me on the topic—I want to know that I'm reading the best truth that we have. I genuinely love what specialization adds to writing, even if I am not a specialist in the topic about which I'm reading. That preference is not wrong or bad. It might be one you also have. It might be why you (or I) would be well served by staying within the particular world-building work of peer review. The best trade nonfiction books, though, accomplish something special, something specialized academic books aren't required to do.

Trade books offer sophisticated accounts of the world using the tools of complex storytelling to justify any specialized language. Trading on the idioms of more or less popular genres, they introduce new understandings to popular audiences, who can use their own skills at navigating genre to absorb argumentative claims. I can tell it's hard to do because it happens so rarely. One of the best at it is Michael Lewis, whom I feel a little awkward about citing because he's such a bro. But if you want a complete masterclass in *dramatizing* an abstract theoretical problem, making its stakes crystal clear, I just don't think you can do much better than reading the first chapter of *The Blind Side*. That this book was made into a super racist movie does not detract from (although it does show some of the risks of) what Lewis accomplishes in his phenomenal act of making NFL funding structures a matter of visceral urgency, felt in your literal bones.[1]

Over the last several years, I've talked to several graduate students and graduate faculty about writing curricula in their programs. Many programs have dramatically expanded what was offered even a few years ago. But some basic skills a good trade nonfiction book requires still seem outside humanist training. Here are a few that I see, from where I'm sitting.

- Humanists are good at interpretation, but not usually dramatization. No matter how lively our prose, most humanities experts aren't trained to describe a scene. In fact, the very same textual qualities that make a scenario compelling to readers both narratively and intellectually—immediacy, viscerality—are those that compelling interpretations can stiff-arm away. This isn't the fault of interpretation. To interpret often means to be distant from a situation even when you're within it, to look at it with an outsider eye. It's an activity and a way of being that I love; it's an art. But it's not the same art, necessarily, as scene setting. This requires a skillful handling of immediacy; of what the writer and editor Meghan O'Rourke has called a "palimpsest voice."[2] Most broad audiences are more skilled at immersive reading than critical interpretation, and to engage those audiences with your prose you need to immerse them, or to find ways to make immersion also interpretive. It's not impossible to do this—an example of an essay that does this brilliantly well is Saidiya Hartman's "The End of White Supremacy: An American Romance," which essentially retells, point by point, the Du Bois short story "The Comet"[3]—but it's not something humanists innately, via their training, have learned how to do.
- Not only do we not know how to *write* an exciting scene, but we're also not experienced in *choosing* a narratively useful one—a moment or encounter that actually serves the story we have to tell. We'll often include personal anecdotes at the beginning of our essays or conference papers, but these personal references, and maybe this is just the conference papers I've presented, tend to drop out as we get going. (My friend Phil says these anecdotes work basically like the "captcha" button you press when you're buying online concert tickets: They disappear after you prove you're not a robot.) A really good piece of narrative nonfiction introduces characters and experiences at the beginning not just because they're cool or fun or compelling,

but rather because the specific interest the characters and conflicts generate can develop into a sustaining structure for the piece. These characters and conflicts come with cultural associations—that's why they work—and thus introduce different representational and political conflicts into a piece of writing than the ones university-trained writers sometimes navigate.

- We're as fascinated by "figures" as we are by characters. Humanities experts have a complex understanding of how culture and people interact. We have well-developed theories of representation; we're good at navigating between individual and type and typology. You can say to a humanities expert, "I'm interested in the figure of the twentieth-century dad," and they'll know what you mean: That people and media and the people who make media have created between them a fluctuating persona, one that exists as metaphor but also partakes of the real. In fact, one of the whole excellent reasons (IMO) to become a humanities expert is because you want to understand and describe culture at this level of sophistication. Doing so makes you—here is another of my strongly held convictions!—a really good reader of life. Our facility with this part of personhood is what we offer, and why more people should take humanities classes! It takes a while to learn how to understand the relation between media and social life in the way the humanities teach us to do. Until more people have done so, we can't write toward readers as though they have. Trade nonfiction needs to be driven by characters, not figures—and, in my opinion, this means trade nonfiction can't accomplish everything we, as humanities experts, might want our nonfiction to do.
- Which means, also, that we might not have training, or even just a personal standard, of what it's like to write about real people. Sometimes these real people might be ourselves, or our friends; other times they are the real people who make the art and media and culture that interests us. I once edited a series of essays about the television show *Dickinson*, a very fun activity that the show's showrunner graciously helped facilitate, before I started to worry: what, then, do we owe this showrunner? I won't speak for the writers in the series, but I know that I personally was somewhat dazzled by the glamour

of knowing a for-real television showrunner, and I wanted her to like me and to think I was smart and insightful, and I didn't really understand in advance that developing a friendship with her, while a totally fine thing to do, wouldn't necessarily serve my ability as a critic to describe how her show succeeded and failed. This problem diminishes somewhat for those of us who are writing in narrative modes about people who died a long time ago or whom, for whatever reasons, we don't mind treating as enemies. And of course, as academics, we *do* often argue in our writing with other real people, about whom we might care. But narrative, because it intensifies the personal, amplifies the emotional stakes of disagreement.

- We proliferate questions more readily than we advocate for answers. I'm not apologizing. I often drill my students that "sides are for lawyers!," and that, as intellectuals, we're here to *go toward* the uncertain. I have spent hours of my one and precious life explaining the word "nuance" to undergraduates and I am not sorry. Complexity is what we give to the world, and the world needs it. And yet: Sometimes what the world also wants is something clear *to do*. It's fair for readers to ask: What's the moral of the story? What steps would make the situation better? As humanities experts writing for a general audience, we should be ready to articulate what outcome or solution, beyond a more complex understanding, our writing can provide.

None of these skills exists beyond our abilities. Any of us who have learned to write within the strange genre of academic argumentation can learn other forms; in fact, some of these forms would help us with our academic argumentation. But wanting a wide readership, for whatever reason you do, doesn't mean that you have the skills those readers desire, and it also doesn't mean that you actually desire to be the kind of writer those readers would want. When academics imagine writing trade books for popular audiences, one thing we often seem to want is to continue doing basically the same things we have done before but freed from the institutions that (for good reasons) can make us feel bad. Trade publication, though, means leaving behind both academic institutions and its shared world of written forms and skills. The question becomes: Would these new narrative forms make us feel good?

There's no actual "us" to answer that question. But here's how I can think through it, in one instance, for me. What if I had started this very chapter in a more narrative way. Let's call this introduction option 2:

> I didn't have much time to answer Aaron's email, but I didn't need it: I knew what I would say. Aaron had asked me a question. It's one I'd heard from so many so many *Avidly* writers before that, by now, my answer was almost rote. Aaron was thinking about writing his next monograph for a trade press. He wanted my advice about how to develop his argument. Sitting in my car after school drop-off, I'd barely skimmed his email on my phone before I started tapping a reply: "For trade books, you can make an argument, but the book needs to tell a STORY." If I'd been talking to Aaron at a bar or over coffee, I would have gestured emphatically; via email, I channeled my enthusiasm into CAPITALS and exclamation marks. Like so many others, Aaron had an idea. What he needed, I jazz-handsed, was "characters! A conflict!" It only took me a few seconds to shoot off the email, but in it I shared some of the most important writing advice I know.

That's an attempt to set a scene, to tell a story. I could have, instead, gone the other direction and doubled down on an argumentative claim. In that case, a third introduction option would be

> Writers choosing between publishing platforms should consider a basic difference between academic and trade publishing. Humanities experts considering trade publication often focus their decision-making on the audiences they hope to reach, wondering if, for instance, they would prefer to write for specialists in their own field or for broader audiences. While the degree of specialization matters, particularly regarding the number of potential readers interested in a given topic, I would argue that academic writers tend to neglect a more structural difference that the two modes demand of the writing

> itself. Because of how the economic procedures, editorial processes, and evaluation standards vary between these two modes of publication, successful trade nonfiction books must, in addition to making a correct argument, tell their readers an engaging story. Writers with academic training, while typically well-versed in research and evidentiary methods, and often skilled at elements of prose style, rarely have committed the time necessary to develop skills of narration, scene setting, and character development. Thus, humanities experts considering whether or not to aim for trade publication should focus not only on their audiences but also and more immediately on their own skills in, and attraction to, storytelling as a conceptual mode.

How can we think about the differences in these three paragraphs, the one with which I really began and these two variants? You'll note immediately how they use (or don't) characters and setting to draw the reader into their claims. In the second introduction, the one mentioning Aaron, I'm trying to drop the ideas and the abstract scenario from this chapter's first, current introduction into an actual time and place. In it, I'm typing at an actual person. To the extent that the paragraph's textual details succeed in getting you into a real-feeling place, those details intensify your readerly response to the claim about stories that this paragraph, like both the others, tries to make. The third introduction, on the other hand, uses the first person, but barely. It lays out the same claims in an abstracted form. This paragraph spends less time on exclamation marks and scene setting and offers more conceptual detail and specificity.

There's no one paragraph that's objectively "the best," outside context and audience. But that's different from the question of what felt "the best" to me as a writer.

The middle-tone paragraph, the one with which I actually began this chapter, was the hardest to write, partly because I did actually write it first (putting it up there isn't just a trick of revision—I produced these paragraphs in the order you're reading them). In this version, which I will refrain from calling the "Goldilocks" version, because my point isn't that the middle tone is "just right," I'm trying to be relatable, authoritative, and clear. By creating a hypothetical encounter, a type of conversation rather than a specific one, I set myself up in the paragraph to use a mode that we might call "semiconversational" or "staged conversational." In this mode, I can set myself up as "saying" something that I've never actually said verbatim to another human person, but that does in fact distill an idea that in real conversations I've tried to express. This "staged conversational" mode works a bit like talking-as-teaching, which is something a lot of academics do, and which is one of the reasons we can be a little annoying at cocktail parties, but effective (if still maybe annoying) in a lecture or seminar. This version includes probably the clearest version of my overall advice, presented in a takeaway form. But, like I said, the professorial tone can be a little annoying. Or at least, I felt a little annoyed with myself while writing it. But I also felt the confidence of knowing that I had something specific to say.

The most argumentative paragraph, the third and most abstracted, slid me toward a familiar kind of thoughtfulness. This was, it's important to say, *enjoyable*. Here I'm doing the genre of academic writing, and when you're practiced, genre feels good. I could feel myself setting up competing ideas in a useful way, evoking the kinds of evidence I would use to explain my point (which helped me realize the kind of information I would need—for instance, about economic procedures, which I started this chapter without thinking much about). The "I" here hints that my claim comes from my personal authority, which the paragraph promises to spell out, but there's the possibility in the paragraph that the "I" could be authoritative because of research and thinking rather than, or in addition to, personality or lived experience. That authority takes me to a confident place. Attaching my expertise to my professional experience (as the first paragraph does) gets me a little worried that I'm actually not the best person to be making this claim, or writing this book, as someone who is only now in the process of writing my first trade book. I'm often less sure of my experience than I am of my thinking. And so, writing the argumentative paragraph made me feel most confident that I was promising the writer something I know how to deliver.

The narrative one, introduction 2: That's different. That's telling the story of a real thing that happened on a real day. I can tell you exactly where I was when I read Aaron's email—at a red light on Coronado Street, which runs through what my friend Sanjukta calls the "demilitarized zone" between the Echo Park and Silver Lake neighborhoods of Los Angeles. I sent Aaron my reply over by King Middle School, on the corner of Manzanita and Fountain, pulled over to the side of the road, as the cross traffic zoomed by, and I felt my email going with the speed of traffic. It was raining. Do these details matter to my story, or to the claim I'm trying to explain to you? They matter to my memory, because it was on that morning, August 17, 2022 (I just checked the email for the date), that I realized, in my emphatic and jazz-handsy reply, in the crush of my busy morning, that I had become someone who really knew something about different modes of writing. I felt that I could give to Aaron—which is the fake name of a real person whom I've edited and deeply respect—some genuinely important advice.

This introduction, #2, the most narrative paragraph, might *not* be the one that's actually most fun for you to read. But, writing it, I was trying to make it fun for you, and to make myself seem like a fun and smart person, and my life and the people in it seem interesting. The self-centeredness of the task suits my low-grade (?) narcissism, and that was a pleasure. I felt, writing, like I could tell you a million more details about my day and that part of Los Angeles and how it feels to be me, in relation to writers whose publishing experience is more squarely academic than mine (the difficulty in choosing among those details illustrates my point above, about the complex skill of dramatization).

But for all these reasons, that paragraph generated the most writing stress. On purpose, I keep Aaron pretty blank in what I'm writing—I didn't want to make him into a fleshed-out character because it's not his job to make my claims. But in this paragraph,

I'm really on display—me, Sarah Mesle, a character coming into focus. Rather than drawing my authority from a well-reasoned argument, I'm pulling it from whatever charm you find in my ALL CAPS, and from whatever respect or identification you have, or don't, with my experience of trying to get some work done in the middle of a caretaking school day.

Note, on this point, that the tension of the argumentative paragraph (introduction 3) comes from competing ideas, from a "they say / I say" structure. There's some of that in the Aaron paragraph. But what ramps up the urgency is my own personal business, the quick tapping on my phone, your own potential experience with dashing off rushed mid-drop-off emails, how your own iPhone's Gorilla Glass feels against your fingers.

Here we get to some important ethical questions of the narrative form of argument, questions that matter for how our writing works and how it feels. Is what I want the authority of character, which is always to some extent the authority of type? Do I want to write in a way that compels you to trust me on this professional, aesthetic point because I'm a rushed mom? I want to add visceral details to make reading my paragraphs enjoyable, and to draw you in to what I'm saying so that your body will help you remember it. But I don't think there's a way to do that, to make writing visceral, to make characters real, that doesn't tie an argument and its convincingness to a range of always-already politicized assumptions about different types of people and their epistemic authority.

The personal story also has a different burden of evidence. To support my claim about economic procedures, I need to know about those procedures. That kind of learning is, by any account, a complex but worthy research task. To support my story about Aaron, I had to go actually look at my emails, counting the exclamation marks and noting what I had, and had not, actually capitalized. I needed, to keep the narrative feeling alive in subsequent analytic paragraphs, to confirm that iPhones are actually still made of Gorilla Glass (mine, a model 14, is). I needed to confirm that it was actually raining on August 17, 2022; in my memory, it's definitely raining. But I have just checked the Los Angeles weather for that date, and now must report to you that the sun was shining. It was a warm and clear day, one that even as I'm describing it to you, I apparently don't seem to remember very well at all.

*

What kind of thing is this chapter? A story, or an argument? Its in-between mode makes it hard to know how to reach a conclusion that feels right. Should I double down on the evidence? Retrace my steps with a different emotional tone, as I often tell my students to do in their academic prose? Should I end with a narrative, about what happened on the day I talked to Aaron, or on the day I was at MLA, or the day I sat down to My Precious Writing Time, making my own genre choice?

The ending of this chapter comes best in a question: What do we want from our books? So many things. It's amazing to fantasize about an experience of book writing that would be fun and unstressful but also somehow career changing, and also fame gathering, and also financially rewarding, and also personally affirming, which are some of the outcomes humanists might hope for when we cast our eyes toward publics, and toward the trade books that are designed for the public to read. I have this fantasy too. But it's not fair to ask nonspecialist readers to step in and affirm us as writers, if our writing selves remain attached to the academic forms through which they came into being.

In this regard, the choice of whether to attempt a trade book or an academic book should be thought of not only as a choice of audience but also and more specifically as a choice about who you want to be, in your words, and whether learning a significant new skill set will bring you closer toward being that person. Because the only thing we know for sure that writing a book can give us is the experience of writing that book, and the skills it takes us to do it.

ELEVEN

The Subject of the Sentence

Put the noun that is your sentence's topic in the sentence's subject position. Or I could put it this way: Make the subject the subject. That's it; that's the advice. Every semester—fifteen weeks of days structured around various practices of writing—there's a moment when I pause at the chalkboard and look at the room full of students. "This thing I'm about to tell you is the main thing I have to say. If you take away one thing from this class, it should be this." I'm always a little apologetic. They're paying a lot to be in this classroom and here I am telling them that they only really need this one principle, this thing it takes me five minutes to explain. But as advice, it really does work. Put the subject in the subject.

For a simple principle, it has a lot of durability. It's the advice I find myself giving to everyone, regardless of writing level. I keep having to give the advice to myself, as a reminder that prose-form writing consists of sentences, and sentences are built out of interacting parts—parts that we can name, and think about, and move around like pieces of Lego. Writing isn't engineering or math, but it's also not *not* engineering or math: each sentence works like a kind of machine or equation, and depending on how you manipulate the variables you'll get something that works more or less efficiently, in a more or less Rube Goldberg fashion, or at all. This "put the subject in the subject" advice draws on the basics of grammar and the basics of writing math to help you make something that you'll find sometimes you want: a simpler, more straightforward sentence machine.

Why do I find this advice helpful? Writing is a game of the reader's attention, the reader's interest. The reader wants to know what the sentence is about; grammatically, the subject is the answer to that question. So, use the strength of that grammatical infrastructure to help you draw the reader's attention toward where you want it to go, the noun that is your topic. Helping your reader focus on the right noun makes things clearer for them. Clarity might not be everything we want, but it's a nice thing to offer your reader, when your reader is tired or distracted or just looking for something simple in this life.

But it's not just my reader I'm helping out with this advice. Once I've got the right noun in the subject position, it's easier to make my writing more stylish across the board. My verbs get more interesting, my sentences less diffuse. Here's why: Putting the central noun in the subject position makes me ask myself what action that noun is performing. A better noun helps me find a more interesting verb than "is." And I can figure out if "my" noun is acting upon another noun. All this, I realize, is basically seventh-grade-level grammar stuff, yet it turns out all that foundational stuff you learned from your seventh-grade language arts teacher (mine was named Mr. Wheate, and he wore all brown, and I can still picture him acting out the difference between direct and indirect objects: "I don't kick Sarah, I kick the ball TO Sarah!") remains foundational until we die, apparently. Anyway, grammar: It involves putting some nouns and verbs in relation to each other with other parts of speech, and in order to do that well we all have to make some decisions about which nouns and their actions are most important to us at a given time. Establishing those hierarchies, by putting the most important noun in the most central position, is the best way to prevent your writing from being, in the words of many marginal comments I have received in my life, "wordy" or "awk."

*

All this may seem like straightforward advice, which it is, but of course thus far I've skipped over the tricky part: knowing, as I have said before, your noun. It's great to focus on your main point of interest, but in order to do so, you need to *have* a main point of interest, and for distractable nerds, this can be a challenge. So here I want to connect this "subject in the subject" advice, which I've offered as a point of style, to the conceptual problem of knowing, at a given time, what you think.

"Writing teaches the writer" is one of those clichés that's annoyingly true—the annoyance comes from my desire, as I've said, to have special unique genius Good Writer writing problems more sophisticated than everyone else's writing problems, rather than the absolutely cliché writing problems by which I am beset—and grammar is a part of writing that teaches me. The advice I gave above was "make the subject the subject"; that's advice, not an equation, but, like an equation, it can be reversed. You can use the sentence's subject position to help you figure out what your subject, your topic, is. Here's how I do it:

1. I take a stab at writing a paragraph, or maybe I'm midway through a paragraph, or maybe I'm in the middle of writing something and I suddenly no longer know what I'm even doing.
2. I rage briefly, yet again, at my failure to be a magical impossible being who always knows what they have to say and never gets stuck and always feels about writing like Emily Byrd Starr does when she's experienced "the flash."[1]
3. Sometimes actually that's it, that's all I do, I give up and dissociate for a while on Instagram, or, on better days, don't so much "give up" as give myself a break and go pull some weeds or walk the dog or another small act of finishing.

4. But other times I take myself in hand, realize that this moment of frustration too shall pass, that it's okay to be stuck, and then I—
5. Make a list of the nouns that seem important in what I'm working on and—
6. Force myself to write at least four different sentences, with different nouns in the subject position.
7. The other rule is that I can't use the verb "to be" in any of the sentences.
8. And then I try to look at this list of sentences to see which has captured an action that matters to me most, and that I most want to explain.

I'm trying to give an honest accounting here, because I really believe in this advice and yet I *always* find it hard to follow, especially at the times I need it most, when I'm tired or (to return to our eternal subject) pressed for time. When I'm trying to *just get it done, get it done already*, the last thing I want to do is to stop and write four sentences like I was back in Mr. Wheate's classroom filling out a worksheet. When I tell myself to make a list of nouns and then write a list of sentences, most of which won't appear in my finished draft, I am literally making work for myself. If I am not literally filling out a form, purple from Mr. Wheate's mimeograph, what I am doing feels spiritually the same, which is to say, a little humiliating. I want to be beyond this. I want, as I have said, to be thinking grown-up Good Writer deep thoughts, not feeling like a middle-schooler working through rules.

Yet every time (more annoyingly true clichés) I slow down and do the work thoughtfully and in a workerlike way, and with some care, I ultimately get my writing done more beautifully and sometimes even faster. I will probably be frustrated by this sorry state of affairs my whole life, and that is okay.

It helps me to remember Peter Stallybrass. Peter Stallybrass, the Marxist book historian, once visited the English department where I got my PhD and gave a truly rousing talk, full of the specific form of slouchy jazz hands only the British can really muster, about how we should stop thinking and start working! (Most exclamation marks in this book are mine, but that one is definitely Stallybrass's.)[2] Stallybrass's point was that "thinking" as an activity feels stressful because of its abstract and thus difficult nature, whereas working involves concrete steps that offer concrete rewards. He was encouraging us, as intellectuals, to regard our labor as work and also craft, which can be practiced and improved.

Worksheets, like the ones I filled out in Mr. Wheate's class, are widely regarded now to be amateurish and bad pedagogy: the opposite of creative thought and the thing that should make you worried about your child's public education. Some are. But worksheets help guide you through work. Worksheets are a kind of *doing,* and doing something feels good, and feeling good is good for writing, and for learning, which may seem to be synonymous with thinking as an abstract action but (key point!) does not need to be.[3]

So I'm a believer in this self-made-worksheet approach to writing. I'm a believer, too, in incorporating similarly mechanical practices into teaching. Several years ago, Elizabeth Freeman, a beautiful prose stylist, recommended the writing practice guide *Style: Ten Lessons in Clarity and Grace,* and specified that it was worth it to track down an out-of-print early version that included exercises (mine is the fifth edition). I promise that if you give your students the *Style* exercise on nominalizations, their writing will become less laborious for you and them. This exercise, which helps students notice the flexible relationship between nouns and verbs, can also help them when they're struggling to write clearly about new, intimidating concepts. It has also, for what it's worth, been helpful in that precise way for me.

That sentence you just read—the one starting "This exercise"—is a sentence I had to work through a few times. Here are a couple of other subject options I tried, just while I was sitting here trying to figure it out:

> Noticing the flexible relation between nouns and verbs can . . .

> Students who are struggling with how to write clearly about concepts . . .

Only in the third attempt did I put "exercise" in the subject position. It was the subject. Normally I like a sentence with a person in the subject position, but this was really a sentence about what the exercise could do for students, rather than the other way around. "Noticing" matters to that sentence, but what I really want to say is that the exercise helps the students notice. (It also helps me notice that gerunds like "noticing" make strange subjects.)

While writing this book and thinking about how to make these practices useful to my students, I've started to deliberately give myself some white space anywhere in a draft I'm thinking through a noun problem. I try to keep all the versions I try. Then I put them in a folder to show my students (a good practice that's awkward the first few times, in the way it's always awkward the first few times you share writing with any new crew). Here's an example. While I was drafting the book proposal summary for the chapter "Burden of Proof," I got stuck on this chunk of prose:

> Online publication makes context impossible to control. Academic disciplines are also renegotiating their own standards of expertise. This means that nearly all expert writers navigate between blurry-edged and sometimes colliding evidentiary systems, like some misfit gang of be-caped nerd-heroes careening through a multiverse. Wrangling information can make the time of writing dilate or contract . . .

Here are some versions of it, in the order in which I produced them:

> The question of how to manage both the acquisition and discussion of information is a place where the time of writing can dilate and contract.

> The question of how to manage information is a place where the time of writing can dilate and contract.

> Managing information can make the time of writing dilate and contract.

> Wrangling information can make the time of writing dilate or contract, precipitously and sometimes petrifyingly. Shifting between standards of expertise feels like moving through an intellectual multiverse.

> For those of us who want our writing to move between worlds, wrangling information can make the time of writing dilate or contract, precipitously and sometimes petrifyingly. Shifting between standards of expertise feels like moving through an intellectual multiverse; the way the internet . . .

This particular writing process was fluid enough that I didn't have to stop and write out my sentences in a notebook, like I often do: typing worked okay. But you can see all my moving parts, and how the subject of the sentence shifted in my drafting. I can also see here a pattern that's typical of my writing: that in my first drafts I'll often start with a noun that needs to be modified with a lot of prepositional phrases; these phrases often contain nouns that are in fact more important to what I'm trying to say than the one my draft uses in the subject position. Where did I get this pattern? From what we sometimes call "academic style." This style is part of why those of us who trained in universities and are hoping to write in other contexts can maybe use this noun advice most of all.

*

In chapter 2, I explained something I'd noticed about a prose style that we sometimes call "academic": that it seemed to mirror a trend in scientific imaging, wherein the goal was to fix—as in, to still—the knowable world for depersonalized observation. I proposed that this might be one way to understand the academic urge to write sentences that begin "this is" or "there was" or, to take a different angle and quote myself from just above, "The question of how to manage both the acquisition and discussion of information is . . ." Our prose style holds our insights precisely, specified by prepositional phrases spooling out like a long string of decimals.

As I've said in other contexts: I'm not apologizing. When you are trying to make a highly specific point, to other experts, about a beloved and well-known poem or city or bug, prepositional phrases offer you a tool to map out your unique angle of vision. The first step of academic writing is often describing a complex situation that we've come, in light of our own expertise, to perceive in some different way from how others have perceived it. Thus our precise, stilled mapping becomes a place of argumentation; the significance of what we say comes from the slightly different conceptual mapping we've gained, which we can outline with prepositional phrases, which others can learn (or, put differently, which others lack).

If your readers have come to your piece of writing hoping to find the most precise poem-city-bug insights available, it will be worth it to them to consider that you do in fact mean "the question of how to manage" rather than simply "managing," which is a simpler but different point (which is to say, the point may be simpler while also being, for a specific audience, less clear).

Here's a demanding sentence, written by Dana Luciano, whose intelligence and command makes the difficulty worth the payoff:

> The conviction that attention to feeling can alter the flow of time marks this PSA as an instance of a distinctively modern affective chronometry: the deployment of the feeling body as the index of a temporality apart from the linear paradigm of "progress."[4]

Luciano might have written this any number of different ways, for instance by explaining to us who feels the conviction. But I don't want this sentence to be any way other than it is. Its complex subject—"The conviction that attention to feeling can alter the flow of time"—keeps its reader waiting a long time for the comfort of a verb. I have to hold a whole series of abstractions in mind, a whole series of guiding numbers. But I have worked really hard to become the kind of thinker who can do just that, much like a mathematician who has studied to not need all equations to register the simplicity of 2 + 2 = 4.

Nonexperts—or experts in contexts where they are hoping primarily to be entertained, or experts in contexts where they don't have the quiet to focus—may be unwilling to sit with us through our carefully crafted noun phrases. But it's not just about willingness. When we ask for a reader's leisure time, we have a kind of obligation to offer them some leisure, something sustaining, in what we write.

In the chapter "Arguments and Other Stories," I described how, in my experience, university-trained writers don't often, in their training, develop the experience of crafting scenes where character-driven action takes place. Instead, we've been spending our time developing the very worthy skill of learning how to write and to understand complex sentences, with elaborate and often abstract noun phrases in the subject position. I find this skill worthy. And, we can't use it to stand in for a different skill, which is habitually and strategically writing sentences that are about subjects (as in topics) who are also subjects (as in people) who can be the subjects (as in grammar) of our sentences, thus becoming *characters*, who can have adventures and fall in love and watch great movies and get annoyed when, after spending their one and precious lives learning how to do one very hard thing, they then discover they also have to learn *other things*.

I don't think there's just one way to write a beautiful, meaningful sentence or to tell a gripping story. I do think it's true that, and here I'm quoting Joseph M. Williams in *Style*, "When you consistently write sentences whose subjects are characters, your readers will judge your prose to be clearer than if you had not."[5] My own spin on this, which I tell my students and which I try to practice, is that a good way to take care of your reader is to make sure that you have a good balance of concrete and abstract nouns in the subject position, and, when possible, to put a person in the subject position, and tell us what they do, what they experience. A human can lead you to a scene, a story, and a different audience for what you write.

TWELVE

Give the Pull Quote

The people want a pull quote, and you should give the people what they want. Who are the people? Reviewers, social media coordinators, interlocutors, friends, anyone who has read your published piece and wants to share it with someone else. All these people need an evocative sentence that captures your claim or your style and offers it up as a morsel, a representative sample. These people want to advocate for your writing. If you want to help these advocates, give them a pull quote. Here's this chapter's pull quote: In any published piece of writing, include a clear, concise sentence that you'd be proud to stand with, a sentence you can get behind.

Academia doesn't really talk about pull quotes (at least, it didn't to me), so helping university-trained writers craft their pull quotes has become one of the most important editorial services I provide. They're not identical with thesis statements, necessarily. "Pull quote," as a term, comes from graphic design. *Avidly*'s CMS, for example, like most digital publications' CMS, allows me to quickly pull a sentence from a piece of writing and turn it into a visual element, setting it apart from the rest of the text. The sentence becomes an illustration designed to attract the reader, to draw them in. This illustrative sentence could be an argument, but it could also be a joke, a hint, a moment. It should work like any other illustration. If the right girl glances at it, the illustration should make her want to read more.

What does this mean, practically speaking, for you? Even if your publication venue won't be using pull quotes as a design feature, considering your sentences visually can help you as a writer, because it can help you understand the qualities a good pull quote should have. A pull quote should be clear enough to be comprehended, or at least intriguing, at a glance. It should have a forcefulness: a narrative quality, a sensory one, a transferability. Questions can be good; so are statements that provoke questions. If your piece of writing tries to be funny, choose a pull quote that makes the reader laugh. If your piece offers beauty, choose lyricism. My general advice for sentences pertains: The more specific the noun and dynamic the verb, the more your pull quote will grip your potential reader.

Your pull quote also needs to work in confined spaces. University-trained writers aren't always trained to be concise, because concision isn't the special value-add we offer. I love long sentences too. But your pull quote must *fit*, and imagining an actual space can help you distill the essentials. Picture a real bubble on a text thread, a real post on social media. You can picture this literally rather than imaginatively, by typing draft sentences into chat or social media. These publishing contexts offer some spatial wiggle room, but you know—you definitely know!—what it's like to get a superlong text or an overly chatty caption on social media. You know how demanding a long text, a long caption, can be. Demands can be appealing but they're also hard work. The point of a pull quote is to entice, not to put off; if you're giving a pull quote, keep it short. If typing into a text thread isn't helping you edit yourself down, an even more constricting (and thus better) space to imagine might be the back of a book cover. Books are real, and they come in certain sizes. No matter how much you love a particular dependent clause, a book cover will not become bigger to accommodate it. Make your point without the dependent clause, here, so it can fit. If you only have space for three nouns, or two, or one, which would you choose? Use the pull quote's limited space to help you make hard choices.

Most importantly of all: By definition, a pull quote needs to make sense when it is pulled out of context. It needs to stand alone. Many, many, academic writers—specifically academic writers who are writing in the genres most available to *new* writers, like reviews—will couch their own claims in a dialogue with a quotation from another source. We will interrupt ourselves with caveats and specifications. I love caveats and specifications. They make for bad pull quotes. To be quoted, a piece of writing should offer a way to stand by itself. Imagine your piece of writing quoted by someone else. Which of your ideas do you want to travel? What is your banner, the flag you wave? What is the style, the way of being with a reader, you'd like to extend as a hand?

Here we rub up against a problem that I find ethically, editorially complex. I feel myself pulled two ways. On the one hand, I value a robust citational practice. I love writing that's collaborative and generous, wearing its relations proudly. On the other, I'm now saying that part of what matters in a piece of writing is its unique position—quotable, transportable, independent. These two orientations toward writing can be at odds. I negotiate between them in every piece I write, every piece I edit. Keeping them both in mind helps each piece find its balance.

What I do want to warn against, however, is a piece of writing in which a writer (myself or someone else) uses a citational practice to avoid the scary work of actually making a contribution. It's hard to make a claim. It's hard to write sentences of aesthetic worth. But if you're not doing either of those things, what are you doing publishing at all? To publish is to make a demand on many people's time (your readers, and also your editors; a whole crew). No matter how deferential your writing style, all publication asserts itself. It should offer something valuable in exchange. That's what a pull quote promises. If you're not adding anything, no pleasure or ideas or style, there's really no reason to be publishing. Maybe you should wait for a while?

Many of us feel the desire to write before we know exactly what we have to say or why anyone else would need to hear it. Many of us also are hesitant about what we have to say. But published writing needs to matter, so revise with the idea of the pull quote in mind. Have you said, somewhere, what you mean? If you haven't yet, do you *know* what you mean? Are you ready to stand with what you mean? It's okay to say no; a successful end to a writing process might be your discovery that your contribution to the conversation isn't really needed, isn't good for you *or* for readers or "the discourse," at this time. An editor shouldn't push you to make a strong claim—*especially* one the people want—that you don't believe. The people want a pull quote, but the person who will get pulled along by the pull quote will be the writer, will be you.

THIRTEEN

Burden of Proof

Research is a place where humanist procrastination goes to hide. Because one value-add of humanist expert writing is its capacity to contribute deep learning and nuanced perspectives, research is a part of how humanists justify our worthiness and desires to take up conversational space. Research is a necessary part of what makes our writing ours. But how much do we need to research? Does more research make us more worthy, or balance other criteria by which we might have less worth? The fact that you *are* working when you are researching, and especially that the work can be anxious and feel bad, means that research becomes an ingeniously effective mechanism for concealing other kinds of avoidance that might be happening. "I need to do more research" is an honorable-sounding way to avoid realizing that you still haven't done the more complex work of determining what you are trying, in your writing, to do, or whether you feel okay about the fact that you're trying to do it.

This chapter takes up some problems of research. It doesn't address database navigation or specific search strategies for learning a new field. These are important capacities that other sources amply address.[1] Instead, it focuses on some emotional struggles that emerge around evaluating research in the process of expert writing, tying those struggles back to the question, raised at the end of the last chapter, about when it is (and isn't) good for you, or the discourse, if you add your writing to that discourse. I'm thinking here about a question I often hear in publication seminars for more advanced students: "How do you know when you're ready to publish?" The question runs parallel to another, one my freshmen often ask me: "How many sources do I need?" These freshmen, whether anxiously or lazily or both, want someone else to place a limit on the amount of labor it's "okay" for them to perform; they want a number that tells them it's okay for their research to stop. Graduate students are less likely than my freshmen to find reading four or six or ten sources onerous. With their broader sense of field and audience, they're more likely to want to read a hundred sources, maybe another hundred after that, or maybe not actually read them, but definitely save them, worry about them, skim them, store them in a teetering digital to-be-read pile. Yet these students, too, want to be told that there's some recognizable sign, some clear marker, that makes what they've done okay. You can stop now, they want to be told, or rather—you're an expert now, an author. You know enough. You can stop researching; you can start taking up space.

Like these graduate students, I pursue writing because, among other reasons, I love my objects and want to better understand them. But often, the research that I love starts to spin out, get anxious. I find myself asking the same question as the freshmen: How many sources is okay? I loved writing as a student, because coursework provided a steady stream of contexts for my writing to be and to be evaluated. A professor would set me the task of mastering everything within a limited circumference, and of saying something that had not been said there, to that person, before. Outside classwork, we have to envision spaces where our work might appear, and then assert our own merits for occupying that space. I can lose track of myself and my standards, of not only what I have to say but whether I'm worth listening too, and in my hesitancy to face that question, I become avoidant: My reading becomes strained and skimmy and I draw out this weird skimmy "research" for longer stretches of time. This happens because I've freighted the scholarly work of building a bibliography with emotional labor: Research carries our worries about how our audiences will receive us and our ambivalences about our space-taking desires. In a moralizing sphere of circulation—such as ours can be—where any bid for attention exposes us to rejection, criticism, general shit-talking, it's especially challenging to determine, for ourselves, that what we're doing is okay.

This has probably always been a problem for research. I remember my panic about my undergraduate honors thesis, which I could hardly write for researching it—my advisor eventually had to sit me down and tell me, "No, you do not need to know that," about a huge stack of books I proposed, at the last minute, to read. But I also think that historical contours place particular pressures on writing and publishing now, and these in turn make the emotions around research more intense. Here are some of these:

- Today, closed systems are rare. It's not simply that we have all regretfully graduated from the soft swaddling of our freshman seminars. We're also in a moment when disciplines, seeking to remedy their own structural blindnesses and also to secure their own relevance, heatedly renegotiate their own methodologies and standards of expertise. Departments and universities cast about for their own authority. Peer review struggles to identify what, in this brave new world, makes someone a peer. These shifts are necessary and productive. They're also uncomfortable. They intensify our difficulty in asserting our own expert values, or in valuing the writers who are enacting them.
- As the standards of authority weaken, the time available declines. The general problem of time crush I've discussed throughout this book matters too—surprise!—for research. Just as I always want to spend my writing time on the "right" thing, I always want to spend my research time doing the right research. It's terrible, absolutely derailing. In the same way that it's impossible to know the crucial

thing to say before you've brought it into words, it's impossible to know what you need to know before you've learned it. And so how can you know in advance if you're reading the "right" thing, in the right way?

- Also the internet just makes everything such a complete and total mess. Everything that's exciting about digital worlds at their best—surprising connections! new readers! stirring insights!—can also, when things are less friendly, which these days is regularly, create conditions of remarkable apprehension, even terror. You simply never know who will be reading your words, what their background or disposition will be, or what *they* think is okay. What is it like to write, in this time of massive and unpredictable contact, reading, and misreading? Nearly all expert writers navigate between blurry-edged or colliding evidentiary systems like some misfit gang of becaped nerd-heroes careening through a multiverse. A claim that looks okay in one system looks absurd, even offensive, in another. There is no certain place to rest. It's like your writing project is an oral exam that's going to be administered by an unknown but definitely persnickety panel of judges, each of whom is tired and themselves desperately clinging to the sphere of their own authority.[2]

A problem here is that if you are writing for potentially anyone, it becomes very hard to write to actually anyone, or also to stop.

Put differently, our current moment augments research's capacity to camouflage avoidance. The difference may be of degree or quality rather than category, but I still feel it acutely. My sense of precarity amplifies my desire to make important exciting claims; it makes it scarier to make the claims; it makes me want more certainty about how those claims will be evaluated. I want more limits and more assurance. And yet, in a perverse twist of fate, my ever-intensifying emotional need for certainty runs up against the cold realities of this postcollapse world, which is ever decreasing in its ability to provide that certainty, at least in the way my training taught me to receive it. In today's evidentiary multiverse, one thing is sure: There will always be someone out there who will find your research inadequate to the space you'd like to take up. This judgy spectator can prevent you from dealing with another very real question, of whether you yourself feel that you deserve to take up the space that you desire.

Here I am really chafing against the fact that there is really only the platitude to deliver: No one can tell you if you're okay but you. This is very irritating, another loathsomely correct cliché. And yet, that is the claim of this chapter: That in the now, it's both harder and more necessary to learn how to stand with your own claims, the space you want to take up, and the criticisms such space-taking may bring to you, which no amount of research can help you avoid.

*

I realized I needed to add this chapter to *Reasons and Feelings* because of a specific research problem I was having in a different writing project. For that essay, I needed to write a paragraph, or maybe two, or maybe three—which is to say, it was unclear how many paragraphs I needed to write in order get what I felt I would actually need—to summarize the state of feminism, and the counterculture more generally, in 1979. I needed a paragraph to give my reader background on how to think about a specific image: the movie poster from the movie *"10,"* featuring the actress Bo Derek running down a beach with her hair in cornrows.

I was writing about this image because of its surprising appearance in a 1981 court case, and later in a law review essay written about that court case (I will mention the essay here, because it's a superlative assertion of research and expertise: Paulette M. Caldwell's "A Hair Piece: Perspectives on the Intersections of Race and Gender.")[3] I wanted to know about the general American moviegoing public, about the people who might have seen the movie, or the poster. What might these viewers have thought about Bo Derek's cornrows, and what connection might they have seen between the cornrows, the poster, and the comically eroticized free-love-ish promiscuity of Derek's character in the movie itself? These questions were not the main focus of my essay, but I needed to answer them, and I felt—as I gave myself two weeks of a holiday break to try and draft this chapter, which it turns out was an absurdly minimal allocation of time—a crushing sense of anxiety. How much of my two weeks should I devote to answering them? A morning? A day? Seventies feminism is a major topic of personal and intellectual interest. You could (and I sometimes wish I had) spend a whole career studying it. I needed to write a couple of paragraphs. How much did I need to know?

On one of the first mornings of that week, I decided to close all my writing files and give myself the gift of just reading, not writing at all. I had the whole day, and it was rainy. I was in my soft pants. I knew I needed to do some reading—why not start there? I love reading and I care about the topic. Here would be an activity I would enjoy.

Yet the reading, despite the soft pants, felt bad. The bad feeling came from being mixed up about what it was I was trying to accomplish. I had thought: It'll be easy to look through these books about feminism and see what they say about feminism and the sexual revolution. But the books had their own questions and arrangements. They were not organized to present me with a clear-cut answer to my personal question. The fate of the counterculture was not something addressed in a paragraph; rather, it was diffused throughout the stories they told. The simple thing I thought I had given myself permission to do—see what these other writers say about the topic on which I'm writing—became complex because it was mixed with other questions: *Is* what they are saying about my topic? How adjacent is it? If there is not a moment in the text that uses the word "counterculture," does that mean I don't need to respond to them? Is there *another* word they are using *besides* "counterculture"? Is the counterculture the thing I am even writing about?

Here I was faced with a limit of my beloved *"They Say / I Say,"* which advises us to craft our arguments in response to other people's ideas on the same topic. Which is really good advice! But in our irritating world, finding a distinguishing principle that effectively limits "the same topic" can be extremely stressful, especially if it is 7:15 in the morning and the gift of reading you thought you were giving yourself has opened into a researchy Pandora's box, with competing keywords flying out like vices. I could feel the contented pleasure I had experienced at the start of a rainy morning, in soft pants, with nothing to do but read and write, start evaporating. An anxious malaise fomented in its place. As I read, I found it increasingly difficult to keep my hands off my phone, where I knew a series of Instagram ads for *different and perhaps more comforting* soft pants awaited me. Soft pants research! Perhaps that is what this scholarly situation needs!

Anyway, I didn't get much reading done. I had to face up to the fact that, although I was telling myself I was setting out to learn about the seventies and its feminisms, what I *really* wanted, in my research, was to find some reputable sources that I could quote as saying what I already believed to be true, which was that by 1979 most radical feminist movements were attenuated in their organizational, cultural force while still being present, for conservative America, as an affective cultural threat. Put differently, while I was telling myself I wanted to learn something, what I also wanted—and wanted more intensely, for the benefit of my work schedule—was for someone important to tell me that I was right, that my ideas were okay.

Writing these paragraphs didn't take two weeks, or three. It took about five months. Spending five months coming to understand a meaningful research topic seems, in retrospect, totally appropriate. What's interesting is that one of the hardest parts about those five months was trying to parse out the difference between, on the one hand, an honest reckoning with what I really did need to know and, on the other, my overly anxious desire to protect myself from the potential accusation that I was wrong.

*

In my desire to know enough that I might avoid accusations of wrongness, my research proliferated. And thus, in a sort of comical way, given that I was writing about Bo Derek in a swimsuit, I came to resemble literature's most iconic failed researcher, George Eliot's Casaubon, in *Middlemarch,* miserably failing to finish his grand research project, "the key to all mythologies."

And this was not the first time. Casaubon's problem is, as they say, relatable, because while "the key to all mythologies" is a patently absurd topic, completely misrecognizing what it is that writing can do, it's also a perfect naming of how research can spin out of control. To stop researching means to create a limit to what you need to know, so that you can finish learning it; to stop researching means to believe that the limit you set, although not a product of the world, can still help us understand the world. No writing project can ever fully represent the world (any more than a map can represent everything in the world without actually being the world). To finish researching means to engage in something like a sleight of hand, making a limit appear where one was not, so that our representational apparatus can function.

What I was feeling, in my research problem, was all three of the dilemmas I outlined in the opening section of this chapter. I was writing outside a specific institutional context, without the disciplinary structures such contexts provide. I felt rushed. And I was worried that my writing, in the wilds of the internet, would be read unsympathetically. In the digital era, it's much easier to feel the pressure to account for all mythologies, and all perspectives on all mythologies, because rapid digital circulation means that anyone with any mythology might well come across your work.

I have sympathy for Casaubon, laboring with increasing miserableness toward his "key to all mythologies," even though I also see him as one of literature's most dreary villains. If I'm honest, I have to admit that I, too, have been made villainous by my failed attempts to stop researching and start finishing. Like Casaubon, my anxiety about my research has, more than once, become extractive. This problem may be common. Casaubon's problem becomes ours when any research project starts to carry the weight of a misaligned psychic need: for an expenditure of time to demonstrate our worthiness of love.

It's tricky: Imagining your reader is a necessary part of writing, and it can also be a debilitating one. In an earlier chapter I pointed out some of the things that can happen when writers don't think *enough* about their girl or where she's going; a thing that can happen with research is that writers think about their girl *too much*, so much that she becomes monstrous and chimera-like, a hydra-headed mean girl grilling you in the cafeteria about your tastes and claims and judgments and scope of information. Some of you can imagine the exact scene I'm talking about: Rachel McAdams rhetorically coiling around Lindsay Lohan's sense of self, like a blond and incisive boa constrictor, in the actual movie *Mean Girls*. Is your reader out to get you, get you by some part of yourself that you had not seen as vulnerable? Is your prose the written equivalent of a bracelet your mom gave you, something that looks one way at home, and a completely different and more humiliating way once exposed to the cruel florescent lights of the cafeteria / Reader #2 / social media? Maybe if you do some more research, you will find out the perfect bracelet, the key to all bracelet mythologies!

What happens, though, when you, or me, or Casaubon spends too much time worrying about our hypothetical readerly Rachel McAdamses is that we start to take on mean-girl qualities ourselves. Imagining ourselves being judged, we become crueler judges. This pressure has significance beyond the problems of research I'm describing in this chapter, but it remains salient here. Projecting judgment onto a hypothetical readership makes me more furtive. When I do so, I have a harder time asserting my own real standards, or evaluating whether I've accomplished them.

In *Middlemarch*, Casaubon takes his worry about "readers" out on the reader closest to him: his wife Dorothea. Hoping to contribute to "the world," he extracts care and energy from the actual world around him. I've done this too. I've worried so much about my research that I've become worse at managing other responsibilities, other relationships; I've become harsh and anxious and unavailable and unable to adequately prepare for class or to cook dinner. The effects spiral from the personal to the professional.

When I'm tangled up in research worry, I become a less responsible editor. I get worse at responding to student papers.

My Bo Derek experience provides an especially good example here, because of an extra problem it caused me. As a white woman writing about another white woman's act of racial appropriation, I had a legitimate intellectual responsibility to do a careful job. But that important concern morphed into a time-consuming and ethically questionable (the consumption of time is part of the questionable ethics) attempt to apologize for my desire to take up space in a particular conversation. I wanted to research my way out of my subject position and the reasonable concerns my subject position raised. Neither of these are problem that can be researched out of. And doing more research into seventies feminism couldn't unlock the answer to the question I really should have asked, which was, What are the grounds that, I, myself, feel would legitimate my decision to take up space? And spinning my research wheels as a way to avoid the real emotional question was mostly another example of the classic white woman move of overproducing anxiety instead of dealing with other, more uncomfortable, situations or questions. I was pouring time (a precious resource) into worrying about how to avoid criticism rather than just doing my best and then taking the criticism, for my research and my writing and my handling of my subject position, that would, inevitably, come my way as a legitimate part of the writing process.

*

Sometimes when I talk to my students about their ideas, they start looking up, and to the side. I can see their shoulders start to tense, pull up toward their ears. What is up there, up where their eyes turn and their shoulders cramp? Are the ideas up there? As their shoulders and eyes rise, their sentences get longer, and their nouns get more abstract; they become more worried about whether their sources are okay; they start offering long explanations of other people's arguments. I recognize the feeling behind my students' posture and the worry behind their long explanations, because I have felt it myself. It's like we are casting upward toward some strange judge in the sky, whose power we can only vaguely imagine.

This Sky Judge is one way—not the only way—writers can imagine their critics. The Sky Judge isn't the same as Regina George, but it's not totally different either. It's an abstract arbiter whose inscrutable will must be accommodated. The Sky Judge is not necessarily malicious, any more than our collective will is necessarily malicious. Yet we often encourage each other, in our language and in our practices, to cultivate a belief in the Sky Judge, a reader full of power in a fickle Old Testament way, and then to write in anxious relation to that authority. I have spent a decent amount of my one and precious life soliciting praise from the Sky Judge. I have also, in my role as an anxious teacher, enjoyed standing in as the Sky Judge's emissary, working like some kind of Metatron, inscribing Judgment From On High. The more we collectively pour our energy into this fantasy Sky Judge, the more power the Sky Judge has.

The more I write from my shoulders, for the Sky Judge, the harder it is for me to say something that matters to me, down here on the ground. And the same thing that happens to my students in their work starts to happen to my own research process—it becomes longer, more uncertain. Rather than finding evidence that satisfies me, and having the confidence that if it satisfies me, it will also satisfy the Sky Judge, I start reaching elsewhere, wondering about all the possible and strange objections the Sky Judge might raise. I imagine standards as judgment as issuing from above, outside the communities of people to whom those standards matter.

But writing requires, always and particularly in our current environment, that we be able to recognize readers that matter to us *here*. I want to thread a particular needle in how I'm recommending that we imagine our readers. Our readers are plural, and they are individual; they read us one by one. The best writing, and the best relation to our authority, comes when we imagine our plural readers as a collectivity of real individuals rather than as a depersonalized, universalized, or abstract "people" or "field." We can't know in advance who any given reader might be, but we can imagine ourselves answering the questions of any given person with standards of evaluation. It's possible to imagine that their standards are ones we find meaningful: that they are standards developed in good faith. If I feel I could explain to that good-faith reader why my contribution matters, why my knowledge is adequate, then I can be square with my writing and the space it takes.

To put this spiritual-sounding advice into a practical research strategy: I'd like to recommend that expert writers, no matter whether we are writing for peer review, a Condé Nast publication, or our own blog, imagine that our writing will be read by a fact-checker. Fact-checking is what happens, with more or less intensity, in news media; sometimes copy editors provide this function as well in academic publishing. A fact-checker combs through a piece of writing, distinguishing between claims stated as opinions and those stated as facts, and confirms that the facts are true by the best available standards. In my own writing, I have had fact-checkers confirm facts ranging from the brand of Gwen Stefani's jeans (J Brand) to Gwyneth Paltrow's specific coffee order from Alfred's (matcha latte with almond milk) to the argument about gender in John Berger's *Ways of Seeing* (trickier than the simple line "men act and women appear"). By confirming these facts, the fact-checker protected the publication and me from accusations of falseness or bias, and they amplified the reader's confidence in both me and the publication. A fact-checker's goal, in other words, is to ask questions in good faith. And I write better—we all might—when I act as though a fact-checker is in my future.

Recently an editor reading a pitch of mine dismissed a historical claim I made as extreme and unsupported. The claim was not about Bo Derek, but it was related: I had claimed that white women's hair had displayed racial privilege since America's founding. The editor was unpersuaded and rejected the pitch. This was annoying, and partly it annoyed me because I knew I had, when writing, dialed up the rhetoric of the claim in order to bring it to the level of intensity I hoped an editor would find compelling. I felt like I had been personally busted for trying to engage in a broken system where only a certain volume of claim could be heard over the general din. But it was also a good opportunity to sit with the claim and consider whether I felt I should dial it back. If this person were a fact-checker, who asked me why I believed my claim was true, what evidence would I marshal? What research would be sufficient? For me, I decided, an adequate piece of evidence that white women's hair mattered to America's founding moment was that, in that founding moment, the poet Phillis Wheatley had written a poem about it. She was one poet, but she was an important one. Her observations about freedom and golden hair were evidence enough for me.[4]

This evidence may not have convinced all editors, or all fact-checkers. But it helped me make the scale of claim I felt I had evidence to present, in good faith, to *any* potential editor or fact-checker. I wasn't trying to fool them or avoid their judgment; if they weren't persuaded, it was because we, in good faith, disagreed. I had the capacity to address a shifting public not as a whole but as a series of individuals. Although this approach does not make the scary Sky Judges or Regina Georges go away—it's still the case that I might face a bad-faith editor or court of public opinion—it gives us a scale of action where we can have integrity, at the level of writing itself.

Such a hypothetical fact-checker might also ask me: Why are you the one to write this? This is a question any pitch or piece of writing should answer, in its insight as well as through the knowledge it displays. Platforms are not an unlimited resource, and attention isn't either. If you're asking to take up space on a platform, you should have a good-faith account of why. It's useful to imagine that a fact-checker asking you this question deserves to hear not only the truth but also the *whole* truth. To give such a person a real, honest, whole-truth answer could include your desire for status and your explanation for why your understanding justified the world giving that status to you, not (at this moment) to someone else. There's no shame in wanting authority and attention. But such motives by themselves aren't enough if we don't have a meaningful contribution to make. Even when we do have some knowledge or insight, and even when an editor would give us space, if we know that our primary motive is self-aggrandizing, it's worth considering whether that space might be better used by someone else. The writing that comes from wanting a specific platform, rather than from genuinely trying to better understand, in public, your specific nerd corner of the world, suffers from such a lack. In this case it's better, I really think, to stop writing this particular thing. Sitting out a conversation—particularly for powerful writers—isn't being silenced. It's listening. You can spend your time doing any number of other useful activities, such as downloading PDFs for someone else's research.

If, on the other hand, you can believe in both your motives and your research, then part of your ethical relation to your knowledge, and to your world of readers, is to take responsibility for your desires. Rather than disavowing them, we can justify them with our work, and our willingness to enter a space by building on what is there. Our job isn't to get the last word. And it's certainly not to clot up our writing and our lives finding citations used mostly to protect ourselves from possible questions, objections, or concerns. Instead, our job is to do our best to make a more interesting structure, a more versatile conversation, for the researcher who comes next.

FOURTEEN

Red Rage

If, on a Friday morning, you're trying to be deliberate in using Your Precious Writing Time, you need to be able to recognize a case of Red Rage. Red Rage is my name for the feeling you get when someone who is *somehow like you* writes something or gets credit for writing something or gets attention for writing something that is somehow similar to what you yourself have written, would like to write, or would like to be more widely praised for having written. By "you" I mean "me." But I also probably mean you. Most writers I know have some version of it. Red Rage transmits like a virus, dormant, the first time you pick up a pen, and then flares up under specific conditions. Some people have very mild variants, some more intense. Here's the bad news: Red Rage is a terminal condition. There's no cure. But proper diagnosis goes a long way toward management. If you can recognize Red Rage for what it is, even a bad flare can be quickly contained. Unmanaged, though, Red Rage can ruin a mood, a situation, even a relation, and definitely the writing time of any given day.

Here's how a Red Rage flare goes. You're peacefully in your day, scrolling on your phone, maybe, or checking your email. You see a headline, a lead image, a mix of title and byline. Someone, not you, has *written something!* While before you had been calm, or at least yourself, you are suddenly, viscerally, activated. A jagged thing twists, hot, somewhere inside you. For me it's often in my shoulders, or the back of my throat. Regardless of where the red heat starts, it pushes you forward, into the words. You read. You simmer. The words, the ideas, they are so bad, so misguided, definitely incorrect, probably unethical. You can't believe this shit. Can anyone else believe this shit? The urge to discuss this shit swells. You text your sympathetic group text; you jump on social media. You stew. You craft razor-sharp rebuttals in your mind. Your nerves, your sentences, percolate with righteous indignation at everyone involved in making this piece-of-shit writing happen—everyone who demonstrated the poor taste and questionable intelligence of soliciting writing from this other person, this person who isn't you.

Red Rage is a feeling. It happens in you. It's a condition that *you* have. Red Rage is about your own worry, your own confidence, your own capacity to be in a day. This is why proximity heightens Red Rage's effects. The closer you are (by whatever metric: age, institution, interest) to the other writer, the more powerfully they can reflect to you your own actions and accomplishments, or comparative lack thereof. Someone else has accomplished something like what you would like to do; in their writing, you see what you have not written. Their piece of writing is not about you, probably. But because it registers internally, their piece of writing feels personal. Encountering their writing leaves your nerves raw and inflamed.

Red Rage isn't attractive. It's an embarrassing feeling, like a psychic rash, and as such it's a feeling most people (that I know anyway, including me) are very likely to misrecognize as righteous fury. In a Red Rageful moment, it takes a lot of self-honesty to say, "I am jealous and ashamed," instead of the much more pleasant emotional claim that "these other writers are wrong and bad." Anger has a noble history; envy, as Sianne Ngai describes it, is an "ugly feeling." So, too, is shame, Red Rage's other component. Sadly, and this is the bad news, you have to learn to admit that you're having Red Rage in order to deal with Red Rage. And if you don't deal with Red Rage, Red Rage will begin to steer Your Precious Writing Time toward its own rage-y ends without your knowing it. Opportunities are not zero-sum, but Red Rage makes it feel like when this other writer took an opportunity, it was an opportunity they took from you, and as though the only opportunity remaining to you is rebuttal. Although Their Precious Writing Time is not Your Precious Writing Time, their use of their time feels like a referendum on yours. They used their time with an efficacy you did not, and now they are taking (rude!) more of your time by writing a thing so atrocious as to basically demand your response, your flurry of texts or tweets or fits of stomping around.

Note! It's possible that the writer or piece of writing that activates your Red Rage actually *does* demonstrate bad taste, intelligence, or ethics. You might be experiencing genuine aesthetic, intellectual, or ethical dismay. But the annoying truth is that a piece of writing can provoke legitimate criticism while also activating your Red Rage. And Red Rage, no matter how it feels, isn't about this annoying other piece of writing, not really. It's about you, and your relationship to your own work. You can't fix how you feel about what you've done yourself by devoting your time to criticizing someone else's work. You have to name the Red Rage for what it is so that you can then decide what you want to do about it. *Especially* if you have a political problem with the piece of writing, you need to be clear about your own Red Rageful relation to it, because even the best political impulses can become marred, dangerous, or ineffective when they're operating as a disguise for unrecognized ugly feelings.

As for all feelings (and many diseases), structural conditions seem to influence Red Rage's etiology. I'm sure this is true but I'm not sure I understand all the ways it's true. I'm genuinely interested in what other people think. I've considered this hypothesis: That the more your demographic markers matter to the opportunities and difficulties that define your writing life, the more the world sets you up to feel competitive with other people who share those markers, and the more work you have to do in order to feel something besides competitive. This thesis has some problems. First, it doesn't correct for the ways being a white woman shapes my perspective. Other communities, I know, do a better job of instilling solidarity practices into their members. White women, on the other hand, who are trained from a young age to see the competition for the power of white men's attention as a charming manifestation of personhood rather than an insidious manifestation of misogyny, seem especially vulnerable to misrecognizing our own emotional relation to competitive systems. Second, it doesn't acknowledge how many people seem to dislike it when women talk to each other at all (see, e.g., Hillary and Huma's email exchanges). And third, it doesn't account for all the extremely toxic behavior of the most structurally privileged. More Red Rage research clearly needs to be done.

Like I said, Red Rage is normal and probably unavoidable. But your flares will be smaller the more comfortable you are with the writing that you *are* doing, on your own terms. The more quickly and honestly you can recognize Red Rage flares, the shorter their duration, and the more efficiently you can decide what to do about them.

And indeed: What to do about it? Here are a few possibilities. First, you can recognize the Red Rage, complain a while to friends who love you and will let you vent, and then go about Your Precious Writing Time as though what the other person has done doesn't actually need to determine your behavior (which, again, it does not).

Second, if someone causes you Red Rage, you have a lot in common. That can make you rivals; it can also make you friends. Consider! Is there a way to join forces? If so, do it. Like the Wonder Twins, frenemies have a power to activate.

But then, there may not be. And I'm not going to pretend the Pollyannaish "rising tides lift all boats" approach is always available, nor is it necessarily the best. So, a third option: If you really have a clear something to say, a position you can stand behind, and also someone you both want to take down and whom you legitimately believe *deserves* to be taken down, I absolutely encourage you to channel your Red Rage purposefully, turning it toward what I have sometimes found to be a lovely intention for a piece of writing: getting revenge.

FIFTEEN

A Short Note About When We Don't Need Your Thoughtful Essay

Because the audience of this book loves writing, its members—and I include myself—are inclined to think that writing might be the best way for us to contribute to the world. I have two points of evidence for this claim. One is my own impulse, at moments of political significance or collective upheaval, to start writing some sort of op-ed or essay or think piece relevant to the occasion. And a second is the number of similar op-eds and essays and think pieces that would appear in my inbox, during my more actively editorial years, in the wake of any disaster. Each one carried the hope that the new idea contained therein would be the magical feather that tips the scales of justice or the court of public opinion in the right direction. Underlying whatever specific claim the essay might make would thrum the fierce conviction that what we need are ideas, ideas that can be brought into being through writing and disseminated through reading.

Lord knows that in these trying times, we do need some new and better ideas. Humanists like to remind ourselves that it's true. To the extent that the world's problems rest in its conceptual frameworks, the solutions fall squarely within humanities experts' skill set. Although the term "thought leadership" carries the blechy taint of its corporate origins, it also names something that people in the humanities might possibly provide, and certainly that many of us would like to provide. Less appealing to many of us (again, definitely including myself) is the truth that in many situations, the world actually *has* some good ideas. Lacking instead are volunteers. It needs people to deliver the meals and lift the sandbags. It needs people willing to muster the daily will to put together call sheets, make a bunch of calls, record the data from calls, and then get yourself (in my case) to Sacramento so you can present legislators with a list of real voters who will act in coalition on behalf of good ideas. It needs people to show up at the city council meeting to make a public comment instead of staying home to write. It needs people, as an *Avidly* listicle once explained, who will "just go do the thing your think piece would tell other people to do, and don't talk about it."[1]

You will not hear me, an author of a writing guide, claiming that writing doesn't matter for political change. It does. I've read things so full of powerful insight that they've caused what you might call a conversion experience in how I spend my time. But listen: Let me give you, in writing, a new idea. Even the best writing about the best ideas requires a lot of grunt work to translate into actual political transformation. Any number of people could read your amazing essay and have a complete change of consciousness, and it still *might not matter* for actual policy, actual conditions, unless someone calls up those readers to ask them about it, so a real practical number of voters can be presented to a legislature or funder or administration.

Is this discouraging news for those who are, in person, awkward and shy? Who believe more or less secretly in our genius writing skills' ability to change the world? Who would have to acquire a whole different skill set, one uncomfortable and seemingly less fancy and less conducive to fame, in order to participate in organizational, rather than intellectual, labor? It's *super* discouraging. Even as I write this I'm imagining the skin-crawling anxiety I feel every time an election draws near and I know the need for phone calls, for *door knocking*, grows nigh. I'm no paragon of good behavior here. So I, too, need the reminder that the world might not really need, at all times, my turn of phrase, my gripping insight. It's possible that it might: It *could* be that your essay is one that will make a difference. But the productively humbling reality is that in most situations, and on balance, boots-on-the-ground labor might be the best resource for all of us writers, even you, even me, to offer.

SIXTEEN

Critical Distance

Writing guides have a lot to say about how hard it is to focus—to stay with a complex intellectual or aesthetic problem until you've worked it through. I've had a hard time developing my focusing skills, and I've also had a hard time finding ways to talk about focus with my students. It's hard because, and I'm just speaking for myself here, my need for focusing help often drives me toward writing guides; just as often, the focusing help on offer leads me to toss that writing guide irritably, if metaphorically, over my shoulder. Often the advice made me feel worse, in ways it was hard to explain, and thus hard to learn how to avoid when I gave focusing advice myself. Reading several writing guides in a row, as I did for this project, made me feel even more reflexive about both my habits and how I describe them to others. By reflexive I mean thoughtful—but in order to get to reflexive, I had to take a long way around through other feelings, like annoyed and hesitant and self-denigrating. Talking about writing is a part of our community-making practice: it shapes how it feels to write, and it can also shape how it feels to read. This chapter is my attempt to take seriously writing talk, especially writing advice about concentration and space, as a part of our collectivizing writing practice.

Most writing guides—this one too—agree that writers need to find some way to create conditions in which they can concentrate. For instance, in his writing guide for humanities experts, Eric Hayot describes his own practice of staying with the writing like this:

> I only write in my office. I begin serious writing days by establishing a sensory space covered by white "noise": I put on headphones . . . I only leave my office to go to the bathroom, but I keep my headphones on and avoid talking to people. I have the phone, internet browser, and e-mail shut down . . . I become fully immersed in the writing task, essentially unaware of the passage of time or of the world outside my work.[1]

I, too, have become a writer of isolated habit. If I have focusing advice (and I have given some already, in the chapter on bodies that keep the score), a lot of it has to do with developing habits around your own focusing needs. I am writing these pages, right now, with my internet blockers on and my phone on a top shelf, there to symbolize its unreachability. I tell my students about this habit: I tell them to turn off their notifications. I tell them to find a regular writing spot. I tell them about my own habit of wearing earplugs even when I'm home alone, in full control of the volume of my music. Hayot creates his white noise by listening to Radiohead over and over; I listen to Kate Bush (specifically her 2005 double album *Aerial*, which, according to my Spotify year-end wrap-up, only 0.05 percent of Spotify users listen to as often as me). The habits that work for me, which I am now sharing with you, are completely in line with typical advice, and also with the tastes of my demographic, which, coincidentally or not, is also a demographic shared by many other writers of writing guides.[2]

I've called this chapter about focus "Critical Distance," a phrase that typically describes a posture toward writing's content. Enacting critical distance means honestly appraising; it means detaching our personal investments from whatever our writing advocates or explores. In one of my favorite books I read for this project, Amanda Anderson beautifully describes detachment as “a set of historically situated, modern practices” we can use to “objectify facets of human existence so as to better understand, criticize, and potentially transform them.”[3] I love this good-faith account of one thing experts can, on the page, achieve. In this chapter, I want to turn Anderson’s account of situated practices sideways, to add another meaning to “critical distance” as a phrase. I want to consider “critical distance” in terms of not just argumentative ethics but also writing practice; not just what happens on the page but also how those words get there.

Here’s the question I’m trying to think through: If we want to write beautifully, meaningfully, ethically, what kind of distance do we, personally, in the act of writing, need? To what extent is it necessary, as Hayot says, to become “essentially unaware” of the world outside your work? If meaningful writing requires quiet and demands space, and if many writers can get neither, what should a professor, or a writing guide, say about that? How should we, as writers and teachers, talk with each other about the isolation, the distance, on which our personal writing practices rely?

Our best guide on the topic may be Gloria Anzaldúa. “The problem,” she writes, “is to focus, to concentrate,” and for many, “the problems seem insurmountable.” In a famous passage, which (even though I know no one reads block quotes) is worth quoting in full, Anzaldúa writes that the problems

> . . . cease being insurmountable once we make up our mind that whether married or childrened or working outside jobs we are going to make time for the writing.
>
> Forget the room of one’s own—write in the kitchen, lock yourself up in the bathroom. Write on the bus or the welfare line, on the job or during meals, between sleeping or waking. I write while sitting on the john. No long stretches at the typewriter unless you’re wealthy or have a patron—you may not even own a typewriter. While you wash the floor or clothes listen to words chanting in your body.[4]

Forget the room of one's own!!! This is remarkable writing guide advice, and it becomes more so when I realize how rarely I've seen guides for writers give advice pitched like this—which is to say, advice attuned to the material conditions of most caretakers in the world.

It's not just Woolf with her room and Hayot with his headphones and me with my on-loop Kate Bush whose writing strategies Anzaldúa's euphoric pragmatism casts aside. So many writers, across genres, talk about personal space as a critical, essential distance. The poet Mary Oliver, for instance, lyrically describes all the ways that creative practice "likes solitude," and claims that "there is no other way work of artistic worth can be done" than by renouncing responsibility to "the ordinary, or the timely."[5] "The most regretful people on earth," she continues, "are those who have felt the call to creative work . . . and gave it neither power nor time."[6] I have seen this advice percolate aphoristically throughout the internet for years. I love Mary Oliver with all the soft animal of my body, yet my body fills with soft animal rage every time I see this passage. Has she read Anzaldúa, I wonder? What does Oliver propose a person should do if they want to create lush images, dramatic narratives, and argumentative force, and yet has neither a table like me, nor an office like Hayot, nor the ability to make sure that no one talks to you?

Is this an unfair question? Maybe, and I'm not sure what to do about that. (As I sometimes tell my students, fair left the building a long time ago.) By juxtaposing Hayot and myself and Oliver with Anzaldúa (who looks good next to Anzaldúa?) I risk making us all look like jerks, even as we all navigate our own versions of distance as a writing problem.

The words you are reading right now have themselves been through a series of engagements that illustrate the question. Right now, I'm writing this in an empty house, trying to focus on working through a complex point that matters. But I first read Anderson's book, and had the idea for this chapter, on an early Saturday morning when I was writing at my dining table and my twelve-year-old son was reading on my bed, in the next room. It was only 7:30 or so, but we had both been up awhile: I get up early every day (routine! distance!), and Asher gets up early on days when he doesn't need to. I felt lucky he had settled in with his book, and I was trying to stay settled in with my thoughts, or rather, swirling with them: Anderson's chapter was helping me, and I could feel the vague shape of a few pages—these pages—beginning to consolidate in my mind. I was thinking about this sentence:

> I want to consider "critical distance" in terms of not just argumentative ethics but also writing practice; not just what happens on the page but also how those words get there.

And I had just added the phrase "in terms of not just argumentative ethics" when Asher began to bundle his way out of bed, still wrapped lumpily in his comforter, toward our dog Luna sleeping on the couch. "Oh Lu," he crooned. "Oh sweet Lulu. Mama, look at Lu's head."

Praising our dog Luna's head has become one of our family's "available practices," to use a term from Anderson, for creating intimacy, for transitioning between scenes. I love Luna's head and I love Asher's appreciation of it, and listening to him croon ("oh Lu, oh Lu") filled me, on this particular morning, with a frantic irritation. I felt my still-inchoate ideas begin to slip back into formlessness; I felt my love for my child and my dog; I felt my ambivalence about my competing desires and ambitions. Why had I made a life in which my gorgeous son's fantastic dog love could ruin my Saturday morning? What was the point of writing anyway? Why would he not be quiet? Where was his volume control?

This was my morning's "set of historically situated, modern practices" (Anderson again) in which I was writing and thinking about writing. This was both a terrible and a perfect occasion to encounter Anderson's ideas, in that nothing makes me value an ideal of detachment more than encountering the limits of my own ability to achieve it. If putting the above writers next to each other seems to show a contrast between Anzaldúa, on the one hand, and Hayot/Oliver/me, on the other, which it does, that contrast shouldn't disable us from seeing an essential similarity, which is that Anzaldúa, like Hayot and all of us, urges her reader to find a way, any way, to *get away*. Driving Hayot and Anzaldúa and me, fleeing from my cozy son, is a writer's decision to, as Anzaldúa says, "make time for the writing." Her time is also a kind of space: a space *away*. She wants some distance.

But still: There is an enormous difference between Hayot's "I only leave my office to go to the bathroom" and my Kate Bush at the table and Anzaldúa's "I write while sitting on the john." The difference isn't in the goal; it's in what's presumed to be available. And thus, for me at least, there's an enormous difference in *what it feels like* to read these different pieces of advice.

When advice about creating isolation is presented as a matter of universally accessible practice, that advice confuses writing discipline with class status, to deleterious effect on my ability to achieve the focused state such advice aims to produce. When writing advice comes from someone with perfect control over their time and space it can be infuriating, especially when it comes off in neutral, "practical," tones. I say this as an economically secure white woman with good health insurance. At the same time, reading such advice can make me feel somehow that if I had more focus or more drive my writing might have enabled me to procure more space, more distance, more childcare—as though the critical difference between the distance I can achieve and what someone else can achieve is a matter of my willpower or talent, rather than economic infrastructure.

For expert writers, the matter becomes intensified when the question of critical distance, as writing habit, merges with critical distance, as an ethics of content, which, in my experience, it often does. There's a whole range of humanities expert writing that emerges from what we might call a "critical closeness," which is to say, conditions of lived pressure that manifest in a compressed, rather than detached, style. I'm not talking about simply writing written in an intimate, first-person voice. (Critical distance, as an ethics of engagement, adheres to neither third-person nor first-person prose: Put differently, tones socially coded as "impersonal" are just as likely to be deployed to shield the writer from thoughtful engagement as intimate, charismatic ones are.) Instead, I'm talking about writing that does in fact refuse particular kinds of objective-seeming engagement.

I'm thinking here about some of the writing I myself have done on the john or in the years spent traveling eastbound on the #2 Sunset Boulevard bus, back from UCLA to Echo Park (my social media handle is @sunsetandecho, the name of the corner of my home bus stop).[7] Writing produced in such conditions isn't always distanced, in the ethical and argumentative sense, or at least mine has rarely been. This doesn't mean it's not smart or right. It may well be. But it typically will also be impatient: either frazzled or, if past that point, aflame. Its stylistic timbre transmits the same fearsomely terse authority as does a mom at the breaking point saying, "Not right now," or "Because I said so," or "STOP TALKING ABOUT LUNA'S HEAD."

Is such writing in good faith, as I have used the phrase in this book? I find so much value in writing that displays a critical detachment, just like I value my own parenting the most when I sit down and talk to my kids rather than, as though I myself were the dog, bark at them. Some of the writing I admire most pushes through the personal with astonishing clarity, opening up new spaces for transformative dialogue. But I also regularly feel the appeal of writing that displays the compressed frenetic energy in which so many of us live, so much of the time, and not because we lack the writerly discipline to get ourselves to our bespoke writing spaces. I respond to writing that refuses particular modes of objectivity, because I feel, in those modes, a reflection of my own lack of distance. Even when such pieces of writing are avowedly biased, I feel how their tone produces a truthful reflection of lived conditions.

Here I remember one of the most popular pieces published in *Avidly*: Susan Harlan's "Things That Male Academics Have Said to Me" (2017).[8] The piece is a short list, including items like "Do you know Rancière? You should read him," "I had this amazing professor when I was in college, and he couldn't have cared less what he looked like. It was great," and "You always come across as so cheery." The piece did so well partly because so many people (women) wanted to comment with their own additions to the list and many other people (both men and women) wanted to argue about whether the listed things male academics had said were troubling, or sexist, or even gendered at all, or, conversely, whether listing insults from male academics reduced feminism to a "mere complaint form," as one comment objected. There were so many comments I got tired of moderating and finally turned them off.

Of the many things to say about Harlan's piece—which I am sitting here chuckling about *still,* all these years later—I want to emphasize the relation between its form and its reception. Harlan generated a list, without any kind of accompanying claim or interpretation. It's the kind of quick composition strategy that does *not* require a bespoke home office. You can (I have) written a list on the bus. The quickness isn't a weakness of the piece. Instead, it presents to her readers a series of floating encounters that replicate the omnipresent, almost atmospheric, experience that many of us have of sexism. It's not incorrect to say (as readers did) that the post displayed some bad faith, a lack of objectivity, toward the particular "academic men" in question. Yet the readers debating whether the lists' items were individually sexist seemed to me to also be mistaking the force behind's Harlan's piece. Her list wasn't a set of arguments to be propositionally debated from a detached position. It was a stylistic manifestation of infrastructural conditions—not the specific crowded intensity of the bus, but the just-as-inescapable reality of gender bias—from which it's so hard to get, ever, any distance. Those who don't regularly experience such sexism, or who experience it differently, might say something like: These words are wrong, or in bad faith. And sometimes such writing *is* in bad faith: selfish, emotionalizing, or reactionary. Yet it's also bad faith to be unwilling to listen more expansively to what such writing has to teach about the worlds in which writing takes place.

I'm using this example to show how the two modes of "critical distance" can merge as a discursive problem for expert humanists. This particular example is a casual and jokey one, if one that nevertheless generated many big, intense feelings. But it stands in for many other pieces of writing with higher stakes and more material consequences for the writer (and the readers).

The struggle, as I see it, is to find ways to value and achieve critical distance, on the page and in process, without casting critical distance as an equal opportunity mode, when it is not. This is not to say that the only writing displaying critical distance comes from privileged writers—in fact, the opposite often seems to be true. But critical distance isn't something that's equally easy for us all to achieve. We shouldn't pretend like it is. It's annoying to have people who have the time and space to consider things slowly tell you that insights produced from compressed lived experience don't hold up under slower inspection, when you never have the luxury of slower inspection, and when slower inspection is the thing of which your life is deprived, but by which it continues to be judged. And it produces shame and stratification when strategies for writing, whether concerning composition or content, that depend on privilege are presented as neutral advice.

Infrastructures we don't choose (and can't white-noise our way out of) shape writing for everyone. In the future, writing contexts and infrastructures, including the resource of distance, are very likely to be more stratified in their distribution. My *Avidly* example suggests that one response is to become better readers of a wider range of forms, including those that are often considered less substantive or serious. "Write and read lists!" is hardly an adequate response to the underlying issues, which will require significant organizational work to remediate. But it is a response that can take place within reading and writing; inasmuch as reading and writing and talking about writing remain central activities for expert humanists, such local responses, for all their insufficiency, may well also be necessary.

I think about my own writing contexts: my Kate Bush, my ear plugs, my son, my dog's head. From these, what advice can I cull to pass on to my students, or other writers? The main advice is to practice remembering that what works for any of us is unlikely to work, proscriptively, for many of us. It's precisely because I value critical distance as an argumentative quality that it seems urgent to have, in my teaching practices and in this book, some critical distance from my own writing practices.

SEVENTEEN

Elements of Teaching Style

When I proposed this book, I felt clear that I would include a chapter about how writing related to teaching. Many of us experts do both, and I had gotten better at seeing them as mutually beneficial. I'd figured out some good strategies for time management and—more importantly—I had deliberately cultivated a more pleasurable relationship to the work of teaching, my teaching job, and thus my students (one of my models in doing so is a specific colleague I'd like to mention here: Stephanie Payne). Plus: I believe that teaching is carework, and that carework is intellectual. Rachel Buurma and Laura Heffernan's fantastic *The Teaching Archive: A New History for Literary Study* provides robust evidence for how classrooms "have made major works of scholarship."[1] So I didn't like it when writing guides or professionalization meetings urged humanities experts to constrain their teaching so that it didn't distract from what was alleged to be the professionally (or intellectually) more significant work of writing. I found myself frustrated by conversations pitting writing and teaching against each other, as though in a "two men enter, one man leaves!" Thunderdome of our intellectual, professional lives. The better approach, I thought, was to find ways for teaching and writing to supplement each other.

Well!

I guess I still think that. But the actual experience of writing this book has made me look at the topic of teach-write balance much less optimistically. I am writing about writing and I teach writing, and even with all my carefully laid plans to connect both the method and the content of my classroom to these pages you are now reading, I still keep confronting the limited hours in a day, the impossibility of really planning how long either teaching or writing will take. I keep not being able to make myself into the efficiency machine that would use all my available hours with rigorous purpose and gracious calm. As the semester wore on and my deadline grew nearer, I kept putting off the writing of this chapter. I kept thinking a solution that would help me, and help the book, would materialize. Instead, teaching and writing felt increasingly out of balance, at odds.

It's not for lack of trying. I used various strategies for connecting my own work to my students'. I built in workshop hours, and participated in those myself, enacting the continuum between student-professor-writer many of us describe in our teaching letters. I built more dedicated working time into my lesson plans, which did help both me and my students in some important ways. But at the semester's end—I am writing this, I should say, at the end of the semester—I could see in student papers the absence of skills they might have developed in the time we spent, instead, quietly working or workshopping. The quiet writing probably helped in other ways, but it was a real decision that meant omitting some important content. Even on days when I was teaching the very writing methods about which I was writing, standing in front of a class takes energy, and I only have so much of that in a day. On many days, teaching and writing did feel like they were battling it out Thunderdome-style, except in the most boring possible version of such a fight, where one man, the teacher, jerks around erratically on his cable, and the other man, the writer, mostly wants to nap.

As my manuscript deadline marched closer, I would lie awake at night and consider ditching this chapter entirely. I couldn't quite do that. It seems impossible to offer up a writing guide for humanities experts without attempting to address a balancing act all of us will need to consider, if not perform. My compromise solution with myself is to keep the chapter and ditch the chipper tone. Even if I don't have a good roadmap, even if I'm not sure how to get back on the road, I feel it's important to hang out together, so we can peer down at the wreck in the ditch together, pointing and scratching our heads. How did we get here? What happened? Could this weird professional car wreck have been avoided? How?

Like I said, my strategies are limited. Here are some things that have, most semesters, helped me. But first a heads-up about the level we're working at: One of these "strategies" is literally a mug.

1. EVERY SEMESTER I GIVE UP ONE THING

Like many of us, my life involves multiple streams of professional (not to mention personal) activities. I'm teaching; I'm planning my teaching; I'm writing; I'm doing a couple of editing projects; I'm preparing for conferences or talks; I'm running a committee or a departmental project; I'm trying to exercise or garden or learn to bake bread or read more. For the last few years, I try at the beginning of every semester to make one activity my priority and take one off my mental workload entirely. It's the scaled-to-teaching version of the "best hour" practice I describe in this book's final chapter, and it's extremely helpful.

I am currently on a complete break from editing, and I miss it badly, but I know it was the right choice. Other semesters I have taken a break from writing. This means that family members and friends and colleagues would ask me, "So what are you working on? What are you writing these days?" and I would say, "Nothing. I am not writing at all." The first couple of times I gave this answer it felt almost shocking. For the last twenty-ish years, people have asked me about writing in much the same way that they bring up my kids: as the steady, ongoing concerns of my life. Saying "I'm not writing right now" wasn't quite as dramatic as saying "I'm not parenting right now," but it felt like giving up a similarly self-making activity, as though I had abandoned part of who I am in the world. But look: even children can go off to summer camp sometimes. Writing, too, can go away for a while. It may feel like it won't come back on schedule, but it will. You're not disowning it, and it won't disavow you, even if it does take a while to get back to your daily relationship. I'm trying to say: You can let things go for a while and not lose them at all. Your identity and your skills and your passions are bigger and more powerful than a semester. And I have found it useful to be clear about what I'm not doing (sometimes writing) so I can be more committed to what I am.

That said, I tried one semester to "give up" teaching, by which I meant not actually playing hooky, but rather letting myself, as I put it, do a "B– teaching job." Given everything else I had going on, this seemed like a good idea at the time: to just admit I wasn't at my teaching best, and not beat myself up for it. But it felt crappy; it was worse than trying and not really getting there. I won't do it on purpose again. But I have had semesters (this is a benefit of teaching one class several times) where I committed to completely repeating the assignments and lesson plans from a previous semester, in an attempt to free myself from some deciding energy. This worked pretty well.

2. I MADE STUDENTS CALL ME "PROFESSOR" AND I MOSTLY STOPPED TEACHING IN JEANS

I love jeans; I love casual authority. I used to always wear jeans on the first day of class; it felt like a flex. My students couldn't out-casual me! But going by Sarah and wearing my casual clothes were joined behaviors that created two problems. It was a display of privilege, number one, and, number two, like all privilege flaunting, it eventually did a disservice to my own well-being. I was devaluing the seriousness of my own scene. Being more formal while teaching students helped teach *me* to feel proud. The prouder I felt to be a professor, the less resentment I felt toward my professorial work.

3. I WORK ON MODERATING MY PIOUS COMPLAINING

Academic chatter about our work, especially our teaching, tends toward two modes. We are often pious: about our compassion, about "meeting the students where they are," about "educating young minds," about our attachment to various political ideals. When we are not being pious, we are complaining. Sometimes we piously complain! We complain as a mode of rote sociality—oh, crap weather we're having, don't you hate grading? We complain as a mode of virtue signaling—oh, I have been BURIED in grading, I've spent hours! We complain as a mode of acceptable bragging—oh, I've been so busy writing that I'm desperately BEHIND on my grading! We complain as a mode of pleasurable "kids today!" ranting. And we complain as a legitimate infrastructural critique—not that any of these other complaints is necessarily illegitimate—because we're asked to do too much with too little for students who are stretched too thin (even most of the privileged ones, many of whom are in my classes, look nearly transparent around the edges), and we're asked to do all this while also making the social case, at every moment, to students and administrators and the public, that what we do is worth doing.

I don't think we should stop complaining, even if we could. We have many reasons to complain! Without complaints, how would we know what could and should be better? Complaint offers a strategy for release, and also for consciousness raising.

I start feeling irritated, though, when complaint begins to mobilize our suffering for needlessly pious ends, as though our suffering were the good thing we were doing, the way we might organize ourselves, the hierarchy that we could meaningfully pit against the absurd institutional hierarchies we navigate. In the contemporary university, humanities experts may suffer the most institutional indignities, but our value doesn't come from our suffering: It comes from our humanities expertise.

Here I'll mention Koritha Mitchell, genius, who has reminded me that "you get better at what you practice." I am trying to practice productive, nonpious complaint.

4. I HAVE A BESPOKE MUG FOR ESPECIALLY IRRITATING DAYS

Instagram sold it to me. On the mug are sketch drawings of several animals, for instance a whale saying "over-whale-med" and a cow saying "moooooo-dy." I use this mug on mornings when I am overwhelmed and moody. On those days, my previous strategy had been to declare, at volume, that "I FEEL FUSSY!" to all my family, first thing in the morning, which also helped, although not as well as the mug. Somehow the mug's mix of diagnosis and absurdity helps me get over the hump of a shitty day, by giving me permission to acknowledge that it *is* a shitty day, and I don't have to pretend it's not, but I still have to get up and face yet another day of absurd demands. When the situation is absurd, so can be our solutions.

Will a poorly fabricated Instagram mug help you? Who can say! But something equally trivial *may* help you. Why not try. I support you.

5. I BELIEVE THE STUDENTS ARE OUR PUBLIC

Look, there's no way around it: Teaching something you don't love (as so many of us have to do) kind of sucks; so does teaching something you love to someone who doesn't love it. Spending time doing either of these teaching activities when you could be writing about what you love for an audience who also loves it feels tedious and rage-y, especially when those students also seem willfully blind, misdirected, and selfish, in addition to being immature, ignorant, and unskilled. That these last qualities are those that it's our job to remedy doesn't make their presence less irksome. Yet here's the thing: Our students are going to leave our classrooms, and when they do, they will be the public—the very same people we imagine our "public-facing writing" will reach. Because this is true, we have to realize that every attempt to communicate with our students *is indeed* practice for journalistic writing in general, even as on a given day spending time on teaching may indeed take time away from working on some specific piece of writing. And, to the extent that we don't enjoy communicating at the generalist level our students demand, we're also learning the helpful lesson that we prefer writing academically. If our students demand clarity we have a hard time delivering, this might be a problem for *all* our communicating, writing included. And in that regard, one of the reasons teaching may *feel* antithetical to writing is that it's showing us the craft skills our writing doesn't yet have, the skills that we need to practice. In this very annoying way, teaching ultimately serves our writing by poking useful holes in our "Good Writer" fantasies.

*

None of these steps contains what I wanted this chapter to deliver, which is a clear program for redesigning the assignments we give so as to better support our own writing. I feel too tired to give a perky pep talk encouraging us to invest ourselves in creatively remaking our assignments and our curricula in order to foster a more collaborative relation between us and our students. Although our current situation clearly calls out for such a creative spirit, it feels impossibly unethical to recommend such an undertaking given the reality of work facing us all.

As against that, though, here's a truth we have to remember: As professors, we wield power, the power of institutions. Even when our particular institutions hamstring what we might do, we still remain that institution's power conduit. The weariness, the irritation, even the delights we feel around teaching can sometimes create affective relations that obscure the key truth that even when we're not feeling creative, even when we're not doing anything new or better, every assignment we give has creative force. No matter how conservative or old-school or from the vaults, every writing-based task we assign to our students creates in a sedimentary fashion the norms of the future.

For those of us who want more freedom, more flexibility, more expansiveness in the writing modes available to us, our classrooms are the places where we exist in a forceful relation to the future toward which we all are traveling. We have to make for our students what we want for ourselves.

On a given day, even today, it can be the right choice to quietly quit our ambitions for our investments in teaching, to preserve our time for the preciousness of our writing. But what makes time precious is holding within it our commitment to what we do and know and the kind of world in which we would like to live, and thus have some responsibility to create.

EIGHTEEN

Elements of Teaching Style, Redux

Against the Thesis Statement

Am I against the thesis? About this polemic claim, already I am unresolved. Do I mean that I'm against arguing? That I'm against a strongly asserted position, against taking a stand? Any of these claims would surely seem out of character, to anyone who has ever hung out with me at a faculty meeting or a bar. I am definitely on record as saying, at one curriculum and diversity meeting, "Thesis statements are the patriarchy," which is a claim that I meant and also, arguably, a thesis statement. Am *I* the patriarchy? Maybe! I love a sweeping truth claim. I love to denounce. I love to issue forth The Word—for instance, these words, about being against thesis statements.

I assign parts of *"They Say / I Say": The Moves That Matter in Academic Writing*, Gerald Graff and Cathy Birkenstein's enormously helpful writing guide, every semester. I have taught college freshman composition for over ten years, which means that I personally am responsible for introducing over nine hundred young writers to the idea that if they want a piece of writing to matter, they need to articulate the unique claim they are making within it—in other words, that they need a thesis. I teach Graff and Birkenstein's book because the thesis statement, which this book frames better than most others I know, genuinely is a "move that matters" in academic writing; perhaps it is the move in academic writing as we've received it that matters most. The blurb (by Patricia Bizzell) on the cover of my copy of *"They Say / I Say"* praises how the book "demystifies academic argumentation," and it does.[1] No single day's reading throughout the semester does so much to level the playing field for my students, who typically come from very different backgrounds and who, regardless of background, have rarely been introduced to the idea that an idea is something that they, let alone a piece of writing, might have. But I'm writing this chapter to propose that the most effective way to make humanities teaching more compatible with our own creative lives would be to de-emphasize the thesis-driven essay as the sine qua non of humanist writing.[2] That, friends, is my thesis. If we want humanist writing to be and feel different, we need to teach it some new moves.

This claim may seem counterintuitive. Thesis statements let a writer—here, our students—provide the standard by which their piece of writing can be judged. That seems fair to them and helpful to us. I have been in so many grade-norming meetings where the thesis statement seemed like the rare compositional quality on which professors with very different evaluation standards could agree. "My teaching priority was that they have a clear thesis," colleagues have said, or "This thesis isn't unified." The thesis is a litmus test most humanists understand how to administer and to communicate about, which makes it useful for grading, and which makes it a clear point of curriculum for me. When I've drilled my students on the elements of a complex thesis statement—and, in so doing, excavate the list-y thesis norms of the five-paragraph essay on which most of them have been previously drilled—I've done so because I believe I'm giving them a tool that will matter to their future experiences of evaluation.

I know not every humanities expert finds themselves in the writing classroom, negotiating how much time to spend helping students to write thesis statements that are, to use the very helpful acronym I learned to use from a colleague, SOFAUN: specific, original, focused, argumentative, unified, and nuanced (if you are going to teach the thesis, this is an effective way to describe their qualities). But most humanist experts who teach seem to find themselves assigning papers, as the better and more intellectually significant evaluation method than tests. I don't have hard data here. I know many professors have developed magical and weird assignments that aren't conventional papers, let alone thesis-driven ones, at all. But judging by the content of some writing center materials, the assignments my students have shown me, and the weary laments I hear from colleagues in person and on social media, many of us assign papers, usually organized around thesis statements more or less implicitly. We do so because we believe in critical thinking, and because we are scholars, and the thesis-driven essay is the form we have been taught will help students think critically, in a scholarly way.

This book you're reading contains a whole manifesto in favor of academic writing; I'm not against it. And I'm not against the thesis statement as one genre through which critical thinking might take place. But as humanists move toward a broader understanding of what critical thinking might be and look like, our assignments need to keep pace. Our students deserve to come with us on the journey, for their own sake, but also for ours. Breaking new writing ground for ourselves—experimenting with forms that display the affective, creative experience of humanities expertise—takes serious work, intellectually and emotionally. Being creative makes a demand. It's true we *can* rise to that challenge while also carrying the weight of older forms and expectations, holding them in balance. But doing so, to some degree, is a form of second-guessing our own creativity. And that tires us out.

A point of clarity: I can imagine the objection that beginners need to learn the basics, through the kind of repetitive practice that I myself have recommended, before they go on to more advanced moves. I agree. Where pedagogy can go wrong is by assuming that the thesis statement is the most important of these basics. That, like first position in ballet, or Daniel LaRusso's waxing on, waxing off in *The Karate Kid*, the thesis is the move most likely to eventually launch the writer into flight. So many students come into my classroom holding this belief—that they need to have the thesis first, in order to get any writing done. But to my mind, this is exactly wrong. Thesis statements are more like a tour jeté or a crane kick. They're the opposite of a basic step; they're an advanced maneuver. And even then, they are only one among many dramatic, winning moves.

Teaching becomes more pleasurable for me, and more compatible with my writing (both intellectually and in terms of my overall energy levels) when I prioritize assignments that focus on the skills that *are* humanist basics: curiosity, risk taking, hunch following, detail noticing, mad question-asking. Many of the forms that encourage these qualities are informal, seemingly less serious. They emphasize what the final chapter of this book refers to as "writing" more than "Writing." But in their playfulness, they too open up a space for rigor. Some of these are:

- **Listicles**: When I rail at my students about their list-y inclinations, one of my lines is "Your thesis can't be '18 Ways to Eat Hummus'!" This is a good joke about a *BuzzFeed* list from 2013 that students are happy to join me in mocking.[3] It's true: A list is the opposite of an organizing claim. But precisely for that reason, lists can offer more capacity to make wide-ranging observations. A thesis, precisely because it sets the parameter for an essay's responsibilities, limits what a piece of writing can know or hold. Often the strangest and most interesting things I find in an object of study—and certainly the things that beginning students find—don't easily fit into the clear argumentative claim I (or they) can make about that object. Lists of "most contradictory moments in this thing" or "moments I loved best and specifically why" help make space for the weird and still unaccounted for, which are the qualities I want my students to go after, rather than ignore.
- **Journaling**: I mean with a notebook and a pen. Students can do it in class. Ask your students to write down three or one or ten concrete details about their object of study, and then to spend some time

speculating about why they find those details interesting, similarities and differences among those details, any connections they see between these details and details elsewhere. You may not want to read it, and you don't have to.[4] Instead, you can have students learn ways to learn from their own journals in class: Ask them to read over their journals and count all the concrete nouns they used, as well as any clichés or generalizations. Students can either self-report or not report at all, depending on whether you'd like to give them a score or simply a check or not do any evaluation beyond repetition of the strategy itself. You can do this too, sharing your own journal with the class as an example. Will a lot of what the students write in their journals be vague and amorphous? Yes. (So will be a lot of their thesis-driven writing.) Does this lead to more advanced work, to Writing? It can, very easily, and it doesn't have to. It emphasizes, in itself, that you as a scholar value your students' curious being in the world.

- **Annotation assignments**: Using printouts, Google Docs, or any other format, ask students to annotate in other pieces of writing the specific elements and decisions relevant to the content of your class: their use of a source, a treatment of an event or performance, a methodological term, or a component of writing. (A great reading to accompany this exercise is Mike Bunn's "How to Read Like a Writer."[5]) I have my students annotate several pieces of writing over the semester: published essays, peer essays, their own essays. Sometimes they annotate or respond to their own or other annotations. I find it far more enjoyable to respond to comments on annotations than to thesis-driven essays, and I find that students take disagreement less personally in this form.
- **Literature reviews**: In order for literature reviews to work nowadays, you need to ask for something different from a simple summary easily generated by AI. But there are all sorts of creative ways to do this. Especially if your students are researching intersecting topics, you can assign second-level literature reviews in which they compare the questions, research, arguments, and methodologies between their reading and their classmates' reading. Doing so is better practice,

usually, for learning how intellectual conversations take place and for thinking critically about them than making, with a thesis, their own interventions.

- **Keyword essays**: Glenn Hendler and Bruce Burgett have been spectacularly effective in developing "keywords" essays as modes of academic writing. The curricular material they have developed remains superb and easily adaptable.[6]
- **Consensus-driven essays**: This is my own term, for a form I've used in conference papers, and that I'll use often for student presentations. This form resembles the thesis-driven essay, but rather than "they say / I say," the approach is more "we know / we're still working." In my writing like this, in the introductory spot where a thesis might be, I include some statements upon which most experts in a field would agree. The body of the essay explains how that consensus helps guide me (or not) through some of my own objects of study. And then the final paragraph includes a list of the other thinkers who are doing the most useful work on these questions and topics. In such a paper, you can make a lot of punchy claims along the way, but you're ceding some important ground; you don't stake out a position at the beginning, and you don't take the chance to deliver your own punchline. So it's a little bit of a blow to the ego, but it leads to a better Q and A.
- **Let them go wild**: Why not. I have never assigned a creative project that didn't lead to pleasurable results, including an unusually high quantity of clearly memorable student delights. One approach would be to offer them, as examples, writing by humanities experts that finds surprising ways to stage encounters with other experts. One gorgeous example is Alexis Pauline Gumbs's reworking of Saidiya Hartman in her book *Spill: Scenes of Black Feminist Fugitivity*; Lauren Berlant and Kathleen Stewart's *The Hundreds* similarly shows the intellectual value of surprising formal constraints.[7]

I teach general education courses with a high level of programmatic oversight. Like many of you, I'm not fully in control of what my courses can contain. But even within those constraints I've been surprised by the flexibility that, when I have the energy, I can move into writing classrooms. As I said in the previous chapter, I often don't have *much* energy. I'm not saying any curricular change is easy. Nothing is easy. Even giving up the malaise of a normal semester can be hard, when you're all wrapped up in its comforting complaints.

One other challenge of new assignments comes from finding new standards of evaluation. I assign thesis-driven papers not only because I am required to but also because I want to be clear on how to evaluate what my students have done and because I want to prepare them for evaluation by other faculty. But this cycle of evaluation stress doesn't serve anyone, especially our students, who are kept by it in an ongoing state of agitation. Most of us, too, also live in a state of ongoing discontent, caused by the knowledge that someday, soon, we will have to *grade* these papers we have assigned. Or, we are in a state of guilt about not having already graded those papers. The faculty who might in the future evaluate whether our students can develop a clear thesis don't want to grade any papers either; they're already dreading the papers we might send their way. Shifting our attention toward new forms of writing doesn't mean we won't have the work of evaluation. But it does spare us the frustration of encountering over and over the paragraphs that seem endlessly to appear on pages 2 to 6 of thesis-driven papers, written by anxious students trying to follow obscure-to-them rules while also being creative and saying something new.[8] What if we tested out new rules, together? What would we lose? Isn't it very possible that better and more interesting thesis statements, somewhere down the line, are something we would gain?

I believe in taking responsibility for your ideas, and that it's good hospitality to let your reader know at the beginning what they can expect your writing to deliver. Yet increasingly, as a teacher, editor, and participant in the (counter)public sphere of the humanities, I'm interested in finding ways to highlight conversation, oddities, collaboration. As much as I like a perfectly executed tour jeté of an argument, I've also come to value writing that admits its own incompletion. What if we foregrounded the collaborative quality of thinking together in words—something that every act of writing invites, yet that most of our editorial and intellectual standards work to constrain? What might we learn from our expertise if we loosened the connection between writing and arguing? What *besides* an argument might our expertise offer, do, or hold? We can develop forms, in the classroom, that highlight the community work of knowledge building, and I guess my real thesis is that we should.

NINETEEN

Small Acts of Finishing

"Writers love to have written," the saying goes, and the saying makes it sound like what writers want is to finish writing. We do. The winding-up feeling of reaching for the perfect last words offers such a rush, a pleasure, my heart soaring like a fountain pen's flourish: *The End*. Finishing feels so good I sometimes forget it's also terrifying. But it must be, because not much else explains my truly amazing capacity to spool out a piece of writing, spinning around in its middle sections, rewriting the introduction, turning at every moment away from the end that I also desperately want to reach. Finishing may be what writers want, but it seems like many of us, on some level, have also absorbed Oscar Wilde's quip that "in this world there are only two tragedies: One is not getting what one wants, and the other is getting it."[1]

Why would finishing be hard? Finishing is an art, like everything else, one hard to master, because its anticipation can feel like a disaster. No matter what's gained by finishing a piece of writing, finishing means losing everything else the piece of writing might have been. So I linger. I dread the moment when I'll have to admit that this is it. *Maybe* I'll get the pen-flourish-finishing feeling, but maybe also everyone will hate it, and I will have to admit I'm not the writer, the talent, the person I thought I was. I will have to go live in a barrel with my shame and some subtweets left for me on X, formerly Twitter, which I will shamefully have checked.

A further problem: The desire to finish and the fear of finishing can work against each other. When I'm worried about finishing a piece of writing, I start putting off—and leaving unfinished—other tasks. The jobs pile. The world around me looks unfinished, and, if this goes on long enough, feels unfinishable. I get overwhelmed and exhausted at the very thought of all I have to do. The dishes! The bibliography! The insurance forms! That one contextualizing paragraph in section two! My psychic finishing muscles atrophy. I dread every task.

So, basically, finishing, the thing I most want to do, remains also, like everything else in this fallen writing world, something I have to practice. My theory, which developed from observing how unfinished writing can leave the rest of life feeling undone, is that the reverse is also true: Doing some practical finishing in nonwriting life helps writerly finishing go better. Somewhere in my score-keeping body, all the finishing connects. What's worked for me is committing to regular small acts of finishing. It gives your psychic finishing muscles strength, and the reminder that letting go feels good.

By a "small act of finishing" I mean a nonwriting activity that quickly gets you to the experience of an end, without becoming so interesting or impressive that it interferes with returning to your intellectual work. A small act of finishing complements writing but doesn't replace it. It helps you manage the delicate balance between sticking with a piece of writing and reminding yourself that, at some point, you'll have to let that piece of writing go. In this way it's different from another thing your psyche might need, which is a complete hard reboot. When you're genuinely lost in an intellectual or compositional problem, it's good to stop writing and chip away at a more tangible complexity. You might, for instance, spend a whole afternoon cleaning out the refrigerator. Doing so, you prove to yourself that you can engage in a hard and not always pleasant and decision-intensive task (Do I need these pickles? Who brought this beer? What price bananas? Are you my Angel?). Hard reboots are useful, but very different from the small act of finishing for which I'm here advocating. A small act of finishing can be done, for instance, on a Pomodoro break, even a short one. Or anytime you look around the room and notice a small thing that could be done, something that makes the room nicer to inhabit.

Here's my ideal small act of finishing: changing a light bulb. This small act satisfies at every level, from the tactile to the symbolic. All the steps of actually changing a light bulb—dragging around a chair, holding smooth glass *not too hard*, twisting, feeling your wrist and arm, maybe a minor contortion of your shoulder, your neck—delight. And when you're done, you have literally enlightened yourself. It perfectly reminds you that finishing feels great. (Here we come to what may be this writing guide's weirdest bit of "practical" advice: When starting a major writing project, stockpile light bulbs on day one, to enable your easy access to this enjoyable small act of finishing and to preclude its counterpart, which is *not* having new light bulbs when needed, and encountering the idea of yourself—myself—as unorganized and unprepared).

Changing a light bulb also works because it requires some initiative. During the day in my apartment, a burned-out light bulb doesn't mean dark, it just means dim. It creates the kind of non-urgent unpleasantness that I'm inclined to just power through, forgetting yet again that most acts of powering through are ultimately enfeebling. Something about my psychic architecture makes it easy for me to substitute "enduring" for "accomplishing," and in this way enduring a dim room runs parallel to enduring a piece of writing's middle section. Gearing up to replace the light bulb reminds me that, in writing too, it's totally okay and actually better to just get to the good part rather than suck up the suffering.

Here are some other small acts of finishing that work for me. If I'm planning to spend a lot of a day writing, I make a list of these on the calendar, next to my other scheduled events, to give them the respect they deserve:

Change the sheets
Take out the trash
Unload, if you are lucky enough to have one, the dishwasher
One sun salutation

Here are some larger but still small acts of finishing:

Fold the laundry
Clean the sink with real cleanser (the powder kind you shake out)
Walk around the block

These activities share a key quality: The activity itself determines what makes the task complete. Once you've begun, your frail finishing psyche has no chance to gum up the works by worrying whether or not you've actually finished. Is the light bulb changed? Is the trash taken out? These are yes or no questions. You know what you need to do, and when you do it, it's done, end of story. Unlike a piece of writing, neither a faulty light bulb nor a full bag of trash offers you the opportunity to consider complex or impressive strategies for reaching the end. You cannot get an A. You can fail, but you always know exactly what to do in order to succeed. These small acts thus give you the chance to move from beginning to finishing with no fuss, and when you know that feeling, you can emulate it in other, trickier contexts. You remind yourself that finishing is something you can do, like to do, and will be rewarded for doing.

Most domestic tasks fail to offer this lesson. My apartment, for instance, is never clean, no matter how much I've cleaned it; my dog, my kids, and my own hoarding habits make my house a self-dirtying situation. Considering whether I've swept up enough dog hair to count my floor as "clean" takes about as much deciding energy as I have most days.

Administrative labor (writing emails, renewing a prescription, making an appointment, submitting reimbursement forms) may or may not offer useful finishing exercise. Appointments and forms seem like they should be rote and thus enjoyable, but too often systems are poorly engineered and thus frustrating. Any person to whom you are writing should be treated like a person, not a task. Writing emails in the morning—even when basically formulaic and easy—can trouble my writing for the rest of the day, because doing so makes more creative writing feel, no less than many administrative encounters, like a poorly engineered system, because that's exactly what creative writing is (if you knew how to do it already, you wouldn't be creating something new). For me, also, anything I do sitting down at the place I write replaces the writing (or Writing, as I'll call it in the next chapter) rather than enhancing it.

Determining which small acts of finishing work for you is a personal matter, so my own list of activities should be taken merely as suggestions (my husband's favorite is filling up the bird feeder). This list also indicates something about my own personal writing system's fragility. For me, finishing up a piece of writing, especially a longer or important one, also means releasing my worries about finishing it, and these worries, though not pleasurable, can become constitutive. The spiral of my worries, their cyclic movement as they tread and retread the same ground, can sediment a kind of self, to the point that I don't know who I'll be without it. I need the small acts of finishing to remind myself there is a version of me besides the one defined by what I can't yet make myself do.

"Lose something every day," writes Elizabeth Bishop. "Practice losing farther, losing faster."[2] Loss is a word that describes the fear of finishing. The bigger the writing (in length, reward, or significance) the more small acts of finishing I need to remind myself that losing also means the lightness of empty hands, nothing to carry, letting the slick fish go.

TWENTY

Writing in Time

You want a social life, with friends
A passionate love life, and as well
To work hard every day. What's true
Is of these three, you may have two.

KENNETH KOCH, "A Social Life, with Friends"

No one has enough Precious Writing Time. That's the writing problem that everyone struggles most to solve. When I asked humanities experts what this writing guide should address, all of them, all of them, regardless of status or position or security, said the same thing: time. These silky-tailed ponies seem to be departing the land, like Elves leaving Middle-earth, or monarch butterflies deprived of habitat. The most pressing problem of the now becomes our moment-by-moment awareness of time's scarcity, which pressurizes our choices, heightening their felt intensity, without offering us the choice we really want, which is *more time*. For people who understand themselves as writers, the dark night of human existential dread looms white, like the blank page we can find no time to face.

In this book's early chapters I wrote about the tension humanists face as they navigate between the institutional and the utopic, the realities of our writing worlds and our hopes for the worlds our writing might make. Here, now, as we near this book's end, I'm trying to think about how to live out that tension in practice. I'm trying to be "practical." I put the word in quotation marks because it's one that travels with "time" when graduate students ask me about writing. "Just being practical," a student asked me recently, "How are we supposed to do all this?" I do have some advice. But the quotation marks also indicate the slipperiness of "practical" as a concept that might apply to humanist writers. None of it is practical at all. And it feels absurd to be all can-do! and task-like about our existential condition, as though we were the momfluencers on Instagram who respond to the absurd expectations on caretakers with the phrase "super cute and easy!" We can change our practices of writing time, but our writing time probably can't transform our existential, infrastructural pressures, because our writing did not cause those pressures, any more than a lack of charming birthday party decorations caused the childcare crisis.

In this chapter, I'm trying to offer some practical ideas about managing our days, without losing sight of the idealism inherent in humanist work. We're all choosing to acquire expert training, and to pursue a writing life that prioritizes that training, in a world that places little value on our training and thus on our lives. Our choices show that we value the idealistic. We're setting ourselves the task of finding a livable, sustainable way to practice an impractical vocation. It's not surprising that we feel weird.

I know I have sometimes turned to writing guides because I want simple, implementable answers to big problems. Some of what follows may sound appealing and straightforward. But even small steps can be hard to take, in my experience. None of what I have to say balances out the bad equations at play, when the amount we want to create doesn't equal the time we have, and the world we want doesn't match the world we're in. For myself, the only way to make the time-writing math work has been to expand what counts as a variable and, more importantly still, to reconsider what feels like a solution.

That metaphor is a little *super cute and easy!* The reality, though, remains hard.

WRITING AND A DAY'S TIME

Most writing guides address the double-edged problem time can cause: Time is both hard to find and, once you find it, hard to use. The writing guide I've personally found the most helpful on these topics is Joli Jensen's *Write No Matter What*. Jensen recommends that to find and use time, we should first "reverse day plan" our days, by which she means that we write down what we actually do, rather than what we plan to do, so that we can see where our time really goes. Write down everything: emailing, walking the dog, snacking, texting with friends. Looking at your days, you can see what might be let go in order to "secure time" (her good phrase for indicating the time's preciousness) for what matters most. *Write No Matter What* makes the reasonable assumption, given the title, that its readers believe writing to matter most. Reverse day planning offers a way to discover what you do *besides* writing that you might do less of, so you could write more. If writing matters most to our goals, our ideas, and our sense of selves, then it takes regular commitments of time, "and the only way we can secure that kind of time is to give writing a place of honor—to make it a true priority, not 'one more commitment' in an overstuffed life."[1] I love Jensen's sense of affect and of agency. I agree with her that even as structural conditions hem in our choices, we need to take control of choices we do have. We have choice in what we prize.

I don't reverse-plan every day, but I've found it's very helpful when either I'm really anxious and busy, or, conversely, when I have "all morning" or "all day" to write and thus am very likely to let the moments seep away in stress and dribbles (a friend calls this latter experience a "want to / should" writing day, when you know you have writing desires but have a hard time finding them under all the ambivalence, fear, and external pressures). In either circumstance, I have a hard time *using* time. Reverse planning helps make me accountable to how I fill my hours.

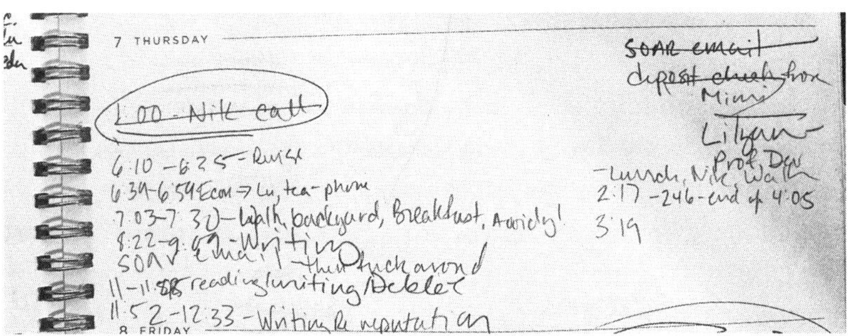

FIGURE 1. Reverse-day-planned calendar

For example, look at my calendar from September 7, 2023 (figure 1).[2]

This was the second kind of reverse-planning day—a sabbatical day when I had no given structure besides a few tasks and a phone call. Looking at it, I can see two hours slipping away between 9:09 ("Writing") and 11 ("reading/writing/Debbie")(Who is Debbie? I honestly don't know). In those two hours, I record that I sent "SOAR email, then fuck around." I don't specify the "fuck around." Maybe I was texting? Scrolling? Shopping for tank tops? I'd guess it was one of those. But there's two hours that I can secure for something I care about. They are hours that could go to writing, if that's what I hope to prioritize.

Jensen uses reverse planning to scope out minutes consumed by an overly busy life. For most humanists, this will be a far more common experience than the "all day free" problem I faced above. Jensen describes how, when she reverse-planned her days, she discovered that a lot of her best energy was going to emailing. She also found that if she reclaimed a portion of the time she gave to emailing and devoted it to her own intellectual projects, everything continued to go on smoothly. The world, it turns out, did not actually need emails to be so substantive or to arrive so soon! With a less urgent response to the writing of email, she got more long-form writing done and felt happier.

Part of what's great about Jensen's book (and, I fear, what's not so readily found in the book currently in your hands) is its clarity of purpose. She describes how not having enough time for writing created a generalized state of discontent that she tried to assuage, ironically, by adding more activities. But securing her time for the writing she cared about improved her overall well-being; knowing that she was definitely doing what she wanted to do (writing) helped her give herself permission to do less generally. It's really inspiring to read about someone who, once she had time for writing, was able—especially when she employed some of her book's other strategies—to use that time to write. And it's worth saying how many writers recommended Jensen's book to me as one that had been truly helpful.

Unfortunately for me, I'm not the kind of person who finds it super easy to use even the time I have. Setting a timer sometimes help me use the hour I've secured for writing, rather than for (as I am otherwise inclined to do) looking around for the right pencil or deciding that I should probably make more tea. Timers can help because if I know when I'll get to stop, it can be easier to start. I sometimes use an online "Pomodoro tracker" that divides a day into twenty-five-minute work segments and five-minute breaks. But I tend to start my day by setting a timer with the clock function on my laptop for seventeen minutes, which for reasons I don't quite understand feels like a lucky number. Sometimes I start with seventeen minutes and slowly ramp up to forty-five minutes or so, before I lose steam and start to wind down.

Timers can help, but not always. Caretaking duties don't care about timers, and having one set can make me crabbier about being in the fluid time of responding to the people I love and for whom I'm responsible. Also, when I'm really not doing well emotionally, I frequently have a hard time being honest about myself. Timers generate bad feelings in this way, too. I belong to an online writing group called Units!!, where members post before starting a forty-five-minute writing unit, and then again after finishing that unit, and other members praise them for both starting and finishing. When I joined the Units!! group I was in a particularly bad place with my avoidance habits. I eagerly told my therapist that I had joined the group: "For forty-five minutes, you do nothing but write!" She gazed at me and very gently asked if I could, in fact, write for forty-five minutes. I could not: *not at all.* Despite how much I wanted to be someone who could productively use my forty-five minutes of secured time, or my twenty-five-minute Pomodoro, this seemingly useful strategy was backfiring. Every time I set the timer all I did was prove to myself that I wasn't the writer I thought I should be.

In order to make good use of a day, I often have to lower my expectations, or change them. I try to remember that it is okay to set my timer for five minutes, or even two, or even thirty seconds. Thirty seconds on a bad day takes as much emotional commitment as forty-five minutes on a better day. And if I reverse-plan my day and find that of whatever time I've secured, only thirty seconds went to writing, maybe that is enough. Maybe there was something else I was doing with my energy that was also significant, if harder to track or see.

WRITING AND YOUR BEST TIME

Every two weeks or so I have a Zoom meeting with my friend Maya that we call "accountability." In our meetings, we make a list of what we want to get done in the next two weeks before we meet again, and we consider what we've gotten done in the last two weeks. It's called "accountability" because we're holding each other accountable for our time, and also because we're holding each other accountable for being honest with ourselves about what we really want to and can do (figure 2). "Accounting" as a name makes it seem mathy and judgy, and it does mean taking responsibility. But it's also the practice that's—and look, I'm going to get a little gushy here—truly transformed my ability to see *actually who I am,* as a writer in time who is also a person in time, rather than *who I wish that I might be.*

Accounting with a good and honest and clear-eyed friend balances out my deeply ingrained habit of overestimating the activities

Next Two Weeks

- ☐ Best Hour: Writing or Exercise
- ☐ This weekend:
  - ☐ Making something that feels like a calendar and stick with it, working backwards from April deadline
  - ☐ For teaching: Open what you did last semester
  - ☐ Write a letter of recommendation
- ☐ Continue practice of saying "No" to everything that's not taking a walk
- ☐ Continue practice of practical, but low-pressure lists
- ☐ Chicago:
  - ☐ Last How Chapter / Voice challenge / Have written a bunch, just needs it to be you.
- ☐ Avidly
  - ☐ Grad students sending essays today
  - ☐ Class is managing it!
- ☐ Teaching
  - ☐ Enjoy that grading is coming and IS NOT HERE YET
  - ☐ Channel Charlotte Web: Never hurry. Never worry.
  - ☐ Planning plus good walk, both of those mornings!
  - ☐ Try not to leave next unit prep til last minute

FIGURE 2. My "accounting" list from January 19, 2024

I can squish into a given period—not just a day, but almost any unit of time. My propensity for overprogramming isn't a marker of my type A effectiveness, of which I have basically none. Instead, it indicates an ideological sense I have (and that maybe you have too) that the people who are the best at my job, the Best Good Writers, and maybe the best people, are the ones that get the most done. I want to be one of the people I imagine, and so I stuff into my days all the activities I imagine such people can perform, even when there's virtually no chance that I will accomplish all of them. Why? Because while you can only do a few things in a day, you can avoid a nearly infinite number of things! Planning to do an impossible amount of work, and then avoiding it, allows me to remain attached to a fantasy of myself as a highly productive person and writer even when I'm not accomplishing any writing or even anything at all, and even when my shame at my unaccomplished to-do list makes me miserable. It's textbook cruel optimism, and accounting with Maya helps me avoid it.

Maya and I have become skilled auditors of each other's lists, noticing when they get too long, or any of the many ways the items on the lists don't equal the days in the week. We've also gotten better at seeing the emotional work behind the work. This has made me better at both planning and reverse-planning my days, because I can better see what I'm actually doing with the time it seems like I haven't secured. Often, I'm using seemingly unsecured time for emotional labor, work I need to do but can have a hard time acknowledging, especially when the emotions causing the labor are shameful ones. When a task is going to cause particular emotional labor, we try to break it into smaller parts (make a list of things that could be in the stressful email you have to send; write a not-going-to-send draft; write a to-send draft, etc.) and maybe only some of those get done in a given two weeks. You'll note that the list I've included as a figure here mentions that I will "try" to not put off my teaching prep. Trying can be its own task.

In accounting, we also try to organize our activities by two important criteria: "best hour" and "back burner." Our goal, which Maya learned from her friend Nikki (friendship here being an abiding source of wisdom), one that takes a lot of practice to implement, is to give ourselves the best hour of the day. We try to specify, for the next two weeks, what part of the day we will be our best selves (it changes based on teaching, deadlines, family, logistics, and health). That's the specific time we hope to secure. Then we try to decide what activity, in a given two weeks, will offer the most reward to our overall well-being, and spend our best hour on *that*, not on the shame emails, unless sending the shame emails really will be the best thing you can do for yourself (it happens). You can see in the accountability list pictured that, for this two-week period, I hope to spend my best hour writing or exercising. January's a busy time of year: I wasn't sure I could do both, given that I also had to start the semester and manage its logistics. But writing and exercise seemed equally valuable as ways to take care of myself. I didn't need to do both in a day, but I would practice giving my best hour (it's usually my first hour) to one of those activities, knowing that as long as I was doing one of them, I was practicing well.

One of the most useful parts of accountability meetings has

become saying out loud to another person: In the next two weeks, "I will best-hour X, and I will back-burner Y." Whatever you put on the back burner is not your job, at all, for two weeks. You don't have to think about it. It will wait on the burner, not going away, and it doesn't need to be stirred or considered or felt bad about. Conversely, the best-hour activity gets your best self, all to itself, for these two weeks only. Here in this book you are reading, I am hoping to communicate this good lesson that accounting with Maya has taught me: In a given two weeks, you might choose to give writing your best hour, and you might choose to back-burner writing while you best-hour yoga, or your kids' end-of-the-year band concert, or gardening, or going for walks with friends. The writing *doesn't go away*, even if you're not prioritizing it for these two weeks, or even longer than two weeks. Nothing goes away. Not everything can be best-houred in the next two weeks, but anything eventually can be best-houred. That is a lesson of long-term accounting, which Maya and I have (*for real!!!*) been doing biweekly for (checks calendar) five years, as of the month I am submitting this manuscript.

Accounting has also helped me reevaluate the relation between the time I give to what we might call "Writing," with a capital *W*, and all the things I do that are also writing but don't always have "Writing" status. It's not ignoring the very real differences between email, texting, and the intellectual and aesthetic labor of creating a sustained writing project to say that writing, whether it's Writing or emailing or responding, *is in fact writing*. You're doing all of it; all of it seeps into your craft affinities. Who you are, in your email prose, can't be fully sequestered from who you are in your larger projects. You are making your writing habits *all of the time*. That's one reason that emailing and sustained projects feel so at odds; to spend your craft energy on one means you have less for the other. And the same for texting with friends.

Our boundaries around what counts as Writing can sometimes serve us, as when we want to secure time for our intellectual lives, not our emails to our health insurance. But as an editor, I often wish the writers with whom I work perceived some of their boundaries differently, so that the wit and humor they revealed in their texts might appear in the prose they hoped to publish. Our low-key writing can be a long-term investment in Writing, and the other way around too.

On my "accountability" list you'll see "continue practice of saying 'no' to everything that's not taking a walk." That meant that my friendships were back-burnered: I was to accept no nonwalking social invitations for the next two weeks. A text from a friend is an invitation. Responding to it may not be on your next-two-weeks list. But texting friends is still writing. Without securing time for friendship (and accounting is a writing practice of friendship) most of the time, I would not have this support for my Writing when I do need it. In the long term, if you want to have friends who read your Writing, whose writing you will read, those friends will sometimes need to get the writing of your best hour, which may not feel like Writing, but in the course of your life will likely serve you more.

What's been best about accounting, finally, isn't how it's helped me become someone who could do more Writing, although it has also done that. More importantly, it's helped me become someone who is okay with doing *less* writing. It's helped me recognize and honor the commitments of time—for myself and other people—it takes to be someone in the world with something worthwhile to say, and with someone to talk to, at all.

WRITING AND GENRE TIME

Let's say I reverse-plan my days and secure five hours a week for writing—not a bad amount in the midst of a busy semester. How should I think about allocating that time, especially if I want to Write?

Here's a claim with some truth to it: Academic institutions, at this time, are best able to validate writing that reaches a substantial length, with single units of prose, such as articles and book chapters, typically clocking in at over five thousand words. This long-genre prose takes a long time to write, and also to publish, and also is expected (by the institution and editors) to be delivered on a long, slow clock, which is also usually predetermined.

Another truth about the world: Journalistic forms of writing exist at a much more flexible range of deadlines and lengths (800 words, 1,200 words, 3,000 words, sometimes longer, sometimes 280 characters). These forms of writing can be edited and published more quickly than most academic forms, if also much more unpredictably, and rarely with the fantastic efficiency and professionalism academics sometimes imagine exist outside academia. Because they are published more quickly, they find an audience faster.

And a final claim: It's hard to have the intellectual breakthroughs that long prose forms require with short bursts of time. I know all the ways that's not necessarily the case. There are whole books about it and I've read them. You can generate a long argumentative essay or chapter in short, daily units of seventeen minutes or forty-five minutes or your own personal bespoke time length. For me, though, holding three or four thousand words in mind, let alone the eight or nine thousand that can make up an academic article, is a deep-dive kind of experience. I can't really get to it without several hours in a row. And I have to have several days in a row, each of which contains several hours, to get to the headspace where I wake up in the night formulating the sentence I needed to crystalize my point or the paragraph change I should make to bring a story into focus. It's like each essay is a new-to-me language I need to immerse myself in in order to speak. I suppose that's what it's like because that's actually what it is.

To the extent that this principle holds true, academic writing—with its long standard lengths—becomes most available to people who can clear long stretches of time. Only some academics can do so, which is unfair. There's no way around that. That's not to say that journalism offers idyllic green fairness pastures. In both academic and journalistic contexts, those with preexisting financial and social resources are most likely to be able to make life- and creativity-preserving choices, with the fewest compromises.

Still, within academia's particular inequities, and within my own busy schedule, I have often chosen—and you too might choose—to write in journalistic forms because they offer me the hope of a reader soon, within easy reach of my five-hour week. I can't always all of a sudden best-hour a piece of timely journalistic writing. But nonacademic publishing feels so good to so many people with academic training partly because of the flexible time of starting, finishing, and being read that nonacademic publishing promises to inject into our five-hour-a-week writing life. A very reasonable choice might be to *not worry* about academic writing during our busiest times. So many short-form projects, and the relationship-building around those projects, can take place without the specific demands of long-form full-brain immersion.

In a better world—one, I'll note, that is within the scope of our agency—academic publication and promotion standards could adapt to better respect and "count" other lengths of writing. In the meantime, shorter genres (and publication processes) can help us get to some rewards of Writing, now.

Yet there are many specific rewards academic writing offers humanist experts that are hard to find elsewhere—things that it *can* offer us, now, even without the prospect of quick publication, and can also offer us in the long term. Academic writing might be worth doing to keep hold of a part of yourself as a participant in a conversation of experts. And it might be worth doing for poem and city and bug reasons of your own devising—because you love your poem or city or bug enough to commit to the long-term investigation of them, over the other things you might do. In many chapters of this book, I've explained why I value the pursuit of these goals. In this chapter let me make the temporal case for committing yourself—your seventeen or forty-five daily minutes of Precious Writing Time, or your five hours a week—to the distant horizon of academic writing, when there are so many desirable destinations closer at hand.

As an academic, one regularly hears the complaint that academic writing, which takes so very long to write and to publish, finds so few readers. The implication seems to be that the number of minutes should balance out to some quantitative measure of readers. Let me say in the strongest terms: This math is bad math. The *number* of readers may matter to publishers, counting clicks for advertising revenue. But to us as writers, comparing the quantity of our minutes to the quantity of our readers is the wrong equation. It misses the quality of readership academic publishing provides.

Academic writing, with its slow process of peer review, makes new knowledge for the world. Doing so, it creates a context for attentive reading like no other in the world. That we don't always or even often achieve that ideal state of attentive academic reading doesn't mean that it's not real. No other system yet established can promise readers—readers driven by poem-city-bug love, or expert-community investments—that their reading labor will be rewarded in such a fundamental, world-knowing way. Thus, in no other publishing system can writers expect readers who are willing to match their level of effort, of commitment. Academic readers are experts of the genre, who understand the genre's value, and who, in the act of reading, give consent to the genre's readerly demands.

All the time I encounter writers with academic training who, for reasons I understand and often share, feel that academic publishing makes too rigorous a demand. *Yet these same writers expect to make academic writing's demand on their readers.* They want to write for readers they can trust to go slow, stay with a complex point or a weedy sentence, weigh evidence, and take the worth of the topic on its own terms. Academic readers may not live up to our hopes for them. They (we) (I) might be distracted, irritable, or otherwise in bad faith, certainly. Yet, writers, let me tell you: There is no more certain way to find the careful readers we long for than to promise them, in our publishing forms, that *we* have been as careful as possible too.

WRITING IN YOUR LIFE'S TIME

I remember thinking, as I was finishing my PhD, that getting a job—and by "job" I meant a specific kind of job, one as a professor of literature—was like catching a train. When I negotiated childcare expenses and responsibilities with my children's father, I would explain how I felt about wanting a ticket on this particular ride. The job train, I explained, would come into a station at a scheduled moment, and then it would go: There was only one chance to buy a ticket, only one train a year, and only so many years (I thought) when the train would consider you a viable passenger at all. How did you buy a ticket? With your writing. How much writing? That was mysterious and shifting, subject to strange inflationary logics. So how much childcare time did I need to budget for or shift away, how many lunches did I need not to pack, to do this writing? That was unclear too. My writing would be competing for golden tickets with people who had more time, who used time better. So no matter how much time I had, I needed more. Always more.

Why did I need to catch this train? I wanted to ride right out of my amateur status, my professional insecurity. I wanted to catch the train toward the future life I longed for, the life in which I could be the person I understood myself as and had trained to be. I had always been warned that the train was unreliable and uncomfortable and *weird* if not cruel in its ticket distribution; that you should not count on getting a ticket, because only a few people did. But my whole life, to that point, I had been one of the people who got the ticket, caught the train. I had always been one of the best; no one who gets into graduate school isn't. I wanted that ticket because I didn't want to face a reality in which I wasn't one of the talented few. I needed a ticket to prove to myself that I was me. To not fight for the ticket was not to fight for my sense of self. Didn't that deserve all the time there was, even if time was something I felt decreasingly able to use?

Reader: Here's what I did. I took a different train.

It didn't seem like a train at the time. I knew I was doing something, but I didn't always feel myself as having direction or momentum. When I was most pinched for time, during the years when my commute was long and my kids were small and babysitting for them was in short supply, and when I had a good friend who was in the same situation, and even though I was (at thirty-six) feeling a real professional-future crunch, we started *Avidly* so we could write short things, in the short time we had.

Starting *Avidly* absolutely took time away, on a daily and monthly basis, from academic writing. I could have been working on a monograph in that time, about my field of scholarly interest. In fact, in 2012, I had some of the most flexible *job* demands that I'll probably ever have, so it really did seem like my monograph moment, especially because my idea for a monograph was good. One of the reasons that particular book has never yet been written is that I secured my time for editing and chatting and social media and production (and writing my own pieces too) instead of academic writing. This was a choice. I did not yet have the language of "securing" time. But I had a sense of worry, and of shame, and of Writing vs. writing. In my internal arguments and my domestic negotiations, I knew I was investing myself in an activity without a future I could see. My choice felt bad, some days, because I worried I was avoiding my real work of Writing and thus losing my career, my ticket. On other days, most days, it felt good and joyful and world-building. It never felt practical.

That choice has earned me, now a decade later with children substantively grown and thus more time in my days, the expertise and perspective and professional status necessary to write *this* academic book. It's not the academic book I thought I would write back then, although it depends on much of the same scholarly expertise. But in the long term, my own life reveals the contest between academic and journalistic publishing, between Writing and writing, to be less zero-sum than it's often described. It's only when I measure my life in the short term (which, of course, is how it's lived) that the two seem dramatically opposed.

Sitting here writing on my Wednesday morning of Precious Writing Time, I find myself genuinely curious about what might be learned or extrapolated from my experience. The choices I made were products of historical conditions, like a particular collapse of the job market and the launch of WordPress's new dashboard, that aren't likely to be repeated. My choices also enact privilege

(I have a strong emotional and familial safety net; my loved ones are physically well; I have never had to manage poverty's many burdens alongside the rest of my workload), as well as some restriction (my kids are not negotiable; in order to keep them near their father and maintain some financial security, I could not pursue various job possibilities). And many of my choices can't fully be described as such. During the early *Avidly* years, my emotional and mental health was quite poor, and I really couldn't sit with myself long enough to write academic prose. So, the writing I did was the writing I could do.

I also know I eventually became a better writer, more focused and ambitious and courageous, by letting myself do all the things that would never show up, in a day reverse-planned, as "writing," let alone "Writing." A lot of what I did might count as "fucking around." I recommitted to cooking after many years of anxiously feeling I couldn't spare any time to cook. I took my dog for longer walks, not trying to crowd time with her in between other "more important" things. I read more novels all the way through, because I wanted to and because they were good. I developed a more ethical practice of gossip. I spent a lot of time with friends. And I spent a lot of time talking to other people about their writing. I edited their writing, platformed their writing, publicized it. I learned to be better at showing up for other people. I learned to show up for myself. I learned by practicing showing up, and by practicing again. I learned how to ask, more responsibly, for people to show up for me. I practice that too.

All this made me a better writer. Being a more honest and consistent participant in my communities helped me have more to say, and to say it more confidently, when I eventually turned back to writing as a best-hour activity. I was less motivated to write by obligation and fear and more by what I was choosing to write about. Being clearer about my motivations helped me feel, like reverse planning did for Jensen, a clearer and thus more abundant sense of time. In this state, the world of words I love so much has become easier for my heart to enter. But more importantly, changing my relationship to time and to my time with friends made me a person I am prouder to be, across the board.

I am writing these words on a Saturday morning. In the time since the Friday morning almost two years ago, a real morning, when this book begins, one of my excellent kids has up and gone to college. One, across the country, has gotten his ears pierced and learned to pitch. The other excellent kid is, really right now as I type, milling about the kitchen. That this revised manuscript comes due two days from now has no bearing on his need for breakfast. Our dog needs to be walked; her head needs to be praised.

I have had some anxious feelings, these last two finishing weeks, that if I wasn't panicking, or shutting everything else out, or otherwise completely in the zone, that this book I have spent so much of My Precious Writing Time traveling toward wouldn't be worth the expenditure. That having some sense of calm meant that I was doing it wrong. That a Good Writer would be more laser focused, and that the result would be a better book. But I am me, and I have written this book. It's the book my life, and my talent, at this now, could contain. So I'm practicing letting the anxious feelings go. I'm trying to absorb this book's central lesson: that building a world in which I actually want to live, with the people I love, is never wasting my precious writing time. The only time to build it is now.

CODA

Hospitality

What I desire, from humanities expert writing, is shelter. I want the job, the space on the page, the resources needed to have good choices. I also want the sense of welcome I find in words that, alongside their intellectual accomplishments, offer a place to think and feel. I want, from writing, a small, safe place. Are these desires obstacles to my flourishing, or ours?

The week that the proposal for this book went to the University of Chicago Press editorial board for consideration was ten years, almost exactly, from when I gave up the tenuous pursuit of a job focused on the nineteenth-century sentimental novel, my area of research expertise. Sending off my proposal, I felt how far I'd come from the mouth-hurting sadness of that decision. But later that very same week, I had to clean out a storage unit my landlords needed for a different tenant. And suddenly I found myself crying over three boxes of files I no longer had space to keep. The files contained printed-out scholarship I hoped to cite in essays I imagined I would write about books I had loved and had hated; the more and less carefully outlined syllabi and writing assignments and sample student writing for courses I had labored over and hoped I'd teach again; conference notes; rough drafts. Opening the files was like unpacking a different version of myself, my expertise, and the writing that my expertise could have led to.

In the grand scheme of things, dumping those files in the trash bin was an unpleasant but exceedingly minor drama. I lost some boxes, one specific future I really wanted but in no way was entitled to have. Others have lost more. Whole departments, whole universities, have been shuttered. Some have been literally razed to the ground. But grief has its own weird sense of proportion. I was so, so sad to let those boxes go.

Loss, at a baffling range of scales and felt textures, surrounds humanities study. I don't mean to be dramatic about it. It's just that in the upheavals of our situation, accurate description gets a little operatic. What I mean is that the past, for humanist writing, held experiences, structures, possibilities, securities that the future won't contain. When one thing leaves a life, others follow, and it's hard to know in advance what those will be. The unpredictable circuitry by which loss travels makes mourning hard, and difficult to share. You think you've gotten over a loss—some files, a job, a friend, a laptop, a venue, a field—I have lost all these—and then all of a sudden you encounter yourself in some place where that lost thing could have been meaningful, and would have been, but now it's not there with you, and is not. And you find that your mourning isn't done, won't ever be done, because you'll never be finished encountering the many futures where your loved lost thing won't be.

Here's something I know: If our future won't contain the same forms as the past, it will contain something new. It won't be empty. It will hold us, and our writing, in some form and in some relation. When I say that I desire shelter, and that I'm worried this desire is an obstacle to flourishing, I mean two things. First, I'm worried that the desire for shelter will keep me pursuing the now-gone structures of the past, pouring effort into old expectations rather than doing the work of revising them for the present and the future. Second, I'm worried about how loss will warp the current work. Grief can build connection, but really, it doesn't always.

I'm worried about the kind of shelter that writing while grieving can provide.

Grief hurts and sometimes it seeks out causes for that hurt. It finds manageable shape in accusation, in self-righteousness. Raising the banner of these feelings, it's really easy to marshal troops to your cause. Academic social media *loves* to feel aggrieved. *I* love to feel aggrieved. It feels so good and easy to stand in phalanx with a crowd of like-grieving people telling you that lashing out in hurt is a noble activity. There, under your locked-in shields, you are sheltered for sure. You are a weapon. That you are legitimately hurt makes it easier to interpret the damage you do as world-making.

Or I guess the damage is world-making. But it's an abrasive and anxious, prepper-like, world. What I sometimes see emerging from the very real bad feelings of our moment is grief thrashing about, looking for objects. We want objects we can hurt. And so we choose each other, the people around us, especially those who are managing their grief differently, making different choices or compromises. For some in the throes of grief, anything new that's organized—a conference, a venue, a curriculum—becomes a cruel manifestation of a past that's no longer possible. Because nothing anyone tries can ever fix everything, anything anyone tries can always be accused of hurting or excluding someone. Any success for some registers mostly as a failure for everyone else who didn't experience it. Writing this account of what grief can do, I'm not describing a hypothetical: I'm thinking about specific polemics, specific people I have seen maneuver, real social media posts I have read, and even some I have written. I regret those posts. I don't want to live in the world any of this grief-waging makes. Its shelter is not hospitable to the future I would like to imagine.

Writing here about grief, I'm also doing something else: using the very expertise in sentimental culture that I felt the crisis in the humanities, the collapsed job market, had taken away from me. There are real losses, for my writing and my humanities expertise: my files, the future in which I would have spent every semester teaching Harriet Beecher Stowe's Lite-Brite sentences and

Harriet Jacobs's true-fire revisions of them, seeing students' wide eyes at the end of *Bleak House*, writing and reading with these students and my colleagues. But my written expertise finds new shape in the shelters made by people who have refused the terms the present seems to impose on them. Sometimes these shelters have been made by Writing, and sometimes by writing. All of them have been forward-looking revisions of what shelter looked like in the past. They have been exercises in hospitality.

Here are some people whom I would like to credit as, in their lives and research and public activity, doing the meaningful work of building worlds where new forms of expertise can take hold: Tom Lutz, Paul Erickson, Meredith McGill, Jackie Goldsby, Meredith Martin, Koritha Mitchell, Christopher Schaberg, Kate Levin, Jonathan Eburne, Rodrigo Lazo, Matt Seybold, Kamran Javaizadeh, Nicholas Dames, and Rebecca Colesworthy. This list skews toward people in fields I know best. Of course it's incomplete.

I would like my praise to be practical. Here are some things the above-listed people have practiced: Starting a bookstore. Starting a prison education program. Starting a new book series. Starting and editing podcasts. Starting a Black studies database and bibliography project. Editing and introducing teaching editions of essential books, and developing the critical methodologies necessary for that editing. Starting a field-redefining digital archive and database. Starting a magazine. Quietly and effectively issuing and depositing the checks, making the Doodle poll, sending the emails, replying to the emails. Writing their names on the spreadsheet, on the ballot, on the line.

None of the above practices were ones I was trained to recognize as "expert writing." But all these people have helped me learn the writing practices this book describes. They have consistently created new shelters that can carry their expertise into the future. They have done so in a way that makes room for so many of us to find new ways of *being* an us, in writing, with them.

Writing that builds is hard, and stinginess can feel so reasonable, so justified. But around us are those who have generously committed to writing into being the worlds in which our ideas and our needs are urgent, legible, worth reading. Hospitality is a practice of relation: It is also a craft of writing, one we can teach and publish and value. This book has argued for that relation—for hospitality's sheltering feeling—as a reason to write.

Acknowledgments

I became someone who could write this book because of so many acts of kindness, acts of care, good jokes, good books, excellent texts (the phone kind), smart observations, good edits, good meals. I am grateful one million ways and to so many people.

First, thanks to Sarah Blackwood, who, with a major practical and emotional assist from Jordan Stein, started *Avidly* with me in 2012, thereby helping me and so many others figure out new ways to feel and reason with the great intensities of this world. This book would not be possible without the turn toward a different way of being with writing that *Avidly* created for me and others. Thank you both, and Sarah especially, for years of getting me through. Thank you to Eric Zinner for all your support of Avidly Reads.

Thanks to Alan Thomas, my editor at the University of Chicago Press, for first asking me if I'd be interested in writing a book like this one, for collaborating with me as it took shape, for telling me when the ropes were too slack, and especially for letting me fly the flags of my sentences into their own strange crosswinds. I'm so grateful to have learned so much about editing from you. Also at the Press, thanks to Sara Bakerman and Randolph Petilos, with deep gratitude for all the writing it takes (emails, nudges, more emails) to help someone else write a book. Stephen Twilley, you are a hero, full stop. Enormous gratitude to my several anonymous readers. Dear Reader #2 especially: Thank you for your readjustments of my Americanist perspective and for telling me about your baby monitor.

Thanks to Tanya McKinnon, my agent and real human genius. Please never stop texting me about important hair.

Thanks to Tom Lutz for starting the *Los Angeles Review of Books* and to Evan Kindley for asking me to join the *Los Angeles Review of Books*. Crossroads of the World!

Thanks to the many graduate students and postdoctoral fellows who discussed these ideas and read some of these pages at Penn State University, Washington University, Northwestern University, University of Wyoming, Rutgers University, the University of Southern California, and the University of Michigan. Thank you especially to the students at Michigan who reminded me that being tired can mean we need and want reading with more beauty, more difficulty, more challenge. This changed my outlook at a crucial time and I'm grateful.

Thanks for taking time to help me talk through my questions in writing this book: Rebecca Colesworthy, Roderick Ferguson, Naomi Greyser, Jonathan Kramnik, Alex Carp, and the many people who suggested things to read. For always being on the lookout for new possibilities, Christopher Schaberg. To all the writers I've edited, who have taught me so much.

Thanks to all my teachers, the people who taught me what the humanities could be and what writing in them might be for. I am grateful especially to Julia Stern; thank you for modeling how to go deep and hold tight and also how to let a project go. To Jay Grossman, for so many reminders about the strangeness of a writer's voice. To Blakey Vermeule, who made an offhand remark I take issue with in these pages, but who made many other offhand remarks in a graduate seminar long ago that continue to guide me. To Chris Looby, who helped (along with many others) turn on the lights at a dark time. Special thanks to Jonathan Freedman for publishing my first essay, and for much more. Looking back further: Doris Witt, Claire Sponsler, Huston Diehl, Kathleen Renk; Ms. Evans, Mr. Wheate, Mrs. Patton, Mrs. Henson. Thank you for the strong foundation.

Thanks to dissertation island, for helping me practice making shelter in expertise: Sarah Blackwood, Katy Chiles, Peter Jaros, and (in the island's evolving coastline) Marcy Dinius. To Catherine Carrigan for excellent dinners over many years.

Thanks to all my writing students over the last decade and more, especially students in my Advanced Writing for Editors classes. Thank you for helping me put it into language.

Thanks for reading and talking over these many pages, as well as these ideas and practices in many different forms: Sarah Ahrens, Hester Blum, Michelle Chihara, Lisa Corrigan, Duncan Faherty, Martin Harries, Virginia Jackson, Greta LaFleur, Dana Luciano, Meredith Martin, Meredith McGill, Mel Micir, Kati Phillips, Jessica Pressman, Jordan Stein, Arielle Zibrak, and Caleb Smith. Thank you so much for your steadiness and insight and always, always for your time.

Thanks to my colleagues at USC, especially Patricia Taylor, Taly Ravid Matejka (for agreeing to be my friend after fifteen minutes in a coffee shop fourteen years ago, and staying true ever since), fearless leaders Norah McNally Ashe and Mariko Dawson Zare, visionaries Nik De Dominic and Kate Levin, and guides Ellen Wayland Smith and Mark Marino, and more. Thanks to USC's Dornsife College of Letters, Arts and Sciences for awarding me an AHSSS sabbatical to support the writing of this book.

To Phil Maciak, my long-term editor and comrade-in-arms and pal—thank you for everything you helped me to cut and everything you encouraged me to keep. MORE HATS! To Maya Gurantz: Thank you for making and sharing our Google Docs archive every two weeks, and for filling the well.

This book happened for many reasons, but one of them is that I totally changed my life so that I could become someone able to do many things differently, including write. The process of changing my life was messy. It made a lot of work, for everyone around me. I am grateful for all the small and large acts of support and care along the way.

Thanks for oysters and real talks in the backyard on two coasts: Eden Osucha, Jason Middleton, Paul North, Caro Baffi, Sasha Rudensky, Eli Huge, Sarah Mahurin, Josh Kamensky, Josh Adams, Jon Zerolnik, Michael Warner, Sean Belman, Kathryn Lofton, David and Jane Kastan, and everyone, everyone there in body and spirit on July 3, 2022.

Thanks for sustaining daily companionship in words and otherwise to Sarah Blackwood, Hester Blum, Claire Jarvis, Kyla Wazana Tompkins, Heather Joy Rosenberg, Lauren Teukolsky, Shoshanna Scholar, Michelle Chihara, Maya Gurantz, Elizabeth Hamilton, Morgan Fahey, Kati Phillips, Becca Lemme, Megan Karsh, Molly Painter, Sarah Ahrens, and Team Jumpies. Thanks to Kate Mann since the very beginning of making worlds of words, and often of Legos. Thanks to Sylviana for first steps.

Thanks to Dan Braun, for all the captaining and all the getting lost. To Kati Phillips, for walking into my life with a reporter's notebook thirty years ago and never leaving. I am so grateful to live this life with both of you. You are golden threads.

Thanks to my family. To everyone in Arkansas who made me feel so at home. To my mother and father, Barbara Hiles Mesle and Bob Mesle: Your steady love is the greatest gift any writer—or person—could receive. To my Grammy, for your pages spread out on the Ping-Pong table. For Grandad's steady clarity. For Gramps' newsletters. For Grams for dreaming of chocolate and explaining freedom. For all my aunts and uncles and cousins, who will sing on cue and who take responsibility for the world. For Mark, my brother, the best there could be, and his astonishing family of mermaids.

Thanks to my boys. To Van Smith, for your determination and your full-throttle embrace of life (and me), and for coaching me through my push-ups. To Elliot Harvey and Asher Mesle, who lived with this book more than anyone. Elliot, so glad to be deine Mutter. I will try to keep this public admiration short, but thank you for loving hard, brave art. Asher, you are such excellent company. Thank you for your exceptional generosity, your questions, your loving companionship in this book's last stages, and for sharing your snacks and your tunes. I love you all so much.

To Caleb Smith: More life! Thank you for turning with me toward the best now, every day, even today. "Thus, though we cannot make our sun / Stand still, yet we will make him run."

Notes

ONE

1. Joli Jensen, *Write No Matter What: Advice for Academics* (University of Chicago Press, 2017), 7.
2. Jensen, *Write No Matter What*, 7.
3. Sianne Ngai, *Our Aesthetic Categories: Zany, Cute, Interesting* (Harvard University Press, 2012), 1.
4. Wayne Bivens-Tatum, "The 'Crisis' in the Humanities," *Academic Librarian*, November 5, 2010, https://blogs.princeton.edu/librarian/2010/11/the_crisis_in_the_humanities/.
5. Natalia Lusin and Mai Hunt, "The MLA *Job List*, 2020–22" (2023), https://www.mla.org/content/download/191179/file/Job-List-Report-20-22.pdf.
6. Lusin and Hunt, "MLA *Job List*, 2020–22." In 2009 the MLA listed a combined 2,122 jobs; this figure rose in 2011, reaching 2,363. In 2020, however, only 1,006 total jobs were listed. Of course, the MLA list is only one metric of humanities hiring.
7. Many consulting firms are notoriously secretive about the advice they actually give. My accusation about classroom cameras seems true to me, based on classroom experience, but the exact source of that decision at my university is likely to remain obscure. I will note, however, that consulting companies like McKinsey certainly tout their own ability to intervene in higher education. McKinsey's "Higher Education" page describes how the company can help universities foster "creative expression that advances humanity and improves our world for the future" while also offering them "strategies that transform operations and strengthen financial

sustainability" ("Higher Education," McKinsey & Company, accessed January 24, 2025, https://www.mckinsey.com/industries/education/how-we-help-clients/higher-education). This language blends moral purpose with economic reorganization. But as *New York Times* journalists Walt Bogdanich and Michael Forsythe show in their book *When McKinsey Comes to Town: The Hidden Influence of the World's Most Powerful Consulting Firm* (Random House, 2022), McKinsey's rhetoric has helped conceal a history of economic practices with dire social stakes, among them exacerbating the opioid crisis (when working for Purdue Pharma), increasing the strain on public welfare systems (when consulting for Walmart), and committing many acts of so-called "right-sizing" and outsourcing jobs. Thus while the results of actions McKinsey might advise in a specific university, whether mine or yours, might not be immediately apparent, there seems just reason for faculty concern.

8. Christopher Newfield, "Have We Wrecked Public Universities? The Case of the American Decline Cycle," *British Journal of Sociology* 69, no. 2 (2018): 485.

9. It's worth saying that one way we might gain control of these metrics is through organized labor. Organizing takes a lot of writing! Such writing—sending the meeting emails, texting reminders about the meetings—may feel like a drain on Our Precious Writing Time, but ultimately sustains it.

10. No amount of writing, for instance, could protect the jobs of humanities faculty at West Virginia University, which at the time of this writing were being cut dramatically by a president guided by so-called market principles rather than by the university's public mission. Some of my friends there focused almost exclusively on scholarly writing; others wrote regularly for social and public audiences. No choice they made could have protected them from Gordon Gee. Very few of us (and fewer all the time!) work at WVU specifically. But WVU's existential threat hangs over us all.

11. That's not what it's called: it's called "Slow Steady," and I have been listening to the same playlist, with minor edits, since the summer of 2009, when I was finishing my dissertation. My relationship to it is close to Pavlovian and I try not to mess that up by overusing it.

12. Sarah Blackwood, "Letter from an English Department on the Brink," *New York Review of Books*, April 2, 2023, https://www.nybooks.com/online/2023/04/02/letter-from-an-english-department-on-the-brink/.

13. Paul Reitter and Chad Wellmon, *Permanent Crisis: The Humanities in a Disenchanted Age* (University of Chicago Press, 2021), 251.

14. Nathan Heller, "The End of the English Major," *New Yorker*, February 27, 2023, https://www.newyorker.com/magazine/2023/03/06/the-end-of-the-english-major.

15. Kandice Chuh, *The Difference Aesthetics Makes: On the Humanities "After Man"* (Duke University Press, 2019).

16. Bennett Carpenter, Laura Goldblatt, and Lenora Hanson, "Unprofessional: Toward a Political Economy of Professionalization," *Social Text* 39, no. 1 (2021): 47–67.

17. The writing support software I have been using the last few Friday mornings, developed by the National Center for Faculty Diversity and Development, tallies up my minutes. Every time I log my hours, the software tells me: "Congrats! You paid yourself first."

18. Nash provides an illustrative history of how often white feminists have presented Black women's experiences as disrupting "feminist collectivity." See her *How We Write Now: Living with Black Feminist Theory* (Duke University Press, 2024), 13–14.

19. Despite its very recent emergence, AI certainly matters to the moment in which I'm revising this book, although *what* it means precisely has shifted dramatically even in the few months between the book's submission and production. Nevertheless, AI makes minimal appearance in these pages, because whatever its virtues, it's not designed to solve the problems this book addresses. If you love writing, it won't help you to have AI write for you; if you're trying to make meaningful decisions about your time and your life, AI can't do that, either. My personal opinion is that it's unethical to turn to AI for any writing assistance a human might provide—whether you are mulling over a direction, an idea, or a sentence—because in such a situation the ethical response is to always take the opportunity to build a human connection. I am here to stand with this arguably extremist position. For one thoughtful account of how AI fits into the temporal economy of humanist work, see Patricia Taylor, "The Imperfect Tutor: Grading, Feedback, and AI," *Inside Higher Ed*, September 6, 2024, https://www.insidehighered.com/opinion/career-advice/teaching/2024/09/06/challenges-using-ai-give-feedback-and-grade-students.

20. We might here align Huerta's work with José Muñoz's account of potentially collectivizing movement toward the utopic: "The 'we' is not content to describe who the collective is but more nearly describes what the collective and the larger social order could be, what it should be." *Cruising Utopia: The Then and There of Queer Futurity* (NYU Press, 2009), 20.

21. Monica Huerta, *Magical Habits* (Duke University Press, 2021), ix.

22. While writing this book and inhabiting the moment of its composition, several other books about formal innovation have been helpful to my thinking. I would like to mention particularly Anahid Nersessian's *The Calamity Form: On Poetry and Social Life* (University of Chicago Press, 2021).

23. Chuh, *Difference Aesthetics Makes*, xi.

TWO

1. Sarah Mesle, "The Unbearable Awesomeness of Lululemon Pants," *Avidly*, June 4, 2013, https://avidly.lareviewofbooks.org/2013/06/04/the-unbearable-awesomeness-of-lululemon-pants/.
2. Christopher Buccafusco and Jeanne C. Fromer, "Fashion's Function in Intellectual Property Law," *Notre Dame Law Review* 93, no. 1 (2017): 107, https://scholarship.law.nd.edu/cgi/viewcontent.cgi?article=4751&context=ndlr.
3. "Feeling" is a messy word, and my use of it here is far from tidy; I purposefully blur the somatic and generic operations of the word. An impressively useful review of the rich mess of "feeling," specifically in relation to the terms "emotion" and "affect," can be found on pages 234–35 of Jordan Stein's recent book, *Fantasies of Nina Simone* (Duke University Press, 2024). Stein's explanation, which appears in a footnote, recalls a similarly essential footnote in the book *Ugly Feelings* (Harvard University Press, 2007), in which Sianne Ngai sorts through Raymond Williams's term "structure of feeling" (359–60). I am indebted to all these writers.
4. Sukhdev Sandhu, "Why We're Hooked," review of *Screen Time*, by Phillip Maciak, *The Guardian*, June 1, 2023, https://www.theguardian.com/books/2023/jun/01/screen-time-by-phillip-maciak-review-why-were-hooked.
5. Molly Worthen, "Stop Saying 'I Feel Like,'" *New York Times*, April 30, 2016, https://www.nytimes.com/2016/05/01/opinion/sunday/stop-saying-i-feel-like.html. Worthen emphasizes the connection between feelings and internal experience, arguing that Americans have abandoned "the Enlightenment quest for universal truth in favor of obsessing over their own internal states and well-being." Other discussions of the phrase "I feel like" appear in venues as disparate as *Jezebel* and *Forbes*. See Katie J. M. Baker, "Ladies, What's Up with the 'I Feel Like' Verbal Tic?," *Jezebel*, August 23, 2013, https://jezebel.com/ladies-whats-up-with-the-i-feel-like-verbal-tic-1184374148; Shane Snow, "I Feel Therefore I Think: If You're a Leader, This Verbal Habit Could Be Undermining You," July 24, 2020, https://www.forbes.com/sites/shanesnow/2020/07/24/i-feel-therefore-i-think-if-youre-a-leader-this-verbal-habit-could-be-undermining-you/.
6. Raymond Williams, *Marxism and Literature* (Oxford University Press, 1977), 132; Audre Lorde, *Uses of the Erotic: The Erotic as Power* (Out & Out Books, 1978), 56.
7. Lorraine Daston and Peter Galison, *Objectivity* (Zone Books, 2007), 22.
8. John Frowe, *Genre* (Routledge, 2005), 102.
9. Daston and Galison, *Objectivity*, 11.
10. Daston and Galison, 11.

11. Daston and Galison, 13–16, 197. The authors are careful to point out that photography didn't cause this epistemic shift, "although the photograph became one of its principal vehicles" (197). Rather, the photograph (which in other contexts was and could be used differently) was turned to historically desirable epistemic ends.
12. Daston and Galison, 16.
13. Take, for example, the sentence from the *Notre Dame Law Review* article I quoted in this chapter's opening section, which "argues that aspects of garment design are functional not only when they affect the physical or technological performance of a garment but also when they affect the perception of the wearer's body" (107). Despite the sentence's focus on wearers and perceivers, no one in this sentence wears or perceives or even functions. Instead, the sentence freezes a precise moment when something, an aspect, "is functional."
14. Heather Radke, *Butts: A Backstory* (Avid Reader Press, 2022), 2.
15. Sander L. Gilman, "Black Bodies, White Bodies: Toward an Iconography of Female Sexuality in Late Nineteenth-Century Art, Medicine, and Literature," *Critical Inquiry* 12, no. 1 (1985): 204–42, http://www.jstor.org/stable/1343468. Note: a reason I'm quoting Gilman, in addition to his insight, is that his association with *Critical Inquiry* and the word "buttocks" rather than "butt" make him feel more reasonable.
16. The paragraph I'm amending with this note makes, I hope, a historical claim that I expand philosophically here. In writing this chapter, and specifically in rereading Fred Moten's discussion of Black radical style in his book *In the Break* (University of Minnesota Press, 2003) against my own knowledge of white American sentimental style, which, like the work Moten discusses, developed in response to slavery, I've come to believe that nineteenth-century debates about the resource worthiness of emerging "objective" and "subjective" styles can best be read as by-products of capitalism's rapacious nineteenth-century spread; I also now think that capitalism helps explain the intensity of our current debates about feelings, reasons, and style. Capitalism, as a world-ordering system, thrives on misdirections and displacements. Just as, famously, commodities conceal social relations, both rationalizations and emotionalizations often conceal the lived lessons of the body. Forms like "objectivity" and "sentimentalism," along with genres training us in those maneuvers, became powerful when they did because the embodied experiences I've been calling "feeling" offer insights into the material world that capitalism doesn't want us to know. I make these claims as someone with a wary and provisional relationship to Marxist thought. I also make them realizing that humanist readers of this book may find them either obvious

or completely unconvincing. But I put this account of my own intellectual transformation here in a good-faith effort to give the best explanation I have for why debates about reason, feeling, and style carry such intensity and why our ongoing negotiations with the style of reason deserve all the resources we can give them.

17. Amanda Anderson, *The Way We Argue Now: A Study in the Cultures of Theory* (Princeton University Press, 2009), 2.

18. Here I'm thinking about Sianne Ngai's account of so-called "ugly feelings" in aesthetic response (see Ngai, *Ugly Feelings*).

19. Jonathan Kramnik, *Criticism and Truth* (University of Chicago Press, 2023), 27.

20. Kramnik, *Criticism and Truth*, 4.

21. Here I'm making a claim for the capacity of criticism to avail itself of different styles in order to know the world differently, a claim that links criticism to art practice. My thinking developed partly by reading several essays about objectivity and fictionality by the critic Anna Kornbluh. For Kornbluh, objectivity enables critique, whereas interiority, identity, and "aboutness"—qualities criticism can take on that I, on the other hand, tend to value and enjoy—often disable it. I went to Kornbluh specifically to read a thoughtful, ethically invested account with which I expected to disagree. In many ways we *do* disagree. But I found Kornbluh's discussion of how literary style can operate socially hugely clarifying. Here's one sentence that was helpful to me in my thinking: in her essay "Objectively Curious Commitments," Kornbluh shows how, "Across setting, tone, and character, Dickens's style ultimately illustrates for Adorno the ways that objectivity can emerge from dissonant blending, from style that limns its own limits, from techniques of representation that deliver representation itself to study" ("Objectively Curious Commitments," *Victorian Literature and Culture* 48, no. 2 [2020]: 449). Creative narration allows Dickens to trouble received norms of interiority by introducing (critique-enabling) objectivity in his novels. My own sense is that creative narration in criticism can work similarly, by pressing the reader to encounter the embedded epistemic values and norms of selfhood that often, in scholarship, go unexamined and unnaturalized.

THREE

1. Ryan Ruby, "A Golden Age?" *Vinduet*, April 25, 2023, https://www.vinduet.no/essayistikk/a-golden-age-ryan-ruby-on-literary-criticism-and-the-internet/.

2. Ruby, "A Golden Age?"

3. That so many sentences produced under such conditions manage to be so beautiful is one mark (among many) of the resilience of humanities scholars and the capacity of our attention to create generative worlds, as I have argued before. See Caleb Smith, Sarah Mesle, and Merve Emre, eds., "No Crisis," special series, *Los Angeles Review of Books* (2015), https://lareviewofbooks.org/feature/no-crisis/. Of special interest, however, may be Evan Calder William's concluding essay, "No, Crisis," which pushes back against the series' framework (*Los Angeles Review of Books*, December 6, 2015, https://lareviewofbooks.org/article/no-crisis-2/).

4. WordPress.com, "New Dashboard Design and March Wrap-Up," April 4, 2008, https://wordpress.com/blog/2008/04/04/new-dashboard/.
5. I would also like to strongly encourage anyone reading this book while spelunking around for a dissertation project to plum the many deep caverns in which this history came to be shaped, because I can only limn the surface of them here. It's hard to even know where to begin as a starting point, when real tech nerds were developing their own platforms of exchange and languages for speaking there since the 1970s and '80s.
6. In a useless but satisfying act of "resistance," I try never to capitalize the name of any Zuckerberg product.
7. I cannot overestimate how powerfully I believe that the turn toward the public humanities grew significantly out of the writing practices developed on several online venues run by women, specifically *Television Without Pity* (1998–2014), by Sarah Bunting and Tara Ariano, the blogs *Dooce* (Heather B. Armstrong) and *Bitch PhD* (Tedra Osell), *Go Fug Yourself* (2004–), by Heather Cocks and Jessica Morgan, and *Bookslut* (2002–2016), by Jessa Crispin. In email interviews, former MLA president Michael Bérubé listed *Bitch PhD* among other political blogs such as Amanda Marcotte's as influences for his own digital practice, and *LARB* founding editor Tom Lutz cited the influence of Crispin.
8. In her essay "The I in the Internet," the critic Jia Tolentino recounts another valuable perspective on the internet history I have told here; she puts the high-water mark of internet writing at around 2012, the very moment when many extra-academic venues were just starting. "The I in the Internet," *CCCB Lab*, February 19, 2020, https://lab.cccb.org/en/the-i-in-the-internet/.
9. Phillip Maciak, personal conversation, June 1, 2023.
10. Here writer Jeffrey Williams paraphrases his own sense of a term used by Brian Edwards at a 2013 MLA session, "The Semi-Public Intellectual." Jeffrey J. Williams, "Empire of Letters: Tom Lutz and the 'Los Angeles Review of Books' Set Out to Create a New Model of Literary Review," *Chronicle of Higher Education*, January 3, 2016, https://www.chronicle.com/article/empire-of-letters/.
11. National Endowment for the Humanities, "Public Scholars," accessed August 25, 2023, https://www.neh.gov/grants/research/public-scholar-program.

12. Ben Smith's recent history of the rise of online news media—a similar history to the one I sketch here—ends by describing the relation of the progressive internet (and many of its failures) to the rise of Trump. "The figures who would create the new American Far Right," he writes, had percolated through digital media from the start. *Traffic: Genius, Rivalry, and Delusion in the Billion-Dollar Race to Go Viral* (Penguin Press, 2023), 290.
13. While it's difficult to condense (or knowledgably describe) the internal business practices of several different websites, this seems to me an accurate description of the problem, as I experienced it anecdotally as a professor and as it was described at the time by editors such as *The Toast*'s Nicole Cliffe. See Mark Scott, "Study of Ad-Blocking Software Suggests Wide Use," *New York Times*, August 10, 2015, https://archive.nytimes.com/bits.blogs.nytimes.com/2015/08/10/study-of-ad-blocking-software-suggests-wide-use/. On the negotiations between advertisers, media, and AdBlock Plus, see Olivia Solon, "AdBlock Plus Launching Platform to Sell 'Acceptable' Ads," *The Guardian*, September 13, 2016, https://www.theguardian.com/business/2016/sep/13/adblock-plus-launching-platform-to-sell-acceptable-ads.
14. "Humanities Research for the Public Good," Council of Independent Colleges, accessed August 25, 2023, https://cic.edu/opportunity/public-humanities/.
15. The website for UBC's Public Humanities Hub lists the scope of issues and ambition: "Society has never needed Humanities scholars' guidance more. We live in a time of crisis: climate change threatens the planet, fake news and extreme populism have put democracy at risk, and racism, war, and wealth disparities have made millions of people around the world incredibly vulnerable. Humanities scholars are a largely untapped resource that can expand public discussions and enrich public understandings beyond our current moment in ways that spark the imagination of different kinds of futures." "Defining the Public Humanities," Public Humanities Hub, University of British Columbia, accessed August 25, 2023, https://publichumanities.ubc.ca/about/what-are-the-public-humanities/.
16. I now teach at a private university; I'm not sure my students there count as "the public," even as some forms of public funding flow into my institution in ways we shouldn't forget. But even if my audience in an academic setting is private, I still think that the value of humanities research writ large comes from its mandate to serve, in a word, *everyone*. And public universities *do* teach and serve and write for the public.
17. Michael Warner, *Publics and Counterpublics* (Zone Books. 2002), 74.
18. Warner, *Publics and Counterpublics*, 114.
19. Warner, 122.
20. Warner, 122.

FOUR

1. Susan K. Harris, "'But Is It Any *Good?*': Evaluating Nineteenth-Century American Women's Fiction," *American Literature* 63, no. 1 (1991): 45.
2. I take the phrase "idea-world" specifically from William Germano's helpful formulation in his book *On Revision*: "The idea-world of scholarship . . . [is] constructed out of institutions and research sites, institutional housing and, above all, people. But the vital fluid that drives the idea-world is simply the insights and claims that people put forward." *On Revision: The Only Writing That Matters* (University of Chicago Press, 2021), 86.
3. See, for instance, Noah Berlatsky, "Why Most Academics Will Always Be Bad Writers," *Chronicle of Higher Education*, July 11, 2016, https://www.chronicle.com/article/why-most-academics-will-always-be-bad-writers/; Victoria Clayton, "The Needless Complexity of Academic Writing," *The Atlantic*, October 16, 2015, https://www.theatlantic.com/education/archive/2015/10/complex-academic-writing/412255/; Stephen Dubner and Angela Duckworth, "Why Is Academic Writing So Bad?," *Freakonomics* (podcast), June 13, 2021.
4. Quoted in Nina Baym, "Rewriting the Scribbling Women," *Legacy* (Amherst, MA) 36, no. 1 (2019): 138.
5. Given my own scholarly interest in fictions of women's hair, I feel compelled to explain that *The Lamplighter* emphasizes the relation of the orphan's hair to her plot by telling us, in the first sentence describing her, that her hair is "long, thick, and uncombed." The adjective "uncombed" illustrates the difficult situation from which she will, by the novel's end, be rescued. Maria S. Cummins, *The Lamplighter* (1854; Project Gutenberg, 2010), chap. 1, https://www.gutenberg.org/cache/epub/31869/pg31869-images.html.
6. Blakey Vermeule, "I've finally figured out why academic writing (the reading and the writing of it) is so awful," Facebook, August 10, 2022.
7. Here and elsewhere I'm influenced by Sara Ahmed's *Complaint!* (Duke University Press, 2021).
8. Lauren Berlant, *The Female Complaint: The Unfinished Business of Sentimentality in American Culture* (Duke University Press, 2008), 13.
9. In this book's chapter "Critical Distance" I argue that humanists should become better readers of claims made in states of irritation, claims that can convey important truth even when they don't withstand the tests we might bring to most truth claims. In my phrasing in this paragraph, I'm trying to be a generous listener, while also strenuously disagreeing, and also being somewhat irritated myself. I am not sure I have achieved that balance, so I leave this note to mark a test case about the limits of my own strategies.
10. I emphasize "findability" based on my experiences as someone who has

written many pieces for wide immediate readership and watched them quickly fall out of circulation. Without good databases, readers investigating your topics can have a hard time finding your work unless they already know it exists; with good databases, a reader pursuing the topics of your mutual concern have a better chance of finding your writing, especially in the long term.

11. Leigh Claire La Berge, *Wages Against Artwork: Decommodified Labor and the Claims of Socially Engaged Art* (Duke University Press, 2019).
12. Michelle Chihara, "Humanities Without Borders," plenary panel at the Modern Language Association Annual Convention, Philadelphia, January 2024.
13. These are all terms taken from this book's "style sheet," compiled by its admirable copy editor, Stephen Twilley. Only by putting writing that uses such terms into peer review could I know the worth of this book's argument, which essentially is that peer review can absolutely be persuaded to read meaning-making styles it had not previously been trained to read.
14. In an early draft, I actually typed "feel out my forms" and didn't realize it for several rounds of revision, because the error is correct too.
15. Virginia Woolf, *A Room of One's Own* (Hogarth Press, 1935), 17, https://archive.org/details/woolf_aroom.
16. Woolf, *A Room of One's Own*, 17.
17. Woolf, 28.
18. Woolf, 28.
19. Audre Lorde, *Sister Outsider: Essays and Speeches* (Crossing Press, 1984), 112.
20. Wikipedia, "Tool," last modified November 19, 2024, 22:34 (UTC), https://en.wikipedia.org/wiki/Tool.
21. Simon Kimani, answer to the question, "What does the expression 'being a tool' mean?," accessed April 5, 2024, https://www.quora.com/What-does-the-expression-being-a-tool-mean/answer/Simon-Kimani. This definition has also appeared on the Wikipedia page.
22. Roderick A. Ferguson, *The Reorder of Things: The University and Its Pedagogies of Minority Difference* (University of Minnesota Press, 2012).
23. Sarah Mesle, "American Studies Takes Care: An Interview with Roderick Ferguson," *Los Angeles Review of Books*, November 6, 2018, https://lareviewofbooks.org/article/american-studies-takes-care-an-interview-with-asa-president-roderick-ferguson/.
24. Conversation with the author, New Haven, CT, February 8, 2024.
25. Emily Lordi, "Why Is Academic Writing So Beautiful? Notes on Black Feminist Scholarship," *Feminist Wire*, March 4, 2014, https://thefeministwire.com/2014/03/academic-writing-black-feminism-krisof/.
26. Fredric Jameson, "Utopia as Method, or the Uses of the Future," in *Utopia/Dystopia* (Princeton University Press, 2010).
27. Jameson, "Utopia as Method," 42.

28. Jameson, 42.
29. Adorno quoted in La Berge, *Wages Against Artwork*, 12.
30. La Berge, *Wages Against Artwork*, 11.
31. Alice Walker, "In Search of Our Mother's Gardens," in *In Search of Our Mothers' Gardens: Womanist Prose* (Harcourt Brace Jovanovich, 1983), 237.
32. Literally five minutes after I finished this last section ("Poems and Cities and Bugs"), two red bulbuls alighted in a tree next to me and burst into song.

SIX

1. According to one *Project Runway* recapper, however, the phrase first came from a contestant, Joshua McKinley. "Project Runway Recap: The Nina Garcia Project (Season 9, Episode 4)," *Cait's a Rough Draft* (blog), August 19, 2011, https://thisisjustaroughdraft.wordpress.com/2011/08/19/project-runway-recap-the-nina-garcia-project-season-9-episode-4/.
2. A word here about girls: You might not imagine your reader to be one. I hope it's clear that I'm talking about a figure, rather than a group of AFAB people. But in any circumstance, "girl" is a fraught word. Some people I know feel "girl" to be a term of intimacy and solidarity; others feel displeasure at how "girl" carries the deeply entrenched American assumption that women can never really be grown. My own mileage varies and so, maybe, does yours. But I like thinking of my reader as a girl, because of how closely I associate reading with girlhood—those who occupy the identity of girl, perhaps more than any other, are trained to understand that their security, as well as their pleasures, hinges on how well they read and can be read. If you believe your self-making depends on your skill at passionate and discerning reading (of texts, other bodies, your interactions), then the identity "girl" might be right for you.
3. Kiese Laymon, "Two Acclaimed Writers on the Art of Revising Your Life," interview by Tressie McMillan Cottom, *Ezra Klein Show* (podcast), November 9, 2021, https://www.nytimes.com/2021/11/09/podcasts/transcript-ezra-klein-show-kiese-laymon.html.

SEVEN

1. Woolf, *A Room of One's Own*, 55.
2. Bessel van der Kolk, *The Body Keeps the Score: Brain, Mind, and Body in the Healing of Trauma* (Viking Penguin, 2015), 235.
3. Writing Program, University of Southern California, *Writing 150 Course Book* (Hayden-McNeil, 2019), 70.
4. Miranda Fricker, *Epistemic Injustice: Power and the Ethics of Knowing* (Oxford University Press, 2007).

5. Fricker, *Epistemic Injustice*, 17, and Cottom, "Dying to Be Competent," in *"Thick" and Other Essays*. Cottom goes on to explain that the "wisdom" of Black women "is only validated by our culture when it serves someone or something else. . . . When, instead, black women are strong in service of themselves, that same strength, wisdom, and wit become evidence of our incompetence" (93).
6. Writing Program, University of Southern California, *Writing 150 Course Book*, 63.
7. Van der Kolk, *Body Keeps the Score*, 87.
8. Van der Kolk, 87.
9. Twyla Tharp, *The Creative Habit: Learn It and Use It for Life; A Practical Guide*, with Mark Reiter (Simon & Schuster, 2003).
10. Tharp's language of ritual finds an echo in the life coach James Clear's recommendation in his best-selling book *Atomic Habits* that we engage in "habit stacking": giving ourselves a specific "cue" that puts a string of desired activities in motion. *Atomic Habits: An Easy and Proven way to Build Good Habits and Break Bad Ones* (Avery, 2018).
11. Sabrina Strings, *Fearing the Black Body: The Racial Origins of Fat Phobia* (NYU Press, 2019).
12. Kate Manne, *Unshrinking: How to Face Fatphobia* (Crown, 2024).
13. Jensen, *Write No Matter What*, 21.
14. Natalie Goldberg, *Writing Down the Bones: Freeing the Writer Within* (Shambhala, 1986), 52.
15. Hayot, *Elements of Academic Style*, 21, 23.
16. Germano, *On Revision*, 100.
17. Anne Lamott, *Bird by Bird: Some Instructions on Writing and Life* (Pantheon Books, 1994), 70.
18. Helen Sword, *The Writer's Diet: A Guide to Fit Prose* (University of Chicago Press, 2016), 1.
19. Jess Row, *White Flights: Race, Fiction, and the American Imagination* (Graywolf Press, 2019), 65.
20. Cottom, "Thick," in *"Thick" and Other Essays*, 6.

NINE

1. I'm drawing the line at *Folklore* not because previously Swift didn't notice the complexities of love, but rather because by *Folklore* she seems to have fully embraced them as a lyrical object.
2. A brief polemic: All scholarly publications should have blogs, and if a venue you care about *doesn't* have a blog, maybe you could propose to start and organize one. If, on the other hand, you're the editor of such a journal, starting

a side publication with a non-peer-review publication process seems to me a practical and important way to increase interest in your field. If you are a chair or dean or administrator, on the other hand, codifying strategies for respecting non-peer-review expert writing seems a politically necessary step.

3. Tressie McMillan Cottom, "Girl 6," in *"Thick" and Other Essays* (New Press, 2019), 203.
4. Ryan Ruby, "The Golden Age of the Working Critic," interview by Matt Seybald, *American Vandal*, August 7, 2023, https://marktwainstudies.com/goldenage/.

TEN

1. The specific bones you will feel are your tibia and fibula as you imagine them bursting, as quarterback Joe Theissman's did, through the skin of your (his) shin.
2. Meghan O'Rourke, "Craft Talk: A Crucial Technique for First-Person Narration," Substack, November 17, 2024, https://meghanorourke.substack.com/p/craft-talk-a-crucial-technique-for.
3. Saidiya Hartman, "The End of White Supremacy: An American Romance," *Bomb*, June 5, 2020, https://bombmagazine.org/articles/2020/06/05/the-end-of-white-supremacy-an-american-romance/.

ELEVEN

1. Special shout-out here to my L. M. Montgomery "girls."
2. Stallybrass later published these ideas in a *PMLA* essay pleasurably titled "Against Thinking" (*PMLA* 122, no. 5 [2007]: 1580–87, http://www.jstor.org/stable/25501804).
3. Around this same time—maybe the same visit—Stallybrass was "working on" a project about the print revolution's relation to the printed "blank," the form, which is what helped make the connection between working and worksheets and writing for me.
4. Dana Luciano, *Arranging Grief: Sacred Time and the Body in Nineteenth-Century America* (NYU Press, 2007), 1.
5. Joseph M. Williams, *Style: Ten Lessons in Clarity and Grace*, 5th ed. (Longman, 1997), 48.

THIRTEEN

1. For the latter topic, I find some of the best advice in introductory guides: I still try to follow the approach formulated in the classic *Craft of Research*, which describes how to move from a topic to a question to its significance.

How Academics Write offers many similar strategies. For the former, the best source is often an information scientist; one at USC whom I've valued working with is Sophie Lesinka. Here I'll note the obvious point that research resources, such as database subscriptions and library staff, are unequally distributed, and that this inequity significantly structures lived experiences of experts (this is one experience that can be missed, it's worth saying, in conversations where "tenure" or "tenure-track" becomes the central mark of security: I don't have tenure but I have a great and well-staffed library). Those of us who do have robust database access should make the time to help out those who don't. Downloading PDFs for someone who could use them, for instance, is a basic and truly helpful form of mutual aid.

2. This list focuses on some common experiences of online pressure, skirting around the very real threats of censorship, harassment, and abuse that some humanists more than others are likely to face.
3. Paulette M. Caldwell, "A Hair Piece: Perspectives on the Intersection of Race and Gender," *Duke Law Journal* 40, no. 2 (1991): 365–96.
4. Phillis Wheatley, "Enclosure: Poem by Phillis Wheatley, 26 October 1775," *Founders Online*, National Archives, accessed May 23, 2024, https://founders.archives.gov/documents/Washington/03-02-02-0222-0002.

FIFTEEN

1. *Avidly*, "51 Things to Do Instead of Writing That Think Piece About Gender," June 8, 2016, https://avidly.lareviewofbooks.org/2016/06/08/51-things-to-do-instead-of-writing-that-think-piece-about-gender/.

SIXTEEN

1. Eric Hayot, *The Elements of Academic Style: Writing for the Humanities* (Columbia University Press, 2014), 21.
2. In a podcast conversation with Kiese Laymon and Deeshaw Philyaw, writer Roxane Gay describes how one of her motivations for publishing a writing guide came from her realization that very few available writing guides have been written by people of color. "Roxane Gay on Criticism, Social Media, and Being Heard," interview by Kiese Laymon and Deeshaw Philyaw, *Reckon True Stories*, July 16, 2024, https://www.reckon.news/podcast/2024/07/roxane-gay-on-criticism-social-media-and-being-heard.html.
3. Anderson, *Way We Argue Now*, 66.
4. Gloria Anzaldúa, "Speaking in Tongues: A Letter to Third World Women Writers," in *This Bridge Called My Back: Writings by Radical Women of Color*, 4th ed., ed. Cherríe Moraga and Gloria Anzaldúa (SUNY Press, 2015), 168.

5. Mary Oliver, "Of Power and Time," in *Upstream: Select Essays* (Penguin Press, 2016), 28, 30.
6. Oliver, 30.
7. This is not at all to say that all bus-writing experiences are equal. I reflect on my own relation to the bus and other women there in the essay "Her Sentimental Properties" (*Los Angeles Review of Books*, June 20, 2020, https://lareviewofbooks.org/article/her-sentimental-properties/).
8. Susan Harlan, "Things That Male Academics Have Said to Me," *Avidly*, November 20, 2017, https://avidly.lareviewofbooks.org/2017/11/20/things-that-male-academics-have-said-to-me/.

SEVENTEEN

1. Rachel Sagner Buurma and Laura Heffernan, *The Teaching Archive: A New History For Literary Study* (University of Chicago Press, 2021), 3.

EIGHTEEN

1. Gerald Graff and Cathy Birkenstein, *"They Say / I Say": The Moves That Matter in Academic Writing*. 3rd ed. (Norton, 2014).
2. This chapter is one that, perhaps more than any other, feels tied to the emergence of generative AI. Given the quick changes of the technology, it's hard for me to forecast what AI will mean for student writing by the time you read this book. However, my sense as of January 2025 is that AI makes the claims of this chapter all the more relevant. Moving away from the thesis will not save us from AI's challenges, but given AI's capacity to produce standard forms, we may be even more motivated to turn toward more creative options.
3. Spencer Althouse, "18 Ways to Eat Hummus All Day Long." *BuzzFeed*, August 6, 2013, https://www.buzzfeed.com/spenceralthouse/ways-to-eat-hummus-all-day-long.
4. Writing by hand can be a disability issue. But when you won't be collecting the journals, the stakes go down.
5. Mike Bunn, "How to Read Like a Writer," *Writing Spaces* 2 (2011), https://parlormultimedia.com/writingspaces/past-volumes/how-to-read-like-a-writer/.
6. Bruce Burgett and Glenn Hendler, "Syllabi and Assignments," in *Keywords for American Cultural Studies*, 3rd ed., NYU Press, accessed May 23, 2024, https://keywords.nyupress.org/american-cultural-studies/in-the-classroom/syllabi-and-assignments/.
7. Lauren Berlant and Kathleen Stewart, *The Hundreds* (Duke University Press,

2019); Alexis Pauline Gumbs, *Spill: Scenes of Black Feminist Fugitivity* (Duke University Press, 2016).

8. Grading contracts can significantly minimize the stress of this process for everyone.

NINETEEN

1. Oscar Wilde, *Lady Windermere's Fan* (1893; Project Gutenberg, 1997), act 3, https://gutenberg.org/cache/epub/790/pg790-images.html.
2. Elizabeth Bishop, "One Art," in *The Complete Poems, 1927–1979* (Noonday Press, 1991), 178.

TWENTY

1. Joli Jensen, *Write No Matter What: Advice for Academics* (University of Chicago Press, 2017), 24.
2. To note here: September 7 is my son's birthday, which I didn't notice when I first snapped this picture. He turned seventeen this day; if he had been turning seven, the day's plan would certainly have involved "buy juice boxes" and "send Evite party reminder."

Bibliography

Ahmed, Sara. *Complaint!* Duke University Press, 2021.

Althouse, Spencer. “18 Ways to Eat Hummus All Day Long.” *BuzzFeed,* August 6, 2013. https://www.buzzfeed.com/spenceralthouse/ways-to-eat-hummus-all-day-long.

Anderson, Amanda. *The Way We Argue Now: A Study in the Cultures of Theory.* Princeton University Press, 2009.

Anzaldúa, Gloria. “Speaking in Tongues: A Letter to Third World Women Writers.” In *This Bridge Called My Back: Writings by Radical Women of Color.* 4th ed. Edited by Cherríe Moraga and Gloria Anzaldúa. SUNY Press, 2015.

Avidly. “51 Things to Do Instead of Writing That Think Piece About Gender.” June 8, 2016. https://avidly.lareviewofbooks.org/2016/06/08/51-things-to-do-instead-of-writing-that-think-piece-about-gender/.

Baker, Katie J. M. “Ladies, What’s Up with ‘I Feel Like’ Verbal Tic?” *Jezebel,* August 23, 2013. https://jezebel.com/ladies-whats-up-with-the-i-feel-like-verbal-tic-1184374148.

Baym, Nina. “Rewriting the Scribbling Women.” *Legacy* (Amherst, MA) 36, no. 1 (2019): 137–50.

Berlant, Lauren. *The Female Complaint: The Unfinished Business of Sentimentality in American Culture.* Duke University Press, 2008.

Berlant, Lauren, and Kathleen Stewart. *The Hundreds.* Duke University Press, 2019.

Berlatsky, Noah. “Why Most Academics Will Always Be Bad Writers.” *Chronicle of*

Higher Education, July 11, 2016. https://www.chronicle.com/article/why-most-academics-will-always-be-bad-writers/.

Bishop, Elizabeth. “One Art.” in *The Complete Poems, 1927–1979*. Noonday Press, 1991.

Bivens-Tatum, Wayne. “The ‘Crisis’ of the Humanities.” *Academic Librarian*, November 5, 2010. https://blogs.princeton.edu/librarian/2010/11/the_crisis_in_the_humanities/.

Blackwood, Sarah. “Letter from an English Department on the Brink.” *New York Review of Books*, April 2, 2023. https://www.nybooks.com/online/2023/04/02/letter-from-an-english-department-on-the-brink/.

Buurma, Rachel Sagner, and Laura Heffernan. *The Teaching Archive: A New History for Literary Study*. University of Chicago Press, 2021.

Bogdanic, Walt, and Michael Forsyth. *When McKinsey Comes to Town: The Hidden Influence of the World’s Most Powerful Consulting Firm*. Random House, 2022.

Bunn, Mike. “How to Read Like a Writer.” *Writing Spaces* 2 (2011). https://parlormultimedia.com/writingspaces/past-volumes/how-to-read-like-a-writer/.

Burgett, Bruce, and Glenn Hendler. “Syllabi and Assignments.” In *Keywords for American Cultural Studies*. 3rd ed. NYU Press. Accessed May 23, 2024. https://keywords.nyupress.org/american-cultural-studies/in-the-classroom/syllabi-and-assignments/.

Cait’s a Rough Draft (blog). “Project Runway Recap: The Nina Garcia Project (Season 9, Episode 4).” August 19, 2011. https://thisisjustaroughdraft.wordpress.com/2011/08/19/project-runway-recap-the-nina-garcia-project-season-9-episode-4/

Caldwell, Paulette M. “A Hair Piece: Perspectives on the Intersection of Race and Gender.” *Duke Law Journal* 40, no. 2 (1991): 365–96.

Carpenter, Bennett, Laura Goldblatt, and Lenora Hanson. “Unprofessional: Toward a Political Economy of Professionalization.” *Social Text* 39, no. 1 (2021): 47–67.

Chihara, Michelle. “Humanities Without Borders.” Plenary panel at the Modern Language Association Annual Convention, Philadelphia, January 2024.

Clayton, Victoria. “The Needless Complexity of Academic Writing.” *The Atlantic*, October 16, 2015. https://www.theatlantic.com/education/archive/2015/10/complex-academic-writing/412255/.

Clear, James. *Atomic Habits: An Easy and Proven way to Build Good Habits and Break Bad Ones*. Avery, 2018.

Corrigan, Lisa. “The Evisceration of a Public University.” *The Atlantic*, August 16, 2023. https://www.thenation.com/article/society/wvu-cuts-higher-education/.

Cottom, Tressie McMillan. *“Thick” and Other Essays*. New Press, 2019.

Cummins, Maria S. *The Lamplighter*. Project Gutenberg, 2010. Originally published in 1854. https://www.gutenberg.org/cache/epub/31869/pg31869-images.html.

Daston, Lorraine, and Peter Galison. *Objectivity*. Zone Books, 2007.

"Defining the Public Humanities." Public Humanities Hub, University of British Columbia. Accessed August 25, 2023. https://publichumanities.ubc.ca/about/what-are-the-public-humanities/.

Delouya, Samantha. "The Rise of Gig Workers Is Changing the Face of the US Economy." CNN, July 25, 2023. https://www.cnn.com/2023/07/24/economy/gig-workers-economy-impact-explained/index.html.

Dubner, Stephen, and Angela Duckworth. "Why Is Academic Writing So Bad?" *Freakonomics* (podcast), June 13, 2021. https://freakonomics.com/podcast/why-is-academic-writing-so-bad/.

Ferguson, Roderick A. *The Reorder of Things: The University and Its Pedagogies of Minority Difference*. University of Minnesota Press, 2012.

Frowe, John. *Genre*. Routledge, 2005.

Fricker, Miranda. *Epistemic Injustice: Power and the Ethics of Knowing*. Oxford University Press, 2007.

Gay, Roxane. "Roxane Gay on Criticism, Social Media, and Being Heard." Interview by Kiese Laymon and Deeshaw Philyaw. *Reckon True Stories* (podcast), July 16, 2024. https://www.reckon.news/podcast/2024/07/roxane-gay-on-criticism-social-media-and-being-heard.html.

Germano, William. *On Revision: The Only Writing That Matters*. University of Chicago Press, 2021.

Gilman, Sander L. "Black Bodies, White Bodies: Toward an Iconography of Female Sexuality in Late Nineteenth-Century Art, Medicine, and Literature." *Critical Inquiry* 12, no. 1 (1985): 204–42. http://www.jstor.org/stable/1343468.

Goldberg, Natalie. *Writing Down the Bones: Freeing the Writer Within*. Shambhala, 1986.

Graff, Gerald, and Cathy Birkenstein. *"They Say / I Say": The Moves That Matter in Academic Writing*. 3rd ed. Norton, 2014.

Greyser, Naomi. "Un/Blocked: Writing, Race, and Gender in the American Academy." *American Quarterly* 75, no. 2 (2023): 335–57.

Guillory, John. *Professing Criticism: Essays on the Organization of Literary Study*. University of Chicago Press, 2022.

Gumbs, Alexis Pauline. *Spill: Scenes of Black Feminist Fugitivity*. Duke University Press, 2016.

Harlan, Susan. "Things That Male Academics Have Said To Me." *Avidly*, November 20, 2017. https://avidly.lareviewofbooks.org/2017/11/20/things-that-male-academics-have-said-to-me/.

Harris, Susan K. "'But Is It Any *Good?*': Evaluating Nineteenth-Century American Women's Fiction." *American Literature* 63, no. 1 (1991): 43–61.

Hartman, Saidiya. "The End of White Supremacy: An American Romance." *Bomb*, June 5, 2020. https://bombmagazine.org/articles/2020/06/05/the-end-of-white-supremacy-an-american-romance/.

Hayot, Eric. *The Elements of Academic Style: Writing for the Humanities*. Columbia University Press, 2014.

Heller, Nathan. "The End of the English Major." *New Yorker*, February 27, 2023. https://www.newyorker.com/magazine/2023/03/06/the-end-of-the-english-major.

Huerta, Monica. *Magical Habits*. Duke University Press, 2021.

"Humanities Research for the Public Good." Council of Independent Colleges. Accessed August 25, 2023. https://cic.edu/opportunity/public-humanities/.

Jameson, Fredric. "Utopia as Method, or the Uses of the Future." In *Utopia/Dystopia*. Princeton University Press, 2010.

Jensen, Joli. *Write No Matter What: Advice for Academics*. University of Chicago Press, 2017.

Kennedy, Bryan, Alec Tyson, and Cary Funk. "Americans' Trust in Scientists, Other Groups, Declines." Pew Research Center, February 15, 2022. https://www.pewresearch.org/science/2022/02/15/americans-trust-in-scientists-other-groups-declines/.

Kimani, Simon. Answer to the question, "What does the expression 'being a tool' mean?" Accessed April 5, 2024. https://www.quora.com/What-does-the-expression-being-a-tool-mean/answer/Simon-Kimani.

Kornbluh, Anna. "Objectively Curious Commitments." *Victorian Literature and Culture* 48, no. 2 (2020): 444–54.

La Berge, Leigh Claire. *Wages Against Artwork: Decommodified Labor and the Claims of Socially Engaged Art*. Duke University Press, 2019.

Laymon, Kiese. "Two Acclaimed Writers on the Art of Revising Your Life." Interview by Tressie McMillan Cottom. *Ezra Klein Show* (podcast), November 9, 2021. https://www.nytimes.com/2021/11/09/podcasts/transcript-ezra-klein-show-kiese-laymon.html.

Lamott, Anne. *Bird by Bird: Some Instructions on Writing and Life*. Pantheon Books, 1994.

Lorde, Audre. *Sister Outsider: Essays and Speeches*. Crossing Press, 1984.

Lorde, Audre. *Uses of the Erotic: The Erotic as Power*. Out & Out Books, 1978.

Lordi, Emily. "Why Is Academic Writing So Beautiful? Notes on Black Feminist Scholarship." *Feminist Wire*, March 4, 2014. https://thefeministwire.com/2014/03/academic-writing-black-feminism-krisof/.

Luciano, Dana. *Arranging Grief: Sacred Time and the Body in Nineteenth-Century America*. NYU Press, 2007.

Lusin, Natalia, and Mai Hunt. "The MLA *Job List*, 2020–22." 2023. https://www.mla.org/content/download/191179/file/Job-List-Report-20-22.pdf.

Manne, Kate. *Unshrinking: How to Face Fatphobia*. Crown, 2024.

Mesle, Sarah. "American Studies Takes Care: An Interview with Roderick Ferguson." *Los Angeles Review of Books*, November 6, 2018. https://lareviewofbooks.org/article/american-studies-takes-care-an-interview-with-asa-president-roderick-ferguson/.

Mesle, Sarah. "Her Sentimental Properties." *Los Angeles Review of Books*, June 20, 2020. https://lareviewofbooks.org/article/her-sentimental-properties/.

Moten, Fred. *In the Break: The Aesthetics of the Black Radical Tradition*. University of Minnesota Press, 2003.

Muñoz, José Esteban. *Cruising Utopia: The Then and There of Queer Futurity*. NYU Press, 2009.

Nash, Jennifer C. *How We Write Now: Living with Black Feminist Theory*. Duke University Press, 2024.

National Endowment for the Humanities. "Public Scholars." Accessed August 25, 2023. https://www.neh.gov/grants/research/public-scholar-program.

Nersessian, Anahid. *The Calamity Form: On Poetry and Social Life*. University of Chicago Press, 2021.

Newfield, Christopher. "Have We Wrecked Public Universities? The Case of the American Decline Cycle." *British Journal of Sociology* 69, no. 2 (2018): 484–93.

Ngai, Sianne. *Our Aesthetic Categories: Zany, Cute, Interesting*. Harvard University Press, 2012.

Ngai, Sianne. *Ugly Feelings*. Harvard University Press, 2007.

Oliver, Mary. "Of Power and Time." In *Upstream: Select Essays*. Penguin Press, 2016.

O'Rourke, Meghan. "Craft Talk: A Crucial Technique for First-Person Narration." Substack, November 17, 2024. https://meghanorourke.substack.com/p/craft-talk-a-crucial-technique-for.

Radke, Heather. *Butts: A Backstory*. Avid Reader Press, 2022.

Reitter, Paul, and Chad Wellmon. *Permanent Crisis: The Humanities in a Disenchanted Age*. University of Chicago Press, 2021.

Row, Jess. *White Flights: Race, Fiction, and the American Imagination*. Graywolf Press, 2019.

Ruby, Ryan. "A Golden Age?" *Vinduet*, April 25, 2023. https://www.vinduet.no/essayistikk/a-golden-age-ryan-ruby-on-literary-criticism-and-the-internet/.

Ruby, Ryan. "The Golden Age of the Working Critic." Interview by Matt Seybald. *American Vandal*, August 7, 2023. https://marktwainstudies.com/goldenage/.

Sandhu, Sukhdev. "Why We're Hooked." Review of *Screen Time*, by Phillip Maciak.

The Guardian, June 1, 2023. https://www.theguardian.com/books/2023/jun/01/screen-time-by-phillip-maciak-review-why-were-hooked.

Scott, Mark, "Study of Ad-Blocking Software Suggests Wide Use." *New York Times,* August 10, 2015. https://archive.nytimes.com/bits.blogs.nytimes.com/2015/08/10/study-of-ad-blocking-software-suggests-wide-use/.

Smith, Ben. *Traffic: Genius, Rivalry, and Delusion in the Billion-Dollar Race to Go Viral.* Penguin Press, 2023.

Smith, Caleb, Sarah Mesle, and Merve Emre, eds. "No Crisis." Special series, *LARB,* 2015. https://lareviewofbooks.org/feature/no-crisis/.

Snow, Shane. "I Feel Therefore I Think: If You're a Leader, This Verbal Habit Could Be Undermining You." July 24, 2020. https://www.forbes.com/sites/shanesnow/2020/07/24/i-feel-therefore-i-think-if-youre-a-leader-this-verbal-habit-could-be-undermining-you/.

Solon, Olivia. "AdBlock Plus Launching Platform to Sell 'Acceptable' Ads." *The Guardian,* September 13, 2016. https://www.theguardian.com/business/2016/sep/13/adblock-plus-launching-platform-to-sell-acceptable-ads.

Stallybrass, Peter. "Against Thinking." *PMLA* 122, no. 5 (2007): 1580–87. http://www.jstor.org/stable/25501804.

Strings, Sabrina. *Fearing the Black Body: The Racial Origins of Fat Phobia.* NYU Press, 2019.

Sword, Helen. *The Writer's Diet: A Guide to Fit Prose.* University of Chicago Press, 2016.

Taylor, Patricia. "The Imperfect Tutor: Grading, Feedback, and AI." *Inside Higher Ed,* September 6, 2024. https://www.insidehighered.com/opinion/career-advice/teaching/2024/09/06/challenges-using-ai-give-feedback-and-grade-students.

Tharp, Twyla. *The Creative Habit: Learn It and Use It for Life; A Practical Guide.* With Mark Reiter. Simon & Schuster, 2003.

Tolentino, Jia. "The I in the Internet." *CCCB Lab,* February 19, 2020. https://lab.cccb.org/en/the-i-in-the-internet/

van der Kolk, Bessel A. *The Body Keeps the Score: Brain, Mind, and Body in the Healing of Trauma.* Viking Penguin, 2015.

Vermeule, Blakey. "I've finally figured out why academic writing (the reading and the writing of it) is so awful." Facebook, August 10, 2022.

Walker, Alice. "In Search of Our Mother's Gardens." *In Search of Our Mothers' Gardens: Womanist Prose.* Harcourt Brace Jovanovich, 1983.

Warner, Michael. *Publics and Counterpublics.* Zone Books, 2002.

Wheatley, Phillis. "Enclosure: Poem by Phillis Wheatley, 26 October 1775." *Founders Online,* National Archives. Accessed May 23, 2024. https://founders.archives.gov/documents/Washington/03-02-02-0222-0002.

Wikipedia. "Tool." Last modified November 19, 2024, 22:34 (UTC). https://en.wikipedia.org/wiki/Tool.

Williams, Jeffrey J. "Empire of Letters: Tom Lutz and the 'Los Angeles Review of Books' Set Out to Create a New Model of Literary Review." *Chronicle of Higher Education*, January 3, 2016. https://www.chronicle.com/article/empire-of-letters/.

Williams, Joseph M. *Style: Ten Lessons in Clarity and Grace*. 5th ed. Longman, 1997.

Williams, Raymond. *Marxism and Literature*. Oxford University Press, 1977.

Woolf, Virginia. *A Room of One's Own*. Hogarth Press, 1935. https://archive.org/details/woolf_aroom.

WordPress.com. "New Dashboard Design and March Wrap-Up." April 4, 2008. https://wordpress.com/blog/2008/04/04/new-dashboard/.

Worthen, Molly. "Stop Saying 'I Feel Like.'" *New York Times*, April 30, 2016. https://www.nytimes.com/2016/05/01/opinion/sunday/stop-saying-i-feel-like.html.

Writing Program, University of Southern California. *Writing 150 Course Book*. Hayden-McNeil, 2019.

Index

Page numbers in italics refer to figures in the text.